Controversy

◆

Issues for Reading and Writing

Controversy

Issues for Reading and Writing

Judith J. Pula

Frostburg State University

Audrey T. Edwards

Eastern Illinois University

R. Allan Dermott

*New Hampshire Community Technical
College at Manchester*

Prentice Hall, Upper Saddle River, New Jersey 07458

Library of Congress Cataloging-in-Publication Data

Controversy : issues for reading and writing / compiled by Judith J.
  Pula. Audrey T. Edwards, R. Allan Dermott
      p.   cm.
    ISBN 0–13–598103–4
    1. College readers.   2. English language—Rhetoric—Problems,
  exercises, etc.   3. Report writing—Problems, exercises, etc.
  I. Pula, Judith J.   II. Edwards, Audrey T.   III. Dermott, R. Allan
  PE1417.C6543   1999
  808'.0427—dc21   98–10093
                                                             CIP

Editor-in-chief: Charlyce Jones Owen
Senior acquisitions editor: Maggie Barbieri
Editorial assistant: Joan Polk
Managing editor: Bonnie Biller
Production liaison: Fran Russello
Editorial/production supervision: Bruce Hobart (Pine Tree Composition)
Cover director: Jane Conte
Cover designer: Bruce Kenselaar
Prepress and manufacturing buyer: Mary Ann Gloriande
Marketing manager: Rob Mejia

This book was set in 10/12 Simoncini Garamond by Pine Tree
Composition, Inc., and was printed and bound by Courier
Companies, Inc. The cover was printed by Phoenix Color Corp.

© 1999 by Prentice-Hall, Inc.
Simon & Schuster/A Viacom Company
Upper Saddle River, New Jersey 07458

Printed in the United States of America
10   9   8   7   6   5   4   2

ISBN: 0-13-598103-4

Prentice-Hall International (UK) Limited, *London*
Prentice-Hall of Australia Pty. Limited, *Sydney*
Prentice-Hall Canada Inc., *Toronto*
Prentice-Hall Hispanoamericana, S.A., *Mexico*
Prentice-Hall of India Private Limited, *New Delhi*
Prentice-Hall of Japan, Inc., *Tokyo*
Simon and Schuster Asia Pte. Ltd., *Singapore*
Editora Prentice-Hall do Brasil, Ltda., *Rio de Janiero*

Contents

Introduction

This book asks you to use what you know to judge an author's ideas and write about them.

You may think you don't know enough to argue with a professional writer. We think you do. For one thing, you have had experiences no one else has had; you and your classmates together have had a great many experiences. For another thing, it's possible to reach different opinions from the same set of facts. In fact, this book gives two opinions on each topic: a short preview article and a longer essay following it. Once you've compared the two, you can draw your own conclusions.

There are 15 major topics in this book, ranging from juvenile justice to reducing the threat of drugs. For each topic, the book has four steps: preview, reading, discussion, and writing.

PREVIEW

During the preview step, you'll be thinking a little about your own beliefs on the topic, discussing your ideas with your classmates, and reading a short preview article. Then you'll be taking a quick look at the essay—the title, the first and last paragraphs, and the author's background—so you can predict the main idea. You'll also look at some quotes from the essay to figure out the meanings of any new words. (To assist you, we've included a list of common word parts in Appendix A at the back of the book.)

READING

After the preview, you'll be ready to read the essay on your own. Following the essay are some reading questions dealing with the main idea, your reactions to it, and the author's writing techniques. As you read, be sure to write down your answers to these questions so that you'll have notes to speak from when you discuss the essay. If an occasional question seems difficult, do the best you can and be prepared to compare ideas in class.

DISCUSSION

Having read the essay and made your notes, you're ready for the discussion. By comparing notes with your classmates, you may find facts you've missed, and you'll certainly hear other people's ideas on the topic. The discussion will help sum up your reading experience and prepare you for writing.

COMPOSITION

When you write, you'll be giving your opinion on the topic you've discussed. At this point, your short answers to the reading questions should help you collect your thoughts and even try out some of the writing techniques used by the authors. Once you've thought about your own experiences, as well as the beliefs of at least two authors and several classmates, you should have something very worthwhile to say.

MAKING DISCUSSIONS EFFECTIVE

Sometimes you're surprised by what you say: Good ideas pop into your mind while you're talking. And sometimes other people's words will give you a new way of looking at things. Good discussion is truly creative.

In fact, discussion has such a strong effect on reading and writing that it's built into the plan for this book—in two places. First, a preview session allows you to think over a topic with other students before you read. Then, after you read, a second session lets you compare notes on the essay and prepare to write about it.

Of course, this class is not the only place where you'll be taking part in discussions. Over the course of a lifetime, you'll sit through many meetings—in classes, clubs, sororities, business groups. These meetings can be a pleasure or an annoyance, and although you can't entirely control the outcome, you can improve the odds—by improving the content and by helping the group to work together more smoothly.

Content

If you've ever felt that you couldn't get a word in—that the discussion went on to something new before you could get your thoughts in order—try forming some opinions ahead of time. (Naturally, these can change when you hear other people's ideas, but at least you'll have a head start.) Before a meeting, thoroughly read anything that's assigned. Mark the key parts and jot down a word or two to remind you of each point you want to make during the discussion. (In using this book, you probably won't be expected to prepare for the preview discussion, but you probably will be asked to write down your answers to the Reading Questions before class.) Then, just before the discussion, quickly look over your notes to refresh your memory. Having prepared, you'll be moving the session along instead of being dragged in its wake. The next question is how to move things along most effectively.

Task and Maintenance Roles

When you think of discussions, you may picture two people trading facts or opinions. Actually, though, a discussion becomes much more interesting when shared by several people playing a variety of roles. People may play either a "task role," helping the group to deal with the task at hand, or a "maintenance role," maintaining group harmony.

Both task actions and maintenance actions are important to the success of your discussions. Listed below are some task and maintenance roles in the form of self-quizzes. Answers are listed after Matching Exercise 2.

Matching Exercise I. To help you learn the task and maintenance roles, match the following terms with their definitions.

Task Roles

___ 1. Information and Opinion Giver

___ 2. Information and Opinion Seeker

___ 3. Direction and Role Definer

___ 4. Summarizer

___ 5. Energizer

___ 6. Comprehension Checker

Maintenance Roles

___ 7. Encourager of Participation

___ 8. Communication Facilitator

___ 9. Tension Releaser

___ 10. Process Observer

___ 11. Interpersonal Problem-Solver

___ 12. Supporter and Praiser

Actions

a. Makes sure all group members understand what each is saying

b. Pulls together related ideas or suggestions and restates them

c. Offers facts, opinions, ideas, feelings, and information

d. Expresses acceptance and liking for group members

e. Uses observations of how the group is working to help discuss how the group can improve

f. Lets members know their contributions are valued

g. Asks for facts, opinions, ideas, feelings, and information

h. Asks others to summarize discussion to make sure they understand

i. Encourages group members to work hard to achieve goals

j. Calls attention to tasks that need to be done and assigns responsibilities

k. Helps resolve and mediate conflicts

l. Tells jokes and increases the group fun

Matching Exercise 2. Match each statement below with the task or maintenance role it seems to fit best.

Task Roles

___ 1. Information and Opinion Giver

___ 2. Information and Opinion Seeker

Statements

a. "Does everyone in the group understand Helen's idea?"

b. "How about giving our report on yoga while standing on our heads?"

Task Roles

__ 3. Direction and Role Definer

__ 4. Summarizer

__ 5. Energizer

__ 6. Comprehension Checker

Maintenance Roles

__ 7. Encourager of Participation

__ 8. Communication Facilitator

__ 9. Tension Releaser

__ 10. Process Observer

__ 11. Interpersonal Problem-Solver

__ 12. Supporter and Praiser

Statements

c. "Edye's idea sounds like Buddy's; I think they could be combined."

d. "I think we should openly discuss the conflict between Dave and Linda to help resolve it."

e. "Before we go on, let me tell you how other groups have solved this task."

f. "We need a time-keeper. Keith, why don't you do that?"

g. "I really enjoy this group. I especially enjoy Roger's sense of humor."

h. "I think we'd find a good solution if we put a little more work into it."

i. "Frank, tell us what we've said so far to see if you understand it correctly."

j. "We seem to be suggesting solutions before we're ready. Let's define the problem first."

k. "I don't understand. What do you mean?"

l. "Helen, I'd like to hear what you think about this; you have such good ideas."

Answer Key. Exercise 1: 1. c; 2. g; 3. j; 4. b; 5. i; 6. h; 7. f; 8. a; 9. l; 10. e; 11. k; 12. d.
Exercise 2: 1. e; 2. k; 3. j; 4. c; 5. h; 6. a; 7. l; 8. i; 9. b; 10. f, 11. d; 12. g.

PLAYING TASK AND MAINTENANCE ROLES: WINTER SURVIVAL EXERCISE

Now that you've seen how many different roles you can play, you know you can contribute in some way to an actual discussion. (You needn't attempt all these roles, of course, and you needn't stick with any one type. Just contribute your thoughts in a way that suits you and perhaps try a new role once in a while.)

Try testing out some of these roles using the following short discussion exercise, "Winter Survival." We recommend the following plan for its use.

First break up into groups of four or five people; move a little way apart from the other groups. Each group should choose one person to record group decisions. Next, read "Winter Survival." (It contains your

xiv   *Introduction*

task and all the information you will need.) As soon as everyone in your small group has finished reading, begin your discussion.

About halfway through the time allowed for discussion, STOP. As a group, consider the following questions. How many people have taken part so far? What went well? How could the discussion be improved during its second half?

Resume your discussion, and try to carry out any suggested improvements.

Once you've concluded the discussion, evaluate it again. What roles did you actually play? Go back over the list of task roles: Check the two or three you found yourself playing most often during the discussion of "Winter Survival." Then pick your two or three most important maintenance roles.

Finally, sum up: How did you help the group—either in getting the job done or in keeping the group going?

What would you like to do differently another time?

Winter Survival: The Situation

You have just crash-landed in the woods of northern Minnesota and southern Manitoba. It is 11:32 A.M. in mid-January. The light plane in which you were traveling crashed on a lake. The pilot and copilot were killed. Shortly after the crash the plane sank completely into the lake with the pilot's and copilot's bodies inside. Miraculously, the rest of you are not seriously injured and you are all dry.

The crash came suddenly, before the pilot had time to radio for help or inform anyone of your position. Since your pilot was trying to avoid a storm, you know the plane was considerably off course. The pilot announced shortly before the crash that you were 20 miles northwest of a small town that is the nearest known habitation.

You are in a wilderness area made up of thick woods broken by many lakes and streams. The snow depth varies from above the ankles in windswept areas to knee-deep where it has drifted. The last weather report indicated that the temperature would reach minus 25 degrees Fahrenheit in the daytime and minus 40 at night. There is plenty of dead wood and twigs in the immediate area. You are dressed in winter clothing appropriate for city wear—suits, pantsuits, street shoes, and overcoats.

While escaping from the plane, the several members of your group salvaged 12 items. Your task is to rank these items according to their importance to your survival, starting with 1 for the most important item and ending with 12 for the least important one.

You may assume that the number of passengers is the same as the number of persons in your group and that the group has agreed to stick together.

Winter Survival Decision Form. Rank the following items according to their importance to your survival, starting with 1 for the most important one and proceeding to 12 for the least important one.

_____ Ball of steel wool
_____ Newspapers (one per person)
_____ Compass
_____ Hand ax
_____ Cigarette lighter (without fluid)
_____ Loaded .45-caliber pistol
_____ Sectional air map made of plastic
_____ Twenty-by-twenty-foot piece of heavy-duty canvas
_____ Extra shirt and pants for each survivor
_____ Can of shortening
_____ Quart of 100-proof whiskey
_____ Family-size chocolate bar (one per person)

Essay Questions: Winter Survival. Choose one of the following questions and answer it in a short essay (about 300 words).

1. Explain why one item on the list created a difficult decision for you. Tell why you finally made the decision you did.
2. Pick one feature (for example, ability to retain heat) that you think is very important in choosing items from the list. Explain what makes that feature so important to your survival.
3. From the items on the list, choose two. Explain why one item is more valuable than the other.

Acknowledgments

Our students contributed many substantive comments to *Controversy*, thereby proving that several heads are better than one at critiquing.

Our teaching colleagues provided advice, information, and warm encouragement.

Our editors at Prentice Hall and their reviewers helped us to see the book clearly as it took shape. Our reviewers were Elaine Chakonas, Triton College; Beth Childress, Armstrong State College; Janet Cutshall, Sussex Community College; Patrick Haas, Glendale Community College; Roberta Panish, Rockland County Community College; and Harvey Rubinstein, Hudson County Community College.

The Maryland chapter of the Delta Kappa Gamma Society International gave us a grant to help defray production costs.

Elizabeth Howell, Elysa Friedman, and Heather Wilkinson served as editorial assistants, and Pamela Williams provided research assistance.

Finally, Sharon Ritchie and Lynn Dermott typed the manuscript, and Michael Pula formatted it, with precision and patience.

Our heartfelt thanks to all who helped make the book a reality.

Judith J. Pula
Audrey T. Edwards
R. Allan Dermott

UNIT
O N E

Overview:
The Processes of Critical
Reading and Writing

The Process of Critical Reading

---◆---

Picture a man who has built some bookshelves but now wants to take on something more ambitious. He wants to build kitchen cabinets for his wife. Our inexperienced cabinetmaker can jump in there with his tools and the best of intentions. If he is persistent, he probably will come up with some kind of cabinets. If he is smart, however, he will get together with an experienced cabinetmaker to pick up a few "tricks of the trade." The result will probably be less time wasted, less frustration, and a better finished product. Likewise, a smart student who knows he is inexperienced at reading may check with a better reader. However, many good readers don't know how to explain what they do in any meaningful way. Allow us, the authors, to be your experienced cabinetmakers.

A good reader doesn't just start sawing and hammering chapter one of a piece of nonfiction. A good reader will preview first—that is, check out a few things before beginning. But what things? These are a few "tricks of the trade" to be discussed in this unit.

Second, what do experienced readers do while reading a chapter? "Read," you say? But what is going on in their thought processes? How do they understand what they are reading if they don't look up every unfamiliar word in the dictionary? Again, we have "tricks of the trade."

Third, let's say that you have "read" the assignment. How comfortable do you usually feel in discussing such assignments when the class meets again? In taking a quiz? In writing an essay on the assignment? If any of these questions make you feel uneasy, you might want to visit your friendly cabinetmakers.

In short, we suggest that you break the process of reading into three steps: previewing, reading to answer questions, and discussing your ideas with others. The results should be a clearer understanding of the ideas involved.

PREVIEWING

Before carpenters begin sawing and hammering, they look over the situation. They get out the measuring tape and jot down a few notes and think some more. Most importantly, they call on past experiences and knowledge to get a better perspective on the current circumstances. The more novel the present situation, the more they need to think through where they are heading. When they understand what the owners want and have integrated the two sets of ideas and possibly recommended changes, then they are ready to proceed.

When it comes to reading, too, past experience and knowledge help. The more we readers can pull together our own ideas before looking at an article, the better. In addition, it often helps if we consider ideas from another author. Therefore, this book begins most units with a short selection having an alternate view to the one in the unit's main reading(s).

Room is provided for you to write your answers to questions. Go through the reading/thinking process and make a clear, written response. If you do, you can be reasonably sure you are on the way to mastering a process that can serve you well for the rest of your life.

In surveying an essay, we as readers prepare ourselves mentally. Before reading the article, we want to know what the writer wants us to get from the paper more than anything else—the main idea. Experienced readers predict the main idea through a two-step process. First, they study the title, which is sometimes the main idea itself or perhaps a modification of it. In any case, as readers we expect the title to at least suggest the topic—that is, tell us what the essay is about.

The second step in predicting the main idea is to read the first and last paragraphs. Often the main thrust is in the first paragraph. If not, it is sometimes in the last. In either case, we should now have a better idea of what the essay is going to be saying.

In writing your statement of a main idea, answer these questions: What does the author want me to believe? What point is the author trying to make? Note that the main idea can be stated in a sentence, unlike the subject matter, topic, or title, which usually is stated in a fragment. Following are some examples of topics and main ideas.

Subject or topic
- Fighter pilots during World War I
- The dangers of flying in World War I

Poor statements of main idea
- It is about fighter pilots during World War I.
- The main idea is about the dangers of flying in World War I.

Good statements of main idea
- Pilots during World War I, who had no parachutes, faced death when their planes were shot down.
- Flying a fighter during the First World War was especially dangerous because the pilots did not have parachutes.

To help you with what might be harder words in each essay, we have added another step to the previewing sections in this book. We could just give you the definitions of words so that you wouldn't have to look them up in the dictionary. Many books like ours do that very thing, but we will be doing something different. In helping you to think the way the very best readers do, we wish to show you how to figure out the meaning of words using a quotation from the essay and Appendix A, Word Parts. You should not have to look up a word in the dictionary unless there are too few meaningful clues. As you learn to use these clues by finding them in the various essays of this book, you should find that increasingly you can use such clues in reading passages in other books.

Now you should be ready to read the preview article. Remember why we included this preview article for you. It presents a point of view different from that of the main essay and thus should help you raise important questions when you read the main selection.

In previewing the unit, you have had a chance to think about the topic and read the preview article. Now it is time to briefly preview the main essay itself. By calling it "the main selection," we do not mean to imply that we think the ideas in the main essay are either more important or better than those in the prereading assignment. It is called that simply because you are going to examine in detail not only what the author says but also how he or she says it. Remember that the way an idea is packaged can greatly influence readers as to the reasonableness of the idea itself.

Once you have a fairly good idea of what the main selection is saying, you then want to turn your attention to the author's background. You may have to check the library for the information. If you already know it or it is given with the article, as in this book, all the better. What you want to determine is what in the author's background may have led him or her to the main idea. Is there anything in the writer's experience that might have influenced him or her? The answer to this question helps you determine what to look at most closely in considering this person's ideas. Even if a writer is qualified, if the essay is subjective—that is, subject to much opinion as with politics—you must proceed with your antennae tuned for detecting prejudices. Equally important, once you know something about the author's attitudes, it's easier to see what he or she is driving at.

Now that you have an idea of what the author's main idea might be and perhaps the experience that influenced this idea, you should pause to ask yourself just what questions you have about this essay before you read it. Is the author going to cover both sides of the issue? What evidence does he or she offer? Does the author think that this idea applies to everybody?

As with the preview article, the main essay may also have some vocabulary that can give you problems. Sometimes you may think you know what a word means, but when checking how it is used in the essay you find that you either have been mistaken or have been using it differently from the way the author has employed it. Remember, you don't need to look up a word in the dictionary unless there are too few clues to the meaning.

Most anthologies, especially collections of essays, have questions following each selection to supplement those that the reader thought of in the preview. This book is no exception. Thus, before reading an essay in a textbook, the good student will study these questions and perhaps generate more questions to be answered by reading.

The questions after each essay are divided into five general areas:

1. The main idea
2. The way the essay is organized
3. The essay's formality
4. Other features of style
5. Reactions to the main idea and the supporting evidence

Following are some typical questions with explanations.

"Where in the essay is the main idea found?"

The main idea is usually found near the beginning of the essay, generally at the end of the last paragraph of the introduction. If not there, it probably is in the conclusion. Sometimes it is in both places. Occasionally, though, the main point, or thesis, appears in the center after the writer has spent much effort building up to it. Then it is followed by still further support.

"Why has the author placed the main idea there?"

Stating the main idea at the beginning gives a framework for organizing the details. If the author repeats the thesis at the end, he or she apparently has felt the need to emphasize it by placing the details in a "sandwich." Sometimes the author will place the main idea at the beginning, in the middle, and at the end. This type of emphasis is a special "sandwich" that we jokingly call the Big Mac. If the main idea does not occur until the center or end, the author may feel the need to build a case with supporting evidence before presenting a thesis that might otherwise be rejected outright.

"In what order are the paragraphs arranged?"

If the author is telling a story, the sequence of events is arranged by *time*. Or sometimes the body of the essay is composed of details or points presented either from *least to most important* or from *most to least important*. If the details seem to be in no special order, then they may be nothing but a *simple listing*. If the author shows that one event is caused by another, the logical explanation is called *cause and effect*. This is not the only kind of logic, however. If the author presents Point A first because it is needed before B can make sense or be convincing—in other words, if the author is reasoning with the reader—the overall organization can probably be called *logic*. If more than one of these organizations seems apparent, underline the pattern that is most obvious overall. Then, so you will be ready for class discussion, jot the other pattern in the margin with the paragraph numbers for reference. For example, an organization based on reasoning or logic may very well include a few paragraphs that tell a story to support the main idea. The overall organization would be *logic*, and a subpattern would be *time*.

"How formal is the essay?"

Indicators of informality include humor, informal expressions and slang, short sentences and paragraphs overall, use of *I* or *you,* and contractions. *Indicators of formality* include seriousness, formal vocabulary, and long sentences and paragraphs overall. On a scale of 1 (very informal) to 10 (very formal), for a 1, consider how you might talk with your friends at a party: "OK, you guys—bet none of you dudes ever got yourselves in a jam like this before." We would give a 10 to writings like the Declaration of Independence, the Constitution of the United States of America, or this example from the Gettysburg Address: "Four score and seven years ago our fathers brought forth on this continent a new nation, conceived in liberty, and dedicated to the proposition that all men are created equal." Most writings, of course, are somewhere between these two extremes. Ask yourself: Does this essay tend to be generally informal, formal, or somewhere in between? Once you have read and rated a few essays, you will have a basis for comparison. Also remember that the ability to judge the tone or style is more important than "getting the right number." Even teachers probably would not agree on the exact number.

"Where do you see the following features of style?"

Here we discuss features such as allusion and metaphor. The terms themselves are not all that important; focus on the writing techniques behind them and the way the author may be using these techniques to communicate something. We have found, however, that these labels make it easier to discuss the essay.

Earlier, we mentioned that an inexperienced reader may want to learn from a "master cabinetmaker" before he finds himself too frustrated or confused. The last sentence of that paragraph read, "Let us, the authors, be your experienced cabinetmakers." If you recognized the comparison between reading and skillful carpentry, then you can grasp what some people call figurative language. You are well on your way to understanding how experienced writers convey their ideas through special techniques.

The key to success lies in taking on only a few of these concepts at a time until you finally have mastered all of them by the end of the course.

When a new term comes up, you can find its meaning in Appendix B, Guide to Literary Terms, and do the accompanying exercise if there is one. For example, turn to the Guide to Literary Terms on page 291 and check out the term *jargon*.

"Does the author propose any change?"

Here you will find questions about the content of the essay. These will help you to clarify the author's views. Three good questions are "Does the author propose any change?" "What would the result be?" and "Do you agree with the author's main idea?"

READING TO ANSWER QUESTIONS

Let's go back to our carpenter who is redoing someone's kitchen. He now knows what the owner's views are and knows how they relate to his own experience, so he can proceed fairly confidently with the job. The end of the preparation does not mean the end of thinking, however. As he progresses, he questions and re-evaluates the situation. Without these questions, he is open to errors that may require some retracing of his steps. Likewise, research shows that people do a better job of understanding what they read if they do it for the purpose of answering questions.

Unlike many other textbooks, this one provides room for you to jot down your answers right after each question given. The advantages of these jottings are fourfold. (1) They are all in one place when you study for a quiz. (2) When a teacher calls on you to answer a certain question you will have notes that can jog your memory. (With a book like this, a teacher is less apt to accept the excuse, "I don't remember.") (3) These spaces after the questions are also good for adding thoughts and examples that occur to you during the class discussion. (4) All these notes are naturally in a well-organized place, ready for you to study for a large exam or to refer to when writing your own essay on the subject.

You should now be ready to read the main essay. As you read it, be certain to keep the preview questions and your responses to them in mind. Read to answer the Reading Questions you just finished looking over. These Reading Questions are reproduced right after the essay itself with space to write your answers in the book.

FOLLOWING UP ON READING

Throughout this unit we have compared reading to building kitchen cabinets. Reading, you see, is more than getting the main idea. It also involves reconstructing the author's plan, the methods of presenting that plan, and, most importantly, the ways these methods help establish the main point. What if a homeowner asks a carpenter to build kitchen cabinets for her? The carpenter now knows the main point: the owner wants new cabinets in her kitchen. But is that all the carpenter needs to know in order to understand the owner's mind? Hardly. He also wants to know her plan: when she wants them done and just where and how high she wants them. Furthermore, he must consider the style she has in mind. Does she want an old rustic barnboard look, or a sleek shine with fancy hinges and knobs, or something—just what?—in between? Likewise, understanding the plan and tone of an essay can help you enter the writer's mind to better understand his or her style and personality. And often it's an aid to finding the meaning.

Writing is also like building cabinets, but there is an important difference. In building kitchen cabinets, you are reconstructing the owner's idea, plan, and style (although it is true that these may be modified according to your suggestions). In writing, however, you are developing your own point (although you are influenced by others' ideas) and shaping this idea according to your own plan and techniques (although you may be influenced by other writers' plans and techniques that you have studied). But what happens if you haven't read all that much or, if you have, you haven't really studied other people's plans and techniques and therefore have only a small collection of such resources to call on in presenting your own ideas? Here is the point where we experienced carpenters can help you. The more you know about various organizational plans and writing techniques, the more easily you can pull together those that best fit your own personality and ideas.

The notes you take in the reading stage will help you to recall the author's facts and writing techniques as well as your reactions to them. These notes will help you during class discussion. Furthermore, notes on your classmates' reactions, combined with your notes made while reading, should aid you in the writing stages. The more time you spend on reading and analyzing, the easier it should be for you to develop your own ideas and to present them effectively.

The Writing Process

---◆---

For most people, writing isn't difficult. It's torture. Yet they do it—to keep up a friendship, to get a job, to pass a course. And if a person must write, there are ways to make the work bearable, the results actually satisfying.

When a task seems to be too much for you, you may be able to manage it by breaking it into parts. One way to break up writing is to set aside a short time for it each day. Your instructor may set aside some class or lab time for writing so you can get help as you go along. Even so, you probably will need to work outside of class, too. Many professional writers schedule morning sessions: Even for them, writing is difficult enough that it requires a clear head. (The best time for you may be different, though.) And it's good to have a place free of tempting distractions: One well-known author goes to the garage and locks herself in the car. This book was written at school, where the authors couldn't develop a sudden interest in washing the dishes, the clothes, the car, and so forth.

Another way of breaking the task into manageable parts is to attack it in stages. A nightmare known to all writers is "The Terror of the Blank Page": They feel that the beautiful white page before them deserves a perfect composition—or at least a composition of some sort, since that's the result they're supposed to produce. But an oil painting may begin as a pencil sketch (or several sketches); a football play may begin as Xs on a chalkboard. Writing, too, can be attacked in stages.

As with painting and football—and not surprisingly, reading—writing proceeds most easily when you go from large to small, when you try to see the major outlines before worrying about the details. In the case of reading, you can move from preview to reading to discussion; in composing, you can move from planning to writing to revising and editing. The process isn't that neat, of course: You may go back and forth between stages. In addition, after using a writing procedure for a while, you add the touches that make it your own. (Some people can think only in tiny, penciled words; you may prefer to use a computer.) Working in stages does help, however.

As you read about each stage below, try it out to see how it works and how important it is to the success of your writing.

PLANNING

The first stage, planning, is getting ideas together before writing a message. Where to begin? In many real-life writing situations, you are responding to someone else's ideas. In this book, you'll be given a reading selection and some questions to discuss after you read. If you jot down your own answers to these reading questions at the time, you'll have some good notes to work from when you plan your writing. These notes will show what the author says about the subject and whether you agree.

You will also be given a composition question or will choose one from a list. Your reply will be your essay. Before looking at these composition questions, try to guess what they'll be. Write down your guesses, then compare them to the questions given. If you can learn to predict, you'll have a useful test-taking skill—and if you come up with a question you like better than what's given, your instructor may prefer it, too.

If you have a choice of questions, take your time deciding; jot down a few words under each one. Which one do you know the most about? Which do you feel most strongly about?

Once you've settled on a single composition question, you have your work cut out for you. You also have quite a few notes on the reading selection, but they won't all help with your particular question. Go back to these notes and copy the few words or phrases that will help answer this one question.

Now you probably will need to make some more notes to plan your answer. Here you have a choice: Some people work from the top down—from main ideas to details—others from the bottom up. (If you've always done it one way, why not try another?) The "top-down" method is to list—far apart—three or four key words showing your main idea and a few points that will help sell that idea to your reader. Then fill in the space beside each word with details from your notes and ideas that occur to you. The more ideas and connections you think of, the more changes you will probably make in the original plan—and that's fine.

Example: For Composition Question 5 in Unit One, The Juvenile Justice System (about whether to reveal the records of guilty children), here are some sample notes made in "top-down" style. The first section is partly filled in. Try completing the other section ("Size of crime?") with your own ideas.

Name juvenile? Dep. on 2 things:

Main Points	Notes
1. Going straight?	How often in trouble? Getting worse/better?
	Any sign that problem is due to temporary upset (death, etc.)?
	Whole pattern of life strange?
	Court psychologist talk with kid—not hired by lawyer
	Look at no. of past crimes
	Secrecy is to help kid go straight—if he isn't going to go straight, name him!
2. Size of crime?	

Another method, the "bottom-up" strategy, is to jot down whatever comes to mind, quickly, without stopping to polish or discard anything. From this wealth of detail, you can decide on the key points that you want to make. If you use this method, try folding your paper lengthwise and writing on only one side. This should help you to write single words or phrases, not "The Perfect Sentence." And it will leave some space to write comments on your ideas when you later sort them.

Example: For another composition question on guilty juveniles, here are some partly-finished sample notes made in "bottom-up" style. Point 1 is already filled in. For point 2, read the detailed notes at the right. Then, at the left, list the major points the student could make in his or her essay.

Main Points	**Notes**
1. Not all kids alike	Allen sounds like my neighbor—"kids rotten these days"—all kids? Sour—trusted wrong kids and got burned?—failure as a parent?
2. _____	H.F. in 1st grade—nice valentine 3d grade—broke windows 5th grade—shooting Not bad to start with—wish he'd gotten help —mother dead What kind of help, when? Don't know—too few answers, but Allen says send 'em all to prison—warehouse

A third method, mapping, is to jot down a mixture of main ideas and details, circling them and connecting them with lines to show their relationship.

Example: For the same composition question, here are some sample notes mapped out with boxes and lines. Try filling in the blank boxes or adding some that will connect to those already shown.

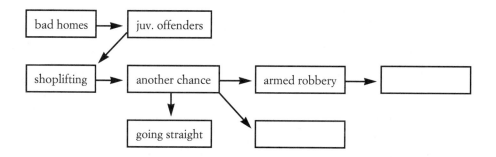

Now that you have thought of a few points you could make in reply to your composition question, you are ready to organize them into an essay. (If, however, you are assigned to write a single-paragraph response instead of a long essay, narrow the topic: you may have two or three points you could use to answer a question, but choose just one of these points to address in your paragraph.)

WRITING

Now for the actual writing. It should proceed more easily once you have notes and a plan, but now that it's time to write the real composition, "The Terror of the Blank Page" may hit with full force. Try to create a situation that allows you to experiment and make changes. One student, Matt, composes on a computer so he can easily add words or change the order of paragraphs. Another student, Amy, leaves large blanks when she's hung up on a point and then comes back to it later. If Shawn has questions about how clear or correct something is, he marks the spot but keeps on writing. Many people write on every other line; that way, whenever they can't choose the right word or sentence, they write both (one above the other) and make a choice later. The idea is to write fairly quickly so as not to lose your train of thought, knowing that you can always make changes later.

Notice that the introduction to a paper gives the kind of information you want when you're meeting someone in person: the first and last names of the authors (and anyone featured) as well as the titles of what they have written. The introduction also gives the authors' main ideas and the question you plan to discuss. (You can give the answer, too, or choose to leave us in suspense for now. Either way will work.)

The other part of the paper that calls for special handling is the conclusion. Just as when you're saying goodbye to someone, don't start the conversation up again with new ideas or details. Instead, tell the reader—briefly—what you really want him or her to remember.

REVISING

Once your paper has been written all the way through to the end, it still is not finished. Now—as with reading—you need to see other points of view. To do this, you should find at least two readers who are friendly but honest.

The first reader can be you—but to really see what you've written, you must first go away from it, preferably overnight. Then return to it, putting yourself in the reader's shoes, and ask yourself these questions:

Revision Questions

  1. Is there any statement the reader might not understand?
     (Explain it.)

2. Is there any statement that might offend the reader?
   (See if you can make it more acceptable.)
3. Is there anything that's not very convincing?
   (Maybe you can add a sentence to strengthen your case.)
4. Have I changed the subject and then changed it back again?
   (Possibly you should rearrange paragraphs so that one idea leads into another.)
5. Have I said the same thing twice?
   (Cross out words or combine sentences where you can.)
6. Do I want to try using any feature of style I've seen in the reading selection?
   (Consider any features discussed in the Reading Questions under style.)

Even after you've made these changes, of course, you still won't know for sure how your composition strikes another person, so mark any places you still have questions about. Then find someone else to read what you've written. This person can be your instructor as long as you make it clear that the composition is not ready for grading. Or your reader may be a classmate. Do not ask any questions at first. Just ask the other person to read the whole essay silently. (If you were to read it aloud, your expression would add clues that aren't available on the page itself. Hold back on the explanations, too.) Your reader could mark the page, placing a "+" beside any sentence that seems especially convincing and a "?" beside any sentence that is unclear or seems to be of doubtful value. Then let the other person tell you what message he or she got. Do not argue. If it's not what you meant, the misunderstanding tells you where to strengthen your writing. Then go over any parts either of you has marked. Ask questions about these parts, and make notes as you go along.

Finally, consider your reader's reactions and decide what changes to make. (Even though another person's ideas can be useful, you have the final say.) Add, subtract, rearrange, and combine to make your paper as clear and convincing as possible.

EDITING

Now that you've decided on your ideas and have put them in order, you are finally ready to edit your writing—to polish it. By leaving the editing until last, you probably have been able to see the overall picture better.

And you've saved yourself work: You don't need to worry about correcting or polishing any words or sentences you've discarded.

To make sure your composition is as clear and easy to read as possible, read each sentence out loud, pause, and ask yourself the following questions.

Editing Questions

1. Does the sentence make sense?

    (Do its parts fit together? Or does it begin as one sentence and change to another in the middle?)
2. Does the sentence use the kind of language that most people consider "good English" these days?

    (*Hint:* Imagine a TV announcer reading it.)
3. Do the periods, commas, and other punctuation show the rise and fall of my voice?

    (A handbook can help you with basic rules, but the more willing you are to try something new, the more questions you'll have that the book can't answer. When in doubt, ask your instructor for an opinion.)
4. Are the words spelled right?

    (Spelling the words right helps you look like an authority. Here again, reading out loud helps: listen to make sure you've written a group of letters for each syllable—each beat, if you're a musician. Then use a spell check, or consult the dictionary, or ask your instructor. You may want to reread your paper backward, word by word, so as to really see each word. But if many of your spelling errors are real words in the wrong place, such as *there* for *they're*, you might better read backwards, sentence by sentence.)

Once all these changes have been made, your paper should be easy to read—if you have been using a computer. If you have been writing by hand, your paper is probably full of crossouts, extra words wedged in at the end of a line, arrows where you've decided to move a paragraph. And the more improvements you make, the harder it is to read. Should you copy it over?

If another person can't read the paper, copy the worst parts over; cut and tape paragraphs in the order you want them. To produce finished copy, of course, you would type or neatly rewrite; find out whether your instructor wants this. If your instructor asks you to copy your paper over, proofread for copying errors before you hand it in.

Some people like to copy the whole thing over just to help themselves remember new rules they've learned. Consider this, however: You could, instead, make a separate list of the sentences that gave you trouble, all neatly corrected, with the troublesome part circled. That way, you'd have the practice and you'd have a personal "handbook" for use in editing your next paper.

You could also make a list of any spelling words you were unsure of so you'll have them for next time; a list is quicker to use than a dictionary. Our student Mike suggested grouping the "a" words and so forth by dividing a sheet of paper into squares—twelve on each side, since very few words start with x or z. We have included such a form for your use as Appendix K, Spelling List, on page 325.

Now you have a finished paper. Do professional writers really go through all these stages? Do they plan, write, revise, edit? Basically, yes. It really is helpful to work on the main points before worrying about the details; it's important not to rush on to the next stage too soon or to skip stages. But sometimes it is necessary to backtrack—you might, for instance, stop editing and go back to add ideas you've just thought of.

It's also important to make the process your own. Some people like to write in pencil so that they can write wherever they are. Many people who are all thumbs prefer a typewriter or computer: It's easier for them to think about ideas when they're not struggling with a pencil. Others dictate to a tape recorder, then play the tape and write out their words.

You may find, after trying out several methods, that you prefer to type instead of write by hand. You'll also know whether you like to plan your writing from the top down (main ideas to details) or from the bottom up. And you'll probably find someone who's a really helpful reader. Whatever methods you use, writing won't suddenly become easy. It can become a little more pleasant, however—and the products can become much more rewarding—if you attack the task by stages: planning, writing, revising, and editing.

UNIT

T W O

The Juvenile Justice System: Does It Work?

PREVIEW STEPS FOR UNIT TWO

In response to questions 1 and 2, try these steps: Write your answers, talk them over with three or four classmates, and then discuss them with the whole class.

1. Have you ever known or heard of a teenager in your neighborhood who was involved in some kind of crime? If so, do you know why the teenager acted as he or she did?

2. In the right-hand column below, check any reason(s) that you think might be a cause for juvenile delinquency. (Leave the columns at left under S and A blank for now.)

S. A.

☐ ☐ ☐ a. lack of jobs (to fill time as well as to get money)
☐ ☐ ☐ b. boredom: desire for excitement
☐ ☐ ☐ c. breakdown of family structure
☐ ☐ ☐ d. lack of parental love
☐ ☐ ☐ e. lack of purpose in life
☐ ☐ ☐ f. feeling that society is against them
☐ ☐ ☐ g. disillusionment about benefits of education
☐ ☐ ☐ h. feeling of being trapped in poverty or ignorance
☐ ☐ ☐ i. peer pressure
☐ ☐ ☐ j. peer comradeship
☐ ☐ ☐ k. experimentation
☐ ☐ ☐ l. need for food, shelter, etc.
☐ ☐ ☐ m. need for street drugs
☐ ☐ ☐ n. desire to defy authority
☐ ☐ ☐ o. viewing crime on TV
☐ ☐ ☐ p. other: _____

3. In light of the causes of juvenile delinquency, place checks beside what might be some of the better ways of solving the problem. (Leave columns at left blank for now.)

S. A.

☐ ☐ ☐ a. imprisonment
☐ ☐ ☐ b. detention halls

S. A.

☐ ☐ ☐ c. court-administered reprimand and warning
☐ ☐ ☐ d. court-administered spanking
☐ ☐ ☐ e. punishment by parents
☐ ☐ ☐ f. roughing up of delinquents in dark alleys
☐ ☐ ☐ g. other punishment by members of the community
☐ ☐ ☐ h. release of names to press as with adults
☐ ☐ ☐ i. probation
☐ ☐ ☐ j. ignoring the incident; problem will go away as teen-agers become adults
☐ ☐ ☐ k. education
☐ ☐ ☐ l. not giving extra chances to young offenders
☐ ☐ ☐ m. part-time jobs
☐ ☐ ☐ n. other: _____
☐ ☐ ☐ o. other: _____

4. a. Read the title of the first essay (page 23). Name the topic. (Who or what is this essay about?)

   b. Now predict the main idea. (What is the main point the author wants to make about this topic?)

   c. Read the first and last paragraphs. Revise your prediction if necessary. (*Note:* The main idea should sum up the smaller ideas of the essay.)

5. Some words from the essay are listed below, accompanied by quotations. Mark any words you do not know and make an educated guess about their meanings using the context supplied by the quotations—and possibly Appendix A, Word Parts, on page 287. You may want to work with a small group of classmates.

anthropologist ". . . Sullivan is an *anthropologist* who instead of heading off to the South Seas has [been] . . . studying [the] youth . . . of Brooklyn."

scavenging ". . . homes . . . , victims of *scavenging* junkies . . ."

ethnic "In a Hispanic [neighborhood] . . . In another *ethnic enclave* he listened to the grandsons of Polish immigrants. . . ."

enclave See above quotation.

irony ". . . . grandsons of Polish immigrants boast without *irony* how they preyed on new refugees. . . ."

predatory ". . . lots of poor teenagers commit *predatory* street crimes. . . ."

incapacitation ". . . the *incapacitation* strategy would . . . *incarcerate* offenders. . . ."

incarcerate See above quotation.

intramural ". . . they . . . moved from *intramural mayhem* to muggings. . . ."

mayhem See above quotation.

abstract "If local residents tolerated burglaries, they drew the line at muggings. . . . [This] was a hard lesson for the young offenders to learn in the *abstract.* . . . Some, like Zap Andrews, weighed the odds and changed course. . . . Not long after one incident he discovered that his victim was his new girlfriend's mother who could easily have identified him. . . . Later he lost more of his bravado after being arrested for assault and landing in jail."

saturated "Zap . . . had *saturated* his market."

implicit "The big question *implicit* in Sullivan's work is how [juvenile delinquents] can learn their lessons sooner."

6. Now read the following essay. As you read, jot down any questions that occur to you.

(*Note:* Question 7 appears after the essay.)

Mapping the Streets of Crime

Mercer Sullivan is an anthropologist who, instead of heading off to the   1
South Seas, has spent the last four years studying youth crime on the
streets of Brooklyn. In housing projects, he hung out with gold-chain
snatchers. In a Hispanic neighborhood, he watched a row of three-story
homes slowly disappear, victims of scavenging junkies and arsonists. In
another ethnic enclave he listened to the grandsons of Polish immigrants boast without irony how they preyed on new refugees who got
drunk on payday and became easy marks. From these field studies Sullivan has emerged with a picture of juvenile crime that any graduate of a
tough urban neighborhood will instantly recognize: Lots of poor
teenagers commit predatory street crimes for a few years—then most
stop, reformed by a combination of jail, growing fear and, most importantly, jobs. . . . What Sullivan's work suggests is that since most teen
crime careers are short, the incapacitation strategy would needlessly incarcerate offenders who are on the verge of going straight.

Sullivan's research grew out of a Vera Institute of Justice pro-   2
ject aimed at testing links between crime and employment. . . . Vera's
researchers, . . . armed with a federal grant, . . . surveyed 900 criminal
defendants and dispatched Sullivan and a team of field workers to
track small groups of young men through three low-income neighborhoods in Brooklyn.

Sullivan found that the youths in the white, black, and Hispanic   3
neighborhoods all began their crime careers as street brawlers, dangerous only to each other. As they grew older, however, they followed markedly different paths. The white teenagers tended to get
part-time jobs through family connections, which filled their time
and provided spending money. The few who experimented with
street robberies quickly found themselves confronted by angry neigh-

bors or businessmen who were prepared either to go to the police or whip the youngsters into line themselves—a form of what anthropologists call local social control.

In contrast, few of the black and Hispanic youths managed to 4
find part-time work. Instead, they took to street corners where most moved from intramural mayhem to muggings. . . . If local residents tolerated burglaries, they drew the line at muggings. "No community will stand for random street attacks," says Sullivan. But he found that was a hard lesson for the young offenders to learn in the abstract. Many of the boys progressed to muggings as they grew bigger. Typically, they struck close to home because they knew the turf. Their victims, however, soon knew them and many were able to identify them to police. Eventually almost all the muggers were arrested, or if they weren't, they knew someone who was. Some, like Zap Andrews, weighed the odds and changed course. His specialty was elevator robberies in housing projects. Not long after one incident, he discovered that his victim was his new girlfriend's mother, who could easily have identified him. Zap, as Sullivan says, had saturated his market. Later he lost more of his bravado after being arrested for assault and landing in jail. Then he turned 17 and found a job in a drycleaning shop, where the money was steady and the risks were few. "Hey," he told Sullivan, "I learned before I got my 20 years."

The big question implicit in Sullivan's work is how Zap An- 5
drews and his friends can learn their lessons sooner. There are no easy answers; but they are more apt to emerge from research that focuses—as the Vera study did—on the processes of crime, and not just on its results. Ignoring those processes may itself be delinquent.

7. State the essay's main idea in your own words. Compare it to your prediction of the main idea. (*Note:* The main idea should sum up the smaller ideas of the essay.)

8. Return to the Unit Preview, question 3, on page 20 and make checkmarks in the S column to show Sullivan's suggestions for solving the juvenile crime problem.

9. What are Sullivan's views on sending juvenile offenders to jail?

PREVIEW STEPS FOR "WHY NOT NAME GUILTY JUVENILES?"

1. a. Read the title of the second essay (page 26). Name the topic. (Who or what is this essay about?)

   b. Now predict the main idea. (What is the main point the author wants to make about this topic?)

   c. Read the first and last paragraphs of the essay. Revise your prediction if necessary. (*Note:* The main idea should sum up the smaller ideas of the essay.)

2. What in the author's background may have led him to the main idea? (See author's background, below title.)

3. Some words from the essay are listed below, accompanied by quotations. Mark any words you do not know and make an educated guess about their meanings using the context supplied by the quotations— and possibly Appendix A, Word Parts, on page 287. You may want to work with a small group of classmates.

assumptions ". . . it has rearranged some of his long-held legal *assumptions*."

transgressions "The theory was for their juvenile offenses not to be made part of their permanent life's record . . . and so we need to protect [them] from [their] own childhood *transgressions*."

hypocritical "That was proper in 1989, but I don't think it's reasonable now. None of these kids is every going to be president of a corporation, and it's *hypocritical* of us to think that keeping things secret is helping anybody."

probation (not **parole**) "So we see kids getting *probation* six or eight times."

4. At the end of the Preview, you may want to go over any new features of style that occur in the following reading selection. You will need to know the terms *jargon, irony of wording,* and *metaphor.* For help, see Appendix B, Guide to Literary Terms (page 291), with accompanying exercises on individual features.

5. Before reading "Why Not Name Guilty Juveniles?" turn to pages 29–31 and skim the Reading Questions. Then read the essay to find answers to these questions. As you read, jot down any questions that occur to you.

Why Not Name Guilty Juveniles?

Michael Olesker

Michael Olesker is a columnist for the Baltimore Sun. *His columns cover everything from sports and ethnic festivals to politics and the ethics of street rumbles. Before joining the* Sun *in February 1979, Olesker was a sports reporter, a film and theater critic in England, an investigative reporter whose stories led to the criminal convictions of several political figures, a journalism instructor at Towson (Md.) State University, and a columnist at the* News American. *His 1995 book,* Michael Olesker's Baltimore, *is a collection of his columns.*

The job takes a little piece out of him every day.   1

He looks down at the children, and wonders where they went   2
wrong. They appear daily in his courtroom, in the city's juvenile system, brought in for offenses that make this the most emotionally
draining job Milton Allen has had in 35 years as a defense attorney,
prosecutor, and judge.

A week ago, it was the 17-year-old girl charged with assault   3
with intent to murder, assault, and child abuse.

That's the legal language. In English, it means she is charged   4
with dumping her newborn down a West Baltimore sewer.

"It's a frightening case," Judge Allen says. "I don't know that   5
the young lady they brought in is guilty, but it's staggering to think
that someone would do something like this. It's almost a miracle the
child was recovered."

The baby girl was found by a man named Maurice Hill. Hill   6
stopped his car at Bloom and Division Streets. His windows were
closed and his radio was on, but Hill thought he heard a baby crying.

He got out of his car, grabbed a tire iron from his trunk and   7
pried open the lid to the sewer, and in the darkness he saw a yellow
plastic bag, and it was moving.

"Almost a miracle," Judge Allen is saying again.   8

He is not accustomed to dealing with miracles. He has been as-   9
signed to Juvenile Court for 16 months now, and it has rearranged
some of his long-held legal assumptions.

For one thing, he thinks Juvenile Court should be open to full   10
media coverage, and he thinks guilty juveniles ought to be identified
publicly.

"The secrecy concept is out of date," says Allen. "We do it to   11
protect the child, and a long time ago, that was proper. I no longer
think it is.

"The theory was for their juvenile offenses not to be made part   12
of their permanent life's record. The idea was that a person might
grow up to become a college president, and so we need to protect
him from his own childhood transgressions.

"That was proper in 1898, but I don't think it's reasonable now.   13
None of these kids is ever going to be president of a corporation, and
it's hypocritical of us to think that keeping things secret is helping
anybody.

"The way to help them is education, which no longer exists. We   14
don't educate these kids. You go on the street; it's loaded with kids.
And they wind up in my courtroom.

"And you hear people refer to it as Kiddie Court. But we aren't 15
dealing with kiddies; we're dealing with murderers, rapists, robbers,
thieves. We find them guilty, only we don't call it guilty; we call it
'delinquent offenses.'

"These kids are never guilty. If he killed the pope, he's never 16
guilty. He's 'delinquent.' But the person is just as dead, and just as
burglarized. Secrecy isn't the answer. We ought to open it up, to let
people know who their friendly neighborhood burglar is. And let
them know how bad the whole juvenile situation is."

It is this bad: Law enforcement people estimate that more than 17
half of all serious crimes today are committed by juveniles.

And it is this bad: The Maryland Training School was once 18
filled with kids who played hooky from school, or stole a car for a
quick joyride, or got caught shoplifting.

Now, it has kids who have committed "delinquent offenses" 19
called murder and rape.

"What appears to be happening," says Allen, "is a trend toward 20
violence, and increasing frequency. They finish one case, and they're
released back to their parents, and then they're back again.

"And it's always the same. After they've been held for a while, 21
they say, 'I've learned my lesson. You'll never see my face in here
again. I'm gonna obey the law.' But then they always come back."

The system attempts to give second chances. And third, and 22
more. It is society's way of trying to deal mercifully with its young, of
giving them enough chances that maybe they will straighten themselves out. But Allen says it is not working.

Much of the problem, he says, is the breakdown of the family 23
structure.

"They have no home training," he says, "and so they live by their 24
own rules, which are often frightening. In 16 months, I think I've had
maybe six cases where both the mother and father were living at home.
In a lot of them, there has never been a father in the house.

"So we see kids getting probation six or eight times. It's our 25
concept of mercy. But probation is one of the worst things in the
world. We get a kid on probation who commits another crime, we've
got to send them away.

"But where? We don't have the institutions. We went down to the 26
legislature, begging them for new facilities. I've invited them to come sit
in my courtroom for one day, but it's way off in a corner to them. They
think juvenile crime is a bunch of kids stealing hubcaps, but it's really
kids carrying big .357 Magnums.

"It's frightening. I don't know what it's doing to me. It's frus- 27
trating. Not enough people understand. The legislature certainly
doesn't. If it did, maybe they would try to do something about it."

READING QUESTIONS FOR "WHY NOT NAME GUILTY JUVENILES?"

Main Idea

1. State the essay's main idea in your own words. Compare it to your prediction of the main idea. (*Note:* The main idea should sum up the smaller ideas of the essay.)

Organization

2. a. Where in the essay is the main idea found?

   b. Why has the author placed the main idea there?

3. In what order are the paragraphs arranged? (Underline one.) Time / Least to most important / Most to least important / Logic: cause and effect / Other logic / Other

Style

4. How formal is the essay? (Circle your choice.)

   [Informal—1—2—3—4—5—6—7—8—9—10—Formal]

   What indicators convinced you? (For a list of possible indicators and two benchmark essays, see Appendix F, The Formality Spectrum, on page 307.)

5. Where do you see the following features of style? List one or two examples of each with their paragraph numbers.

   Features (For definitions, see Appendix B, page 291.)

   a. jargon

   b. irony of wording

   c. metaphor

   Content

6. Return to the Unit Preview, question 2, on page 20, and place checkmarks in the A column beside Allen's explanations for the causes of juvenile delinquency.
7. Return also to Unit Preview, question 3, on page 20, and place checkmarks in the A column beside Allen's suggestions for the solutions to juvenile delinquency.
8. Are Sullivan and Allen discussing the same kind of juveniles?

9. How effective is probation for guilty teenagers? Compare the views of Allen to those of Sullivan.

10. How much are Sullivan and Allen concerned with the right of society to be protected from becoming victims of teenage crimes?

11. To what degree would you agree with Judge Allen? Why?

COMPOSITION QUESTIONS

Listed below are the writing questions. Choose one and write an essay that answers it. Whichever question you choose, think of the person who will read your answer. The question may tell who your audience is. If not, think of a person you know and respect—preferably your instructor or a fellow student who will read your essay. Try to convince that person to believe you.

Bring in useful details from the selection(s) you have read and perhaps other incidents you know of. For ideas, review your answers to questions in the Preview and Reading Steps. When you first refer to a reading, give its title (in quotation marks) and the author's full name. Also, give the full name of anyone featured in the article the first time you mention that person.

Note: If you are assigned to write a one-paragraph essay, think of your answer to the question, and list several key points you could make to support your answer. Then choose just one of the points and explain it in detail.

1. Judge Milton Allen argues that society overprotects juvenile offenders by maintaining secrecy about their records. Analyze the issues involved; agree and/or disagree with this point.

2. Judge Milton Allen argues that probation is no longer an effective means of dealing with juvenile crime. Analyze the issues involved; agree and/or disagree with this point.

3. Mercer Sullivan suggests that the rights of society must be balanced equally with the needs of the offender. Analyze the issues involved; agree and/or disagree with this point.

4. Judge Milton Allen suggests that juvenile offenders are unredeemable and will rarely straighten out. By contrast, Mercer Sullivan indicates that juvenile offenders often do reform. Compare their views and explain why you think one is more realistic than the other.

5. Many people believe that society deserves to know the records of offenders, both juvenile and adult. Analyze the issues involved; agree and/or disagree with the present policy of secrecy for all but the most serious crimes.

6. Some people may feel that Judge Allen's attitude toward juvenile offenders is too harsh. Analyze the issues involved; agree and/or disagree with this point.

7. According to an African saying, "It takes a village to raise a child." After reading Mercer Sullivan's and Milton Allen's views, we might take "a village" to mean either the juvenile's neighborhood or the justice system. Explain which one you think has the greater influence in reforming juveniles.

REVISION QUESTIONS

Once you have finished writing your essay, ask yourself the following questions.

1. Is there any statement the reader might not understand?
2. Is there any statement that might offend the reader?
3. Is there anything that's not very convincing?
4. Have I changed the subject and then changed it back again?
5. Have I said the same thing twice?
6. Do I want to try using any feature of style I've seen in the reading selection?

EDITING QUESTIONS

Once you've made changes, ask someone else to read your essay. Change it again as needed. Then read your essay out loud and answer the following questions.

1. Does every sentence make sense?
2. Does every sentence use the kind of language that most people consider "good English" these days? (*Hint:* Imagine a TV announcer reading it.)
3. Do the periods, commas, and other punctuation show the rise and fall of my voice?
4. Are the words spelled right?

If your instructor asks you to copy your paper over, proofread for copying errors before you hand it in.

UNIT
THREE

◆

Bystanders Witnessing a Crisis

PREVIEW STEPS FOR UNIT THREE

1. Have you seen or heard of incidents in which someone needed help right away? What did bystanders do? Why did they act as they did?

2. a. If you saw a murder being committed, what are some things you might do?

   b. What do you think most people would do?
      - ☐ run to the victim's rescue
      - ☐ shout or throw things to scare off the murderer
      - ☐ call the police
      - ☐ do nothing, assuming other witnesses would act
      - ☐ choose not to act, fearing the killer might harm them—then or later
      - ☐ choose not to get involved for fear of police or public notice
      - ☐ choose not to get involved to avoid the bother of going to court
      - ☐ freeze from indecision
      - ☐ other:_____

   c. Why might some people act differently than others do?

   d. Do you think people's decisions are affected by whether they live in a city?

3. a. Read the title of the first essay (page 37). Name the topic. (Who or what is this essay about?)

b. Now predict the main idea. (What is the main point the author wants to make about this topic?)

c. Read the first and last paragraphs. Revise your prediction if necessary. (*Note:* The main idea should sum up the smaller ideas of the essay.)

4. Some words from the essay are listed below, accompanied by quotations. Mark any words you do not know and make an educated guess about their meanings using the context supplied by the quotations—and possibly Appendix A, Word Parts, on page 287. You may want to work with a small group of classmates.

abduction "It was a massacre," said [the police commissioner], adding that the victims had come upon an "*abduction* or *altercation*."

altercation See above quotation.

5. Now read the following essay. As you read, jot down any questions that occur to you.

(*Note:* Question 6 appears after the essay.)

Triple Slaying Probed

New York (AP)—A man trying to force a woman into a van shouted   1
"What did you see?" at three men picking up their cars in a parking lot, then chased them down one by one and shot them in the head at close range, killing them, police said.

    With the woman slumped inside, the gunman drove the van   2
down a winding ramp and left the lot, police said, quoting a witness who hid under a car. Police were searching for the van early today.

"It was a massacre," said Deputy Police Commissioner Alice   3
McGillion, adding that the victims had come upon an "abduction or
altercation."

The witness said the three men, all technicians at a nearby CBS   4
television network studio, were heading to their cars at dusk Monday
when they saw a man struggling with a woman in the parking lot,
which is atop a pier that juts into the Hudson River, Chief of Detectives James T. Sullivan said Monday.

The three approached and the man asked what they had seen,   5
but without waiting for an answer, he drew a pistol and shot the first
victim in the back of the head as the man started to flee, the witness,
also a CBS employee, said.

The gunman chased the other two around parked cars and   6
across the lot and killed them by shooting each behind the right ear.

"It appears as though they were coming to the assistance of the   7
woman who was being accosted," Sullivan said of the three victims—
Leo A. Kuranuki of Great Neck, N.Y., and Edward M. Benford of
Clifton, N.J., both managers of studio maintenance, and Robert W.
Schulze of Bergen County, N.J., a technician.

One of the victims lay with his car keys clutched in his hand,   8
the detective said.

Police said the woman, whom they could not identify, may have   9
been injured. There was blood near the spot where the van had
stood, Sullivan said, and the witness, who escaped unnoticed by the
gunman, reported seeing her slumped inside the late-model van.

A scarf, sunglasses, a plastic headband, and a pair of high-   10
heeled shoes were found, left behind after the woman's struggle with
the gunman, police said.

The victims had just left work at the CBS Broadcast Center a   11
few blocks away and were approaching their own cars at about 6
p.m. on the roof of Pier 92, which stands in a waterfront area where
cruise ships dock.

After the gunman shot the first victim, the gunman chased the   12
two other CBS employees as they fled toward the river end of the
pier, which is 75 feet wide and has spaces for 700 cars. It was not
known why the victims fled toward the lot's river end, which has no
exit.

The gunman caught up with the second victim and shot him,   13
apparently also at point-blank range, about 30 feet from the first victim. The gunman caught the third man near a waist-high concrete

wall at the end of the pier, about 100 feet from the first victim. The third victim also was believed to have been shot at close range.

Police also found three .22-caliber shell casings near the bodies,   14 apparently from the handgun used to kill the men.

6. State the essay's main idea in your own words. Compare it to your prediction of the main idea. (*Note:* The main idea should sum up the smaller ideas of the essay.)

PREVIEW STEPS FOR "37 WHO SAW MURDER DIDN'T CALL THE POLICE"

1. a. Read the title of the second essay (page 40). Name the topic. (Who or what is this essay about?)

   b. Now predict the main idea. (What is the main point the author wants to make about this topic?)

   c. Read the first and last paragraphs of the essay. Revise your prediction if necessary. (*Note:* The main idea should sum up the smaller ideas of the essay.)

2. What in the author's background may have led him to the main idea? (See author's background, below title.)

3. Some words from the essay are listed below, accompanied by quotations. Mark any words you do not know and make an educated guess about their meanings using the context supplied by the quotations—

and possibly Appendix A, Word Parts, on page 287. You may want to work with a small group of classmates.

shrouded "At night the quiet neighborhood is *shrouded* in the slumbering darkness. . . ."

distraught "Today witnesses . . . find it difficult to explain why they didn't call the police. . . . A *distraught* woman, wiping her hands on her apron, said, 'I didn't want my husband to get involved.' "

4. At the end of the Preview, you may want to go over any new features of style that occur in the following reading selection. You will need to know the terms *metaphor, irony of situation, irony of wording, restraint,* and *symbol.* For help, see Appendix B, Guide to Literary Terms (page 291), with accompanying exercises on individual features.

5. Before reading "37 Who Saw Murder Didn't Call Police," turn to pages 44–45 and skim the Reading Questions. Then read the essay to find answers to these questions. As you read, jot down any questions that occur to you.

37 Who Saw Murder Didn't Call the Police

Martin Gansberg

Martin Gansberg (1920–1995) lived in the New York area all his life except for a three-year assignment in Paris. After receiving a Bachelor of Social Sciences degree, he joined The New York Times, *where he served as a reporter and later as assistant managing editor. He also taught journalism at Fairleigh Dickinson University for more than 20 years and wrote for several magazines, including* Catholic Digest, Diplomat, *and* Facts. *The article below won wide recognition, including three special awards.*

Apathy at Stabbing of Queens Woman Shocks Inspector

For more than half an hour 38 respectable, law-abiding citizens in   1
Queens watched a killer stalk and stab a woman in three separate attacks in Kew Gardens.

Twice the sound of their voices and the sudden glow of their   2
bedroom lights interrupted him and frightened him off. Each time he
returned, sought her out and stabbed her again. Not one person tele-
phoned the police during the assault; one witness called after the
woman was dead.

That was two weeks ago today. But Assistant Chief Inspector   3
Frederick M. Lussen, in charge of the borough's detectives and a veteran of 25 years of homicide investigations, is still shocked.

He can give a matter-of-fact recitation of many murders. But   4
the Kew Gardens slaying baffles him—not because it is a murder,
but because the "good people" failed to call the police.

"As we have reconstructed the crime," he said, "the assailant   5
had three chances to kill this woman during a 35-minute period. He
returned twice to complete the job. If we had been called when he
first attacked, the woman might not be dead now."

This is what the police say happened beginning at 3:20 A.M. in   6
the staid, middle-class, tree-lined Austin Street area:

Twenty-eight-year-old Catherine Genovese, who was called   7
Kitty by almost everyone in the neighborhood, was returning home
from her job as manager of a bar in Hollis. She parked her red Fiat in
a lot adjacent to the Kew Gardens Long Island Rail Road Station,
facing Mowbray Place. Like many residents of the neighborhood, she
had parked there day after day since her arrival from Connecticut a
year ago, although the railroad frowns on the practice.

She turned off the lights of her car, locked the door and started   8
to walk the 100 feet to the entrance of her apartment at 82-70 Austin
Street, which is in a Tudor building, with stores on the first floor and
apartments on the second.

The entrance to the apartment is in the rear of the building be-   9
cause the front is rented to retail stores. At night the quiet neighborhood is shrouded in the slumbering darkness that marks most residential areas.

Miss Genovese noticed a man at the far end of the lot, near a   10
seven-story apartment house at 82-40 Austin Street. She halted.
Then, nervously, she headed up Austin Street toward Lefferts Boule-

vard, where there is a call box to the 102d Police Precinct in nearby Richmond Hill.

"He Stabbed Me!"

She got as far as a street light in front of a bookstore before the man 11 grabbed her. She screamed. Lights went on in the 10-story apartment house at 82-67 Austin Street, which faces the bookstore. Windows slid open and voices punctured the early-morning stillness.

Miss Genovese screamed: "Oh, my God, he stabbed me! Please 12 help me! Please help me!"

From one of the upper windows, in the apartment house, a man 13 called down: "Let that girl alone!"

The assailant looked up at him, shrugged and walked down 14 Austin Street toward a white sedan parked a short distance away. Miss Genovese struggled to her feet.

Lights went out. The killer returned to Miss Genovese, now try- 15 ing to make her way around the side of the building by the parking lot to get to her apartment. The assailant stabbed her again.

"I'm dying!" she shrieked. "I'm dying!" 16

A City Bus Passed

Windows were opened again, and lights went on in many apart- 17 ments. The assailant got into his car and drove away. Miss Genovese staggered to her feet. A city bus, Q-10, the Lefferts Boulevard line to Kennedy International Airport, passed. It was 3:35 A.M.

The assailant returned. By then, Miss Genovese had crawled to 18 the back of the building, where the freshly painted brown doors to the apartment house held out hope of safety. The killer tried the first door; she wasn't there. At the second door, 82-62 Austin Street, he saw her slumped on the floor at the foot of the stairs. He stabbed her a third time—fatally.

It was 3:50 by the time the police received their first call, from a 19 man who was a neighbor of Miss Genovese. In two minutes they were at the scene. The neighbor, a 70-year-old woman and another woman were the only persons on the street. Nobody else came forward.

The man explained that he had called the police after much de-   20
liberation. He had phoned a friend in Nassau County for advice and
then he had crossed the roof of the building to the apartment of the
elderly woman to get her to make the call.

"I didn't want to get involved," he sheepishly told the police.   21

Suspect Is Arrested

Six days later, the police arrested Winston Moseley, a 29-year-old   22
business-machine operator, and charged him with the homicide.
Moseley had no previous record. He is married, has two children and
owns a home at 13319 Sutter Avenue, South Ozone Park, Queens.
On Wednesday, a court committed him to Kings County Hospital
for psychiatric observation.

When questioned by the police, Moseley also said that he had   23
slain Mrs. Annie May Johnson, 24, of 146-12 133rd Avenue, Jamaica,
on Feb. 29 and Barbara Kralik, 15, of 174-17 140th Avenue, Spring-
field Gardens, last July. In the Kralik case, the police are holding
Alvin L. Mitchell, who is said to have confessed to that slaying.

The police stressed how simple it would have been to have got-   24
ten in touch with them. "A phone call," said one of the detectives,
"would have done it." The police may be reached by dialing "0" for
operator or SPring 7-3100.

Today witnesses from the neighborhood, which is made up of   25
one-family homes in the $35,000 to $60,000 range with the exception
of the two apartment houses near the railroad station, find it difficult
to explain why they didn't call the police.

A housewife, knowingly if quite casually, said, "We thought it   26
was a lover's quarrel." A husband and wife both said, "Frankly, we
were afraid." They seemed aware of the fact that events might have
been different. A distraught woman, wiping her hands on her apron,
said, "I didn't want my husband to get involved."

One couple, now willing to talk about that night, said they   27
heard the first screams. The husband looked thoughtfully at the
bookstore where the killer first grabbed Miss Genovese.

"We went to the window to see what was happening," he said,   28
"but the light from our bedroom made it difficult to see the street."
The wife, still apprehensive, added: "I put out the light and we were
able to see better."

Asked why they hadn't called the police, she shrugged and   29
replied: "I don't know."

A man peeked out from a slight opening in the doorway to his   30
apartment and rattled off an account of the killer's second attack.
Why hadn't he called the police at the time? "I was tired," he said
without emotion. "I went back to bed."

It was 4:25 A.M. when the ambulance arrived for the body of   31
Miss Genovese. It drove off. "Then," a solemn police detective said,
"the people came out."

READING QUESTIONS FOR "37 WHO SAW MURDER DIDN'T CALL THE POLICE"

Main Idea

1. State the essay's main idea in your own words. Compare it to your prediction of the main idea. (*Note:* The main idea should sum up the smaller ideas of the essay.)

Organization

2. a. Where in the essay is the main idea found?

   b. Why has the author placed the main idea there?

3. In what order are the paragraphs arranged? (Underline one.) Time / Least to most important / Most to least important / Simple listing / Logic: cause and effect / Other logic / Other

Style

4. How formal is the essay? (Circle your choice.)

   [Informal—1—2—3—4—5—6—7—8—9—10—Formal]

What indicators convinced you? (For a list of possible indicators and two benchmark essays, see Appendix F, The Formality Spectrum, on page 307.)

5. Where do you see the following features of style? List one or two examples of each with their paragraph numbers.

    Features (For definitions, see Appendix B, page 291.)

    a. irony of situation

    b. irony of wording

    c. metaphor

    d. symbols

    Content

6. Does the author propose any change? If so, what do you think would be the result of such a change?

7. Do you agree with the author's main idea? Why or why not?

If you have not already read the essay and answered the Reading Questions, be sure to do so before you proceed.

COMPOSITION QUESTIONS

Listed below are the writing questions. Choose one and write an essay that answers it. Whichever question you choose, think of the person who will read your answer. The question may tell who your audience is. If not, think of a person you know and respect—preferably your instructor or a fellow student who will read your essay. Try to convince that person to believe you.

Bring in useful details from the selection(s) you have read and perhaps other incidents you know of. For ideas, review your answers to questions in the Preview and Reading Steps. When you first refer to a reading, give its title (in quotation marks) and the author's full name. Also, give the full name of anyone featured in the article the first time you mention that person.

Note: If you are assigned to write a one-paragraph essay, think of your answer to the question, and list several key points you could make to support your answer. Then choose just one of the points and explain it in detail.

1. Why is it that some people, like the thirty-seven witnesses, don't get involved and others, like the thirty-eighth, do? Consider some of the following: emotional stability; physical strength; background (upbringing, education, and training); previous experience in a crisis, either as a victim or as a rescuer; seeing or hearing of someone else's experience; reasons to avoid the police; and anything else you think is important.

2. If you had been Kitty's neighbor and knew her slightly, do you think you would have acted differently from the 37 witnesses who did not act? Consider some of the variables in question 1.

3. Write to a person who would choose not to assist someone else in distress. Imagine his reasons. Argue that he should become a more involved sort of person. Remember that he may be on the defensive;

if you suggest, for example, that he is a bad person, he may tune you out. What reasoning would appeal to this person?

4. Write to a person who would choose to help someone else in distress. Consider her reasons. Using evidence from "Triple Slaying Probed," argue that she should become more cautious and more self-protective. Remember that her beliefs may be part of her sense of who she is (a strong person or a moral person). Your appeal will have to fit her self-concept.

5. Imagine that Kitty Genovese's relatives are suing the 37 witnesses for "wrongful death," saying she would be alive today if they had intervened. You are defending one of the witnesses. Argue that he had good reasons not to get involved. You may want to use evidence from "Triple Slaying Probed."

6. Propose a plan for bystanders to use in responding to violence. The plan should offer a balance between risk to the bystander and risk to the victim. Show how your plan would fit the situations in both "Triple Slaying Probed" and "37 Who Saw Murder Didn't Call the Police."

7. Explain what psychologists call the "bystander effect," in which people's sense of responsibility is diluted in a crowd. Discuss ways of reducing the bystander effect.

REVISION QUESTIONS

Once you have finished writing your essay, ask yourself the following questions.

1. Is there any statement the reader might not understand?
2. Is there any statement that might offend the reader?
3. Is there anything that's not very convincing?
4. Have I changed the subject and then changed it back again?
5. Have I said the same thing twice?
6. Do I want to try using any feature of style I've seen in the reading selection?

EDITING QUESTIONS

Once you've made changes, ask someone else to read your essay. Change it again as needed. Then read your essay out loud and answer the following questions.

1. Does every sentence make sense?
2. Does every sentence use the kind of language that most people consider "good English" these days? (*Hint:* Imagine a TV announcer reading it.)
3. Do the periods, commas, and other punctuation show the rise and fall of my voice?
4. Are the words spelled right?

If your instructor asks you to copy your paper over, proofread for copying errors before you hand it in.

UNIT
FOUR

---◆---

American Attitudes
Toward Aging

PREVIEW STEPS FOR UNIT FOUR

1. a. You probably know several people who are over 65 years old. Think of the three you know best. Jot down their initials to the left of the three numbers below. Then beside each number, write three words that describe that person.

1. _____   _____   _____
2. _____   _____   _____
3. _____   _____   _____

   b. For the first person, did you write more positive (+) than negative (–) words—or the reverse? At the left of that person's number write a + or – sign. Now label the other two people you listed.

2. Sometimes people are treated in a special way because of their age. Choose one of the three people above and write about a time when that person was treated with extra respect or disrespect. Would a young person ever be treated that way?

3. a. Read the title of the first essay (page 51). Name the topic. (Who or what is this essay about?)

   b. Now predict the main idea. (What is the main point the author wants to make about this topic?)

   c. Read the first and last paragraphs. Revise your prediction if necessary. (*Note:* The main idea should sum up the smaller ideas of the essay.)

4. Some words from the essay are listed below, accompanied by quotations. Mark any words you do not know and make an educated guess about their meanings using the context supplied by the quotations—and possibly Appendix A, Word Parts, on page 287. You may want to work with a small group of classmates.

radically "The territory of the 50s, 60s, and beyond is changing so *radically* that it now opens up whole new stages of life. . . ."

legions ". . . the number of Europeans over 60 has risen by half over the past 30 years, and their *legions* will swell by half again in the next 30 years."

disorientation "This reality does not easily compute with our old timetables. Along with any surprise, of course, comes *disorientation. . . .*"

serial "Young men are likely to have two marriages. *Serial* families will be the norm."

5. Now read the following essay. As you read, jot down any questions that occur to you.

(*Note:* Question 6 appears after the essay.)

Am I an Adult Yet?

Gail Sheehy

Middle age has already been pushed far into the 50s—if it is acknowledged at all today. The territory of the 50s, 60s, and beyond is changing so radically that it now opens up whole new stages of life that are nothing like what our parents or grandparents experienced.   1

Fifty is now what 40 used to be.   2

Sixty is now what 50 used to be.   3

Europeans, just like Americans, are marrying later, having fewer children, and living longer. A European Community study found that the number of Europeans over 60 has risen by half over the past 30 years, and their legions will swell by half again in the next 30 years.   4

Certain pacesetters among the 45+ population are already ea-   5
gerly remaking themselves to start again, sensing that they are probably going to live far longer than their parents. And they're right.
For the first time in the history of the world most people in advanced societies can expect to live into the long late afternoon of
life. Two-thirds of the total gains in life expectancy accomplished
since the human species emerged have been made in this century
alone! . . . [R]ecent experiments have shattered our common notions about life expectancy. Scientists have uncovered the first evidence suggesting that there may be no inborn limit to how old people can grow. The new research, led by James Carey of the
University of California at Davis and James Vaupel of Duke University, suggests that given good health practices, the current life expectancy of about 75 years may rise to 90 and 100 in the foreseeable
future.

With luck, then, once baby boomers pass 45, another whole   6
adult lifetime lies before them: 30, 40, even 50 years. This reality does
not easily compute with our old timetables. Along with any surprise,
of course, comes disorientation and a certain amount of anxiety. We
now have not one but three adult lives to be anticipated, prepared
for, mapped out. For clarity of discussion, I have given titles to these
overarching periods: provisional adulthood (18 to 30), first adulthood (30 to 45), and second adulthood (45 to 85+).

Each presents its own struggles and begs for a new dream.   7
The ages at which we enter and leave each period will vary; it is the
very presence and possibilities of these three different territories of
the adult life cycle that are important. It is likely that we will share
these three lives with different partners or journey through one or
more of them alone. Young men are likely to have two marriages.
Serial families will be the norm. A third partner, to share the mellow years after 55, is also increasingly common for a man, but he
often doesn't marry her. And all along, we have new opportunities
for development. Stop and recalculate. Imagine the day you will
turn 45 as the infancy of another life. It amounts to a second adulthood.

Have you asked yourself: What can you make of your next life?   8
Whom do you want to share it with, if anybody? What new ventures
or adventures can you now dare try? What old shells can you slough
off? Are there fatal traps you should avoid? What about those ex-

ploratory spiritual journeys you keep putting off? How can you best give back? What investments in learning and changes in lifestyle are you willing to undertake to make all these extra years ahead livable? How long do you *want* to live?

6. State the essay's main idea in your own words. Compare it to your prediction of the main idea. (*Note:* The main idea should sum up the smaller ideas of the essay.)

PREVIEW STEPS FOR "OLD BEFORE HER TIME"

1. a. Read the title of the second essay (page 55). Name the topic. (Who or what is this essay about?)

   b. Now predict the main idea. (What is the main point the author wants to make about this topic?)

   c. Read the first and last paragraphs. Revise your prediction if necessary. (*Note:* The main idea should sum up the smaller ideas of the essay.)

2. What in the author's background may have led her to the main idea? (See author's background, below title.)

3. Some words from the essay are listed below, accompanied by quotations. Mark any words you do not know and make an educated guess about their meanings using the context supplied by the quotations—

and possibly Appendix A, Word Parts, on page 287. You may want to work with a small group of classmates.

donned "In all, she *donned* her costume more than two hundred times. . . ."

gerontology "They were all attending a *gerontology* conference . . . a throng of men and women who devoted their working lives to the elderly. . . ."

nonentity ". . . the room was filled with animated chatter. But no one was talking to Pat. . . . She began to feel like a total *nonentity*."

condescended " 'Just because I looked different, people either *condescended* or they totally dismissed me.' "

manipulate ". . . she struggled to hold her threadbare coat closed with one hand and *manipulate* her cane with the other."

anathema ". . . she was stunned to find others who had stayed together unhappily—because divorce was still an *anathema* in their middle years."

nattily "He was a thin man, rather *nattily* dressed, with a hat that he graciously tipped. . . ."

abysmally "Society often did treat the elderly *abysmally*. . . . they were sometimes ignored, sometimes victimized, sometimes poor and frightened. . . ."

4. At the end of the Preview, you may want to go over any new features of style that occur in the following reading selection. You will need to know the terms *cliché, metaphor,* and *simile.* For help, see Appendix B, Guide to Literary Terms (page 291), with accompanying exercises on individual features.

5. Before reading "Old Before Her Time" turn to pages 62–64 and skim the Reading Questions. Then read the essay to find answers to these questions. As you read, jot down any questions that occur to you.

Old Before Her Time

Katherine Barrett

Katherine Barrett (1954–) was a contributing editor and senior editor at Ladies' Home Journal, *where she worked from 1980 to 1997. A graduate of the Medill School of Journalism at Northwestern University, she has been a newspaper reporter and has written for many major national magazines. She and her husband Richard Greene work as collaborative freelance writers. They are columnists for* Glamour *magazine and authors of* The Man Behind the Magic, *a biography of Walt Disney.*

This is the story of an extraordinary voyage in time, and of a young woman who devoted three years to a singular experiment.   1

In 1979, Patty Moore—then aged twenty-six—transformed herself for the first of many times into an eighty-five-year-old woman. Her object was to discover firsthand the problems, joys, and frustrations of the elderly. She wanted to know for herself what it's like to live in a culture of youth and beauty when your hair is gray, your skin is wrinkled, and no men turn their heads as you pass.   2

Her time machine was a makeup kit. Barbara Kelly, a friend and professional makeup artist, helped Patty pick out a wardrobe and showed her how to use latex to create wrinkles, and wrap Ace bandages to give the impression of stiff joints. "It was peculiar," Patty recalls, as she relaxes in her New York City apartment. "Even the first few times I went out I realized that I wouldn't have to act that much. The more I was perceived as elderly by others, the more 'elderly' I actually became. . . . I imagine that's just what happens to people who really are old."   3

What motivated Patty to make her strange journey? Partly her career—as an industrial designer, Patty often focuses on the needs of the elderly. But the roots of her interest are also deeply personal. Ex-   4 tremely close to her own grandparents—particularly her maternal grandfather, now ninety—and raised in a part of Buffalo, New York, where there was a large elderly population, Patty always drew comfort and support from the older people around her.

When her own marriage ended in 1979 and her life seemed to   5
be falling apart, she dove into her "project" with all her soul. In all, she donned her costume more than two hundred times in fourteen different states.

Here is the remarkable story of what she found.   6

Columbus, Ohio, May 1979

Leaning heavily on her cane, Pat Moore stood alone in the middle of   7
a crowd of young professionals. They were all attending a gerontology conference, and the room was filled with animated chatter.

But no one was talking to Pat. In a throng of men and women   8
who devoted their working lives to the elderly, she began to feel like a total nonentity. "I'll get us all some coffee," a young man told a group of women next to her.

"What about me?" thought Pat. "If I were young, they would   9
be offering me coffee, too."

It was a bitter thought at the end of a disappointing day—a day   10
that marked Patty's first appearance as "the old woman." She had planned to attend the gerontology conference anyway, and almost as a lark decided to see how professionals would react to an old person in their midst.

Now, she was angry. All day she had been ignored . . . counted   11
out in a way she had never experienced before.

She didn't understand. Why didn't people help her when they   12
saw her struggling to open a heavy door? Why didn't they include her in conversations? Why did the other participants seem almost embarrassed by her presence at the conference—as if it were somehow inappropriate that an old person should be professionally active?

And so, eighty-five-year-old Pat Moore learned her first lesson: 13
The old are often ignored.

"I discovered that people really do judge a book by its cover,"   14
Patty says today. "Just because I looked different, people either condescended or they totally dismissed me.

"Later, in stores, I'd get the same reaction. A clerk would turn 15
to someone younger and wait on her first. It was as if he assumed
that I—the older woman—could wait because I didn't have anything
better to do."

New York City, October 1979

Bent over her cane, Pat walked slowly toward the edge of the park. 16
She had spent the day sitting on a bench with friends, but now dusk
was falling and her friends had all gone home.

She looked around nervously at the deserted area and tried to 17
move faster, but her joints were stiff. It was then that she heard the
barely audible sound of sneakered feet approaching and the kids'
voices.

"Grab her, man." "Get her purse." Suddenly an arm was 18
around her throat and she was dragged back, knocked off her feet.

She saw only a blur of sneakers and blue jeans, heard the 19
sounds of mocking laughter, felt fists pummeling her—on her back,
her legs, her breasts, her stomach. "Oh, God," she thought, using her
arms to protect her head and curling herself into a ball. "They're
going to kill me. I'm going to die. . . ."

Then, as suddenly as the boys attacked, they were gone. And 20
Patty was left alone, struggling to rise. The boys' punches had broken
the latex makeup on her face, the fall had disarranged her wig, and
her whole body ached. (Later she would learn that she had fractured
her left wrist, an injury that took two years to heal completely.) Sob-
bing, she left the park and hailed a cab to return home. Again the
thought struck her: What if I really lived in the gray ghetto . . . what
if I couldn't escape to my nice safe home . . . ?

Lesson number two: The fear of crime is paralyzing. 21

"I really understand now why the elderly become homebound," 22
the young woman says as she recalls her ordeal today. "When something like this happens, the fear just doesn't go away. And the elderly
often can't afford to move if the area in which they live deteriorates,
becomes unsafe. I met people like this and they were imprisoned by
their fear. That's when the bolts go on the door. That's when people
starve themselves because they're afraid to go to the grocery store."

New York City, February 1980

It was a slushy, gray day and Pat had laboriously descended four   23
flights of stairs from her apartment to go shopping. Once outside,
she struggled to hold her threadbare coat closed with one hand and
manipulate her cane with the other. Splotches of snow made the
street difficult for anyone to navigate, but for someone hunched
over, as she was, it was almost impossible.

The curb was another obstacle. The slush looked ankle-deep—   24
and what was she to do? Jump over it? Slowly, she worked her way
around to a drier spot, but the crowds were impatient to move. A
woman with packages jostled her as she rushed past, causing Pat to
nearly lose her balance.

If I really were old, I would have fallen, she thought. Maybe   25
broken something. On another day, a woman had practically
knocked her over by letting go of a heavy door as Pat tried to enter a
coffee shop. Then there were the revolving doors. How could you
push them without strength? And how could you get up and down
stairs, on and off a bus, without risking a terrible fall?

Lesson number three: If small, thoughtless deficiencies in de-   26
sign were corrected, life would be so much easier for older people.

It was no surprise to Patty that the "built" environment is   27
often inflexible. But even she didn't realize the extent of the problems, she admits. "It was a terrible feeling. I never realized how difficult it is to get off a curb if your knees don't bend easily. Or the
helpless feeling you get if your upper arms aren't strong enough to
open a door.

"You know, I just felt so vulnerable—as if I was at the mercy of   28
every barrier or rude person I encountered."

Ft. Lauderdale, Florida, May 1980

Pat met a new friend while shopping and they decided to continue   29
their conversation over a sundae at a nearby coffee shop. The woman
was in her late seventies, "younger" than Pat, but she was obviously
reaching out for help.

Slowly, her story unfolded.   30

"My husband moved out of our bedroom," the woman said   31
softly, fiddling with her coffee cup and fighting back tears. "He
won't touch me anymore.

"And when he gets angry at me for being stupid, he'll even sometimes . . ." The woman looked down, embarrassed to go on.

Pat took her hand.

"He hits me . . . he gets so mean."

"Can't you tell anyone?" Pat asked. "Can't you tell your son?"

"Oh, no!" the woman almost gasped. "I would never tell the children; they absolutely adore him."

Lesson number four: Even a fifty-year-old marriage isn't necessarily a good one.

While Patty met many loving and devoted elderly couples, she was stunned to find others who had stayed together unhappily—because divorce was still an anathema in their middle years. "I met women who secretly wished their husbands dead, because after so many years they just ended up full of hatred."

Patty pauses thoughtfully and continues. "I guess what really made an impression on me, the real eye-opener, was that so many of these older women had the same problems as women twenty, thirty, or forty. Problems with men . . . problems with the different roles that are expected of them. These issues aren't age-related. They affect everyone."

Clearwater, Florida, January 1981

She heard the children laughing, but she didn't realize at first that they were laughing at her.

On this day, as on several others, Pat had shed the clothes of a middle-income woman for the rags of a bag lady. She wanted to see the extremes of the human condition, what it was like to be old and poor, and outside traditional society as well. Now, tottering down the sidewalk, she was most concerned with the cold, since her layers of ragged clothing did little to ease the chill.

She had spent the afternoon rummaging through garbage cans, loading her shopping bags with bits of debris, and she was stiff and tired.

Suddenly, she saw that four little boys, five or six years old, were moving up on her. And then she felt the sting of the pebbles they were throwing.

She quickened her pace to escape, but another handful of gravel hit her and the laughter continued.

They're using me as a target, she thought, horror-stricken. They don't even think of me as a person.

Lesson number five: Social class affects every aspect of an older   46
person's existence.

"I found out that class is a very important factor when you're   47
old," says Patty. "It was interesting. That same day, I went back to
my hotel and got dressed as a wealthy woman, another role that I occasionally took. Outside the hotel, a little boy of about seven asked if
I would go shelling with him. We walked along the beach, and he
reached out to hold my hand.

"I knew he must have a grandmother who walked with a cane,   48
because he was so concerned about me and my footing. 'Don't put
your cane there, the sand's wet,' he'd say. He really took responsibility for my welfare.

"There's no question that money does make life easier for older   49
people, not only because it gives them a more comfortable life-style,
but because it makes others treat them with greater respect."

New York City, May 1981

One spring day she found herself sitting with three women, all wid-   50
ows, and the conversation turned to the few available men around.

"It's been a long time since anyone hugged me," one woman   51
complained.

Another agreed. "Isn't that the truth. I need a hug, too."   52

It was a favorite topic, Pat found—the lack of touching left in   53
these women's lives, the lack of hugging, the lack of men.

In the last two years, she had found out herself how it felt to   54
walk down Fifth Avenue and know that no men were turning to look
after her.

Or how it felt to look at models in magazines or store mannequins   55
and know that those gorgeous clothes were just not made for her.

She hadn't realized before just how much casual attention was   56
paid to her because she was young and pretty.

She hadn't realized it until it stopped.   57

Lesson number six: You never grow old emotionally. You al-   58
ways need to feel loved.

"It's not surprising that everyone needs love and touching and   59
holding," says Patty. "But I think some people feel that you reach a point
in your life when you accept that those intimate feelings are in the past.

"That's wrong. These women were still interested in sex. But more than that, they—like everyone—needed to be hugged and touched.

"Yet, I also saw that there are people who are afraid to touch an old person . . . they were afraid to touch me. It's as if they think old age is a disease and it's catching. They think that something might rub off on them."

New York City, September 1981

He was a thin man, rather nattily dressed, with a hat that he graciously tipped at Pat as he approached the bench where she sat.

"Might I join you?" he asked jauntily.

Pat told him he would be welcome and he offered her one of the dietetic hard candies that he carried in a crumpled paper bag.

As the afternoon passed, they got to talking . . . about the beautiful buds on the trees and the world around them and the past.

"Life's for the living, my wife used to tell me," he said. "When she took sick she made me promise her that I wouldn't waste a moment. But the first year after she died, I just sat in the apartment. I didn't want to see anyone, talk to anyone or go anywhere. I missed her so much."

He took a handkerchief from his pocket and wiped his eyes, and they sat in silence. Then he slapped his leg to break the mood and change the subject. He asked Pat about herself, and described his life alone. He belonged to a "senior center" now, and went on trips and had lots of friends. Life did go on.

Lesson number seven: Life does go on . . . as long as you're flexible and open to change.

"That man really meant a lot to me, even though I never saw him again," says Patty, her eyes wandering toward the gray wig that now sits on a wigstand on the top shelf of her bookcase. "He was a real old-fashioned gentleman, yet not afraid to show his feelings—as so many men my age are."

Society often did treat the elderly abysmally . . . they were sometimes ignored, sometimes victimized, sometimes poor and frightened, but so many of them were survivors. They had lived through two world wars, the Depression and into the computer age. "If there was one lesson to learn, one lesson that I'll take with me into my old age, it's that you've got to be flexible," Patty says. "I saw my friend in the park, managing after the loss of his wife, and I met countless other people who picked themselves up after something bad—or even something catastrophic—happened. I'm not worried about them. I'm worried about the others who shut themselves away. It's funny, but seeing these two extremes helped me recover from the trauma in my own life, to pull my life together."

Today, Patty is back to living the life of a single thirty-year-old,   71
and she rarely dons her costumes anymore. "I must admit, though. I do still think a lot about aging," she says. "I look in the mirror and I begin to see wrinkles, and then I realize that I won't be able to wash those wrinkles off."

READING QUESTIONS FOR "OLD BEFORE HER TIME"

Main Idea

1. State the essay's main idea in your own words. Compare it to your prediction of the main idea. (*Note:* The main idea should sum up the smaller ideas of the essay.)

Organization

2. a. Where in the essay is the main idea found?

   b. Why has the author placed the main idea there?

3. In what order are the paragraphs arranged? (Underline one.) Time / Least to most important / Most to least important / Simple listing / Logic: cause and effect / Other logic / Other

Style

4. How formal is the essay? (Circle your choice.)

   [Informal—1—2—3—4—5—6—7—8—9—10—Formal]

What indicators convinced you? (For a list of possible indicators and two benchmark essays, see Appendix F, The Formality Spectrum, on page 307.)

5. Where do you see the following features of style? List one or two examples of each with their paragraph numbers.

Features (For definitions, see Appendix B, page 291.)

a. cliché

b. metaphor

c. simile

6. In each section, where does the author place the "lesson" sentence? (For example, see "Lesson number two: The fear of crime is paralyzing.") Why?

7. The author often uses a string of one- or two-sentence paragraphs. What is the effect? And do you like it?

Content

8. What are the seven lessons?

9. Does the author propose any change? If so, what do you think would be the result of such a change?

10. Do you agree with the author's main idea? Why or why not?

11. Can you really find out about other people's problems by playing a role?

If you have not already read the essay and answered the Reading Questions, be sure to do so before you proceed.

COMPOSITION QUESTIONS*

Listed below are the writing questions. Choose one and write an essay that answers it. Whichever question you choose, think of the person who will read your answer. The question may tell who your audience is. If not, think of a person you know and respect—preferably your instructor or a fellow student who will read your essay. Try to convince that person to believe you.

Bring in useful details from the selection(s) you have read and perhaps other incidents you know of. For ideas, review your answers to questions in the Preview and Reading Steps. When you first refer to a reading, give its title (in quotation marks) and the author's full name. Also, give the full name of anyone featured in the article the first time you mention that person.

Note: If you are assigned to write a one-paragraph essay, think of your answer to the question, and list several key points you could make to support your answer. Then choose just one of the points and explain it in detail.

1. Many people would rather care for a helpless baby than for a helpless but alert old person. What does their reaction say about their feelings

_____

*In referring to "Old Before Her Time," identify both the author (Katherine Barrett) and the woman she describes (Patty Moore).

toward aging or about old people's feelings toward the stage they are in? In answering, consider Sheehy's positive portrait of the last stage of life and people's attitudes toward Patty Moore.

2. Consider the two essays' pictures of older people's lives in America. How are these pictures influenced by an older person's national/ethnic group or social class?

3. Sheehy says older people these days have many more years to look forward to than they once did, although she says these added years may be good or bad. Barrett paints a picture of disrespect toward older people that makes us wonder whether old people were given more respect in earlier times. Overall, is it better or worse to be an old person in America today than it was 30 years ago?

4. Changes in prevention and care of illness may change the picture presented by Sheehy or Barrett or both. Do you think life will be better or worse for older people in the future?

5. Compare the two essays in this unit. Use your own observations or experiences to show why one essay is more accurate than the other.

6. When you are 75, will you be more like the people in Sheehy's essay or the people in Barrett's? How much control do you have over the outcome?

7. Patty Moore learned several lessons about aging by playing the part of an 85-year-old. Sheehy, on the other hand, has already entered the third period she describes. In your opinion, how much can you tell about other people's problems by "walking in their footsteps" when you have not actually lived the experience?

8. Sheehy divides life into three periods. She describes "second adulthood" (the third period) as starting at roughly age 45. Yet she mentions "the mellow years after 55," suggesting that 55 is an important dividing line. And Barrett describes Patty Moore, when playing an 85-year-old, as having severe problems in getting around, suggesting that 55 and 85 may not belong in the same period. Based on Sheehy's and Barrett's essays, how would you divide adulthood into stages?

REVISION QUESTIONS

Once you have finished writing your essay, ask yourself the following questions.

1. Is there any statement the reader might not understand?
2. Is there any statement that might offend the reader?
3. Is there anything that's not very convincing?
4. Have I changed the subject and then changed it back again?
5. Have I said the same thing twice?
6. Do I want to try using any feature of style I've seen in the reading selection?

EDITING QUESTIONS

Once you've made changes, ask someone else to read your essay. Change it again as needed. Then read your essay out loud and answer the following questions.

1. Does every sentence make sense?
2. Does every sentence use the kind of language that most people consider "good English" these days? (*Hint:* Imagine a TV announcer reading it.)
3. Do the periods, commas, and other punctuation show the rise and fall of my voice?
4. Are the words spelled right?

If your instructor asks you to copy your paper over, proofread for copying errors before you hand it in.

UNIT
FIVE

Aggression in Sports

PREVIEW STEPS FOR UNIT FIVE

In response to questions 1 and 2, try these steps: Write your answers, talk them over with three or four classmates, and then discuss them with the whole class.

1. List at least three sports in each of the following areas.

Contact Sports	Sports That Are Supposed to Be Noncontact but Often Involve Contact	Noncontact Sports

2. a. Read the title of the first essay (page 69). Name the topic. (Who or what is this essay about?)

   b. Now predict the main idea. (What is the main point the author wants to make about this topic?)

   c. Read the first five short paragraphs and the last one. Revise your prediction if necessary. (*Note:* The main idea should sum up the smaller ideas of the essay.)

3. Some words from the essay are listed on page 69, accompanied by quotations. Mark any words you do not know and make an educated guess about their meanings using the context supplied by the quotations—and possibly Appendix A, Word Parts, on page 287. You may want to work with a small group of classmates.

resignation ". . . to break down the protection and reach the quarterback, to loom over him, seeing the last quick frantic turns of the passer's helmet before it ducks in *resignation* . . ."

4. Now read the following essay. As you read, jot down any questions that occur to you.

(*Note:* Question 5 appears after the essay.)

Mr. Hyde and Dr. Jekyll

George Plimpton

[Ed. note: Following are two excerpts from George Plimpton's book Paper Lion. *Plimpton is the "paper" football player who tells how he was given permission to practice with the Detroit Lions a number of years ago and to then go through a few plays during a game so that he could experience the life of a pro football player. The headings below and title above Plimpton's name are ours; the title was taken from one of the passages below.]*

Big Daddy Lipscomb

They were watching the rookies substituting at their positions. "That's crud," one of them said, gauging his replacement. "Look at that!" he said scornfully. Their attention was completely taken up by it. He pointed at some maneuver the rookie had made which was too subtle for me to catch.   1

I asked, "Will you straighten him out—whatever it is he did wrong?"   2

"You must be kidding," Brettschneider said. "They're after our jobs, boy."   3

"But they're your teammates—common cause," I said tentatively. I was startled.   4

"Crap," one of them said.   5

Wayne Walker pointed at the rookie who had taken over at his   6
position. "Look at Clark's stance," he said. "It's wrong for a linebacker. He's got his arms hanging down as he waits. When the line-
man busts through to him he's got to bring those hands up to stave
him off, which loses him half a second or so of motion. He should
wait with those hands up—all set to fend. . . ."

"But you won't tell him?" I asked.   7

"Hell no," said Schmidt. "He'll learn quick enough. He'll get   8
hit on his ass and he'll learn."

"That's the damnedest thing," I said.   9

Schmidt looked across. He could sense my disillusionment, par-   10
ticularly after the display of the regulars coming into the scrimmage to
help me. "I'll tell you," he said. "When I came up in 1953 the team was
hot off the 1952 championship. But it was a team getting on, long in the
tooth, and Buddy Parker traded some of the regulars to put in rookies
and first-year men. When he traded Flanagan, the middle linebacker, a
lot of the regulars broke down and *cried*, I want to tell you, and when I
took over his position they took it out on me as if I was responsible.
They wouldn't have anything to do with me. I went through six league
games as a regular and no one talked to me. I played the game, dressed,
and then I went home to my apartment and looked at the wall.

"Veterans don't love rookies," he went on. "It's as simple as   11
that. You always read in the paper that some young rookie coming
up says he couldn't've done it if it hadn't been for some ol' pappy-
guy veteran who took him aside and said: 'No, son, up here we do it
this way,' and then showing him. Well, that's crap, you'd better believe it. A regular, particularly an old-timer, will do almost anything
to hold on to his position short of murder. They say that Big Daddy
Lipscomb used to get into these horrible fights, close to *kill* these
guys during the training season when he was with Los Angeles, really
beat up on them, and everybody'd say, 'Boy, Big Daddy's got a mean
temper this year.' Then the coaches look around and find that cooler
than hell he'd been beating up on the guys trying for his position so
that finally there wasn't anybody at his position *but* Big Daddy."

Roger Brown

That provides the highest satisfaction—to break down the protection   12
and reach the quarterback, to loom over him, seeing the last quick

frantic turns of the passer's helmet before it ducks in resignation, and the quarterback's body begin to jackknife over the ball tucked in the belly for protection as Brown enfolds and drops him. Brown does not feel he has had a good game unless he has been able to do this once or twice during the afternoon.

"Well, what sort of pleasure is it?" I asked him. The Dinah   13
Washington records were going and Night Train Lane was lying on his belly on the next bed, watching them turn.

Brown shrugged.   14

"Well, what about rage?" I asked.   15

He blinked behind his spectacles. It was strange to think that   16
his vision was poor. I remembered him one night trying to slap a big moth that was hammering around the overhead light. He shouted, "Fly *still*," flailing at the moth with a big towel so wildly that he drove Night Train out of the room.

"No," he said. "I don't go around growling. But the feeling's   17
there. You know what I feel, Train," he said to Lane. "I think back on all the guys I know who have been injured, and I say to myself those guys across the line are trying to do it to me. Well, they aren't *going* to do it," he said.

Night Train nodded. "You got . . . er . . . a great communion to   18
get to the Hall of Fame," he said.

Brown stared briefly at him, and continued: "It's not hatred.   19
You feel deep you want to win. It feels good to get to the quarterback, but you never want to *disjoint* him. Mind, you want to let him know you're there. For sure. So I get plenty worked up. Home with the wife and then on the field, I'm two different people—like Mr. Hyde and Dr. Jekyll. On the field—" he began laughing—"I don't know that I'd like to meet myself on the field. . . . I mean I can think of other folks around that I'd *prefer* meeting."

5. State the essay's main idea in your own words. Compare it to your prediction of the main idea. (*Note:* The main idea should sum up the smaller ideas of the essay.)

6. The title of this essay is an allusion to a nineteenth-century book by Robert Louis Stevenson, *The Strange Case of Dr. Jekyll and Mr. Hyde*, about a man who was sometimes gentle but was at other times a

monster. Which of the two players is described as both a Mr. Hyde and a Dr. Jekyll?

7. a. What evidence does Plimpton give that a good football player must see his opponent as an opponent, not as a fellow sportsman?

   b. What statements of Plimpton's players show that they enjoy treating their opponents as opponents?

8. Pro football is a contact sport. How much roughness do you think is needed in order to keep pro football interesting to its fans?

PREVIEW STEPS FOR "A HUMANISTIC APPROACH TO SPORTS"

1. a. Read the title of the second essay (page 74). Name the topic. (Who or what is this essay about?)

   b. Now predict the main idea. (What is the main point the author wants to make about this topic?)

   c. Read the first and last paragraphs of the essay. Revise your prediction if necessary. (*Note:* The main idea should sum up the smaller ideas of the essay.)

2. What in the author's background may have led him to the main idea? (See author's background, below title.)

3. Some words from the essay are listed below, accompanied by quotations. Mark any words you do not know and make an educated guess about their meanings using the context supplied by the quotations— and possibly Appendix A, Word Parts, on page 287. You may want to work with a small group of classmates.

mayhem "[Negative remarks can] influence behavior in such a way as to lead to bloodshed and *mayhem*."

humanistic ". . . words having certain connotations may cause us to react in ways quite foreign to what we consider to be our usual *humanistic* behavior."

mutual "It is possible to experience this new dimension when players enter the court with a set of values based on *mutual* trust."

supersede "In the fun dimension the enjoyment of playing would *supersede* the strong desire to win at any cost, but the desire to win would not *wane*."

wane See above quotation.

antagonistic "Avoid *antagonistic* counterattacks."

disparaging ". . . in the fun dimension . . . participants are enjoying themselves. No harsh words are spoken. No *disparaging* remarks are voiced—about yourself or your *colleague*."

colleague See above quotation.

deleterious "To grow from a level at which the *deleterious* effects of anger, frustration, and regret ran rampant to the level of the fun dimension . . ."

aesthetic "As you play for fun . . . , a . . . more subtle transformation takes place . . . in what I call the '*aesthetic* dimension.' "

repertoire ". . . you try things you never tried before. . . . Your *repertoire* [pronounced *rep'* er twar'] of choices increases. You develop techniques and strategies . . ."

innovation "Spectators . . . delight in seeing the unexpected emerge . . . and at that time *innovation* is applauded."

dexterity ". . . a player's *dexterity* on the handball court and his execution of plays as 'poetry in motion.' "

4. At the end of the Preview, you may want to go over any new features of style that occur in the following reading selection. You will need to know the terms *cliché* and *jargon*. For help, see Appendix B, Guide to Literary Terms (page 291), with accompanying exercises on individual features.

5. Before reading "A Humanistic Approach to Sports" turn to pages 79–80 and skim the Reading Questions. Then read the essay to find answers to these questions. As you read, jot down any questions that occur to you.

A Humanistic Approach to Sports

Irving Simon

Irving Simon (1920–) graduated from UCLA in 1978 at the age of 58 with a B.A. in philosophy. Simon grew up in Brooklyn playing handball on any available wall. He did not compete at the national level until he was 40. As a handball player, he has, with the help of nine different partners, won 15 national doubles championships. In 1980 he won the National Invitational singles for ages 60 to 64. In 1982 he won the Super Golden doubles, partnered with his brother (also over 60). Simon is in the Handball

Published July 1983 by *The Humanist* magazine. Copyright © 1983 by the publisher, having since reverted to the author. Reprinted by permission of Irving Simon.

Hall of Fame. He no longer plays handball, although he continues to teach the sport.

"Tear 'em apart!" "Kill the bum!" "Murder the umpire!" 1

These are common remarks one may hear at various sporting 2
events. At the time they are made, they may seem innocent enough.
But let's not kid ourselves. They have been known to influence behavior in such a way as to lead to bloodshed and mayhem. Volumes
have been written about the way words affect us. It has been shown
that words having certain connotations may cause us to react in ways
quite foreign to what we consider to be our usual humanistic behavior. I see the term *opponent* as one of those words. Perhaps the time
has come to delete it from sports terminology.

The dictionary meaning of the term *opponent* is "adversary"; 3
"enemy"; "one who opposes your interests." Thus, when a player
meets an opponent, he or she may tend to treat that opponent as an
adversary, and therefore beating the enemy becomes the foremost
purpose for playing the game. At such times, winning may dominate
one's intellect, and every action, no matter how gross, may be considered justifiable. For example, in my favorite sport, handball, intentional hinders become routine, skip-balls and two-bounce plays are
argued, efforts are made to emotionally upset one's opponent, and
using every method possible to stall a game becomes a pastime. I recall an incident when a referee refused a player's request for a time
out for a glove change because he did not deem them wet enough.
The player proceeded to rub his gloves across his wet tee shirt and
then exclaimed, "Are they wet enough now?"

In the heat of battle, players have been observed to hurl themselves 4
across the court without considering the consequences that such a move
might have on anyone in their way. I have also witnessed a player reacting to his opponent's intentional and illegal blocking by deliberately hitting him with the ball as hard as he could during the course of play. Off
the court, they are good friends. Does that make any sense? It certainly
gives proof of a court attitude which is alien to normal behavior.

The Fun Dimension

In this age of "concerned awareness," I believe that it is time we ele- 5
vated the game of handball to the level where it belongs, thereby set-

ting an example to the rest of the sporting world. Replacing the term *opponent* with *associate* could be an ideal way to start.

The dictionary meaning of the term *associate* is "colleague"; 6 "friend"; "companion." Reflect a moment! You may soon see and possibly feel the difference in your reaction to the term *associate* rather than *opponent*. When you realize that your associate is the most important aspect of the game, because without him or her there is no game, it is no longer possible to think in terms of "one who is opposing your interests."

When you see yourself and your opponent as associates, a new 7 dimension to the game emerges. I like to think of it as the "fun dimension." All of us who are involved in the game know that there is something more one derives when playing than just the benefits associated with a physical workout. When referring to "fun," I am referring to that something which at times we may vaguely sense but which in actuality is the essence of what we look forward to when we suit up to play.

It is possible to experience this new dimension when players 8 enter the court with a set of values based on mutual trust. At that time a number of things will become evident. Bickering will not take up valuable time. Referees will be given every possible assistance in determining the accuracy of their calls so that the part they play will become more meaningful. Avoidable hinders will be at a minimum, and there will no longer be any need for the intentional hinder to remain part of the rules.

Friendly competition makes it possible to develop our skill and 9 improve our game in general without creating up-tight feelings. This is what may happen when playing for fun in a relaxed and trusting atmosphere. But many players believe that it is necessary to evoke the "killer instinct" in order to bring out one's best, and anything short of a psyched-up feeling would lead to a what's-the-difference-who-wins attitude. It is assumed that competitiveness would diminish. On the contrary, I maintain that mutual trust will heighten competitiveness. It puts responsibility on all players to do their best. Since your associate is dependent on you for the opportunity to compare and improve his or her game, you would be betraying a trust if you should "dog it." One would sense a hollow victory knowing that his or her associate was intentionally not playing up to par.

In the fun dimension the enjoyment of playing would supersede 10 the strong desire to win at any cost, but the desire to win would not wane. Every good play and volley would be pleasing to all players and spectators, who, in a way, are also participating. Sensing the "felt-relatedness" of the players, they may no longer feel a need to take sides. They may find themselves completely involved in watching the game for the game's sake.

You may ask, "How can I put myself in a position of trust when   11
it may not be mutual?" "How can I overcome the bad habits of those who do not read articles like this or who just don't give a damn?" I say, "Take a chance! Avoid antagonistic counterattacks." It may take time, but I sincerely believe that playing in the fun dimension is contagious. Your attitude will eventually be noticed by your associate, and he or she will want to join with you in making the new experience a joint adventure.

The Game as Art

When playing in the fun dimension, it is understood that the partici-   12
pants are enjoying themselves. No harsh words are spoken. No disparaging remarks are voiced—about yourself or your colleague. Smiles on the part of the participants acknowledge the use of a clever strategy. Jests are made about goofs, and even hearty laughter can be heard after associates end a long volley of trying to "out-fox" one another.

The underlying desire to play has more meaning now. Competi-   13
tion is seen as the basis for measuring your ability as a player, an opportunity to improve your skill, and a fundamental requirement for the additional pleasure one derives from winning.

To grow from a level at which the deleterious effects of anger,   14
frustration, and regret ran rampant to the level of the fun dimension may have required a transformation. As you play for fun in an atmosphere of mutual trust, a similar but more subtle transformation takes place, and you may soon find yourself in what I call the "aesthetic dimension." You will realize that you are playing at this new level when, among other things, some of the following are noted:

1. You find that you do not dwell on misses or so-called "bad plays," but accept mistakes as part of the game. You consider them non-learning experiences.

2. You do reflect on good plays—momentarily or for a longer period of time after the game. You do not take for granted specific (possibly lucky) plays which you rarely execute. You consider them learning experiences. Eventually those plays will become routine.

3. You realize that becoming skillful at the game takes time. But since time is being spent on having fun, you won't mind how long it takes.

4. You become aware that you can improve your game by participating fully as a player, referee, or spectator. As a referee or spectator, you have a neutral opportunity to learn by watching others play the game.

Playing for the sheer enjoyment of participating with your colleagues at the level of aesthetics brings to light the aspect of novelty. Just for the fun of it, you try things you never tried before. Your obvious pattern of playing disappears. Your repertoire of choices increases. You develop techniques and strategies that test the ingenuity of your associate and vice versa. Spectators as well as players delight in seeing the unexpected emerge from a difficult situation, and at that time innovation is applauded. 15

I have heard others remark and I have also referred to a player's dexterity on the handball court and his execution of plays as "poetry in motion." I compare it to the movements executed by a ballet dancer. In such a context, playing handball or any other sport can be as artistic as any other art form, and the more expert one becomes, the better his or her performance of the art. 16

It may take a great deal of devotion to the game before one can play as an expert. However, even while we are learning we can direct our creative talent toward newness, and newness in this context implies artistry. 17

Yet how have the spectators changed who used to yell, "Kill the bum!"? In the fun dimension, they have learned to enjoy every play as it unfolds and no longer find the need to take sides. In the fun dimension, they have given up the need to cast disparaging remarks at the players or the referee. At the esthetic level, they sense their involvement with the game. At this level we may find the players, the referee, and the spectators participating in the production of a work of art. 18

READING QUESTIONS FOR "A HUMANISTIC APPROACH TO SPORTS"

Main Idea

1. State the essay's main idea in your own words. Compare it to your prediction of the main idea. (*Note:* The main idea should sum up the smaller ideas of the essay.)

Organization

2. a. Where in the essay is the main idea found?

   b. Why has the author placed the main idea there?

3. In what order are the paragraphs arranged? (Underline one.) Time / Least to most important / Most to least important / Simple listing / Logic: cause and effect / Other logic / Other

Style

4. How formal is the essay? (Circle your choice.)

   [Informal–1–2–3–4–5–6–7–8–9–10–Formal]

   What indicators convinced you? (For a list of possible indicators and two benchmark essays, see Appendix F, The Formality Spectrum, on page 307.)

5. Where do you see the following features of style? List one or two examples of each with their paragraph numbers.

Features (For definitions, see Appendix B, page 291.)

a. cliché

b. jargon

Content

6. Does the author propose any change? If so, what do you think would be the result of such change?

7. Do you agree with the author's main idea? Why or why not?

8. To what extent can Simon's ideas be applied to pro football or boxing? Why or why not?

If you have not already read the essay and answered the Reading Questions, be sure to do so before you proceed.

COMPOSITION QUESTIONS

Listed below are the writing questions. Choose one and write an essay that answers it. Whichever question you choose, think of the person who will read your answer. The question may tell who your audience is. If not, think of a person you know and respect—preferably your instructor or a fellow student who will read your essay. Try to convince that person to believe you.

Bring in useful details from the selection(s) you have read and perhaps other incidents you know of. For ideas, review your answers to questions in the Preview and Reading Steps. When you first refer to a reading, give its title (in quotation marks) and the author's full name. Also, give the full name of anyone featured in the article the first time you mention that person.

Note: If you are assigned to write a one-paragraph essay, think of your answer to the question, and list several key points you could make to support your answer. Then choose just one of the points and explain it in detail.

1. Irving Simon proposes that we take part in sports with a new attitude. Does either of the two football players in the Plimpton selection have a personality that might make him more likely to accept at least some of Simon's humanistic concepts concerning sports? Why? Why would the other player be less likely to agree with Simon?

2. Can you think of any football players' nicknames (such as "Monsters of the Midway" and "Bulldog" Turner) that suggest violence? Simon discusses at some length the connotations of certain terms such as "opponent." Just how much do our words influence our attitudes— and in turn our behavior? Or are our words just symptoms of our attitudes?

3. You may have seen one of the movies in the *Rocky* series, starring Sylvester Stallone. If Rocky had embraced Simon's philosophy, would his career have been the same? Can a boxer accept such a philosophy and still be a champion? Why or why not?

4. In the first Preview Step, you were asked to list three sports in each of the three areas: (a) contact sports, (b) sports that are supposed to be noncontact but often involve contact, and (c) noncontact sports. Consider one or more of these divisions. What would it take for players to live by Simon's philosophy? Would the results be favorable or unfavorable? Why?

5. Plimpton suggests that some football players have a split personality. Draw up a profile of a typical football player's personality. Could such a player follow Simon's philosophy?

6. Can a player or spectator find psychological relief by expressing aggression under controlled conditions? If Simon's ideas were put into practice, would society be losing a useful safety valve?

7. According to Simon, would competition decrease if his proposal went into effect? Do you agree?

8. Compare amateur players, such as Simon, to professional players, such as those in the Plimpton article: Would one type of player have more trouble than the other in carrying out Simon's philosophy?

REVISION QUESTIONS

Once you have finished writing your essay, ask yourself the following questions.

1. Is there any statement the reader might not understand?
2. Is there any statement that might offend the reader?
3. Is there anything that's not very convincing?
4. Have I changed the subject and then changed it back again?
5. Have I said the same thing twice?
6. Do I want to try using any feature of style I've seen in the reading selection?

EDITING QUESTIONS

Once you've made changes, ask someone else to read your essay. Change it again as needed. Then read your essay out loud and answer the following questions.

1. Does every sentence make sense?
2. Does every sentence use the kind of language that most people consider "good English" these days? (*Hint:* Imagine a TV announcer reading it.)
3. Do the periods, commas, and other punctuation show the rise and fall of my voice?
4. Are the words spelled right?

If your instructor asks you to copy your paper over, proofread for copying errors before you hand it in.

UNIT
SIX

Controlling Our Own Health

PREVIEW STEPS FOR UNIT SIX

In response to questions 1 and 2, try these steps: Write your answers, talk them over with three or four classmates, and then discuss them with the whole class.

1. When something bad happens to you—illness, an accident, a rejection—what do you usually tell yourself? (Check one or two.)
   a. It must be something I did.
   b. It was my attitude.
   c. There must be something wrong with me.
   d. Somebody was out to get me.
   e. Somebody made a mistake.
   f. It was meant to be.
   g. These things just happen at random.
   h. Other: _____

2. a. When something bad happens to you, what is the most useful way for you to look at the situation? That is, what will help you most in the long run?

   b. Do you think people can change their attitudes to more useful ones? Explain.

3. a. Read the title of the first essay (page 85). Name the topic. (Who or what is this essay about?)

   b. Now predict the main idea. (What is the main point the author wants to make about this topic?)

   c. Read the first and last paragraphs. Revise your prediction if necessary. (*Note:* The main idea should sum up the smaller ideas of the essay.)

4. Some words from the essay are listed below, accompanied by quotations. Mark any words you do not know and make an educated guess about their meanings using the context supplied by the quotations—and possibly Appendix A, Word Parts, on page 287. You may want to work with a small group of classmates.

omnipotence "Psychologists speak of the infantile myth of *omnipotence*. A baby comes to think that the world exists to meet his needs, and that he makes everything happen in it."

gratuitous "It is *gratuitous*, even cruel, to tell the person who has been hurt . . . 'Maybe if you had acted differently, things would not have turned out so badly.' "

5. Now read the following essay. As you read, jot down any questions that occur to you.

(*Note:* Question 6 appears after the essay.)

God Helps Those Who Stop Hurting Themselves

Harold Kushner

I had an experience some years ago which taught me something   1
about the ways in which people make a bad situation worse by blaming themselves. One January, I had to officiate at two funerals on successive days for two elderly women in my community. Both had

---

died "full of years," as the Bible would say; both succumbed to the normal wearing out of the body after a long and full life. Their homes happened to be near each other, so I paid condolence calls on the two families on the same afternoon.

At the first home, the son of the deceased woman said to me, "If only I had sent my mother to Florida and gotten her out of this cold and snow, she would be alive today. It's my fault that she died." At the second home, the son of the other deceased woman said, "If only I hadn't insisted on my mother's going to Florida, she would be alive today. That long airplane ride, the abrupt change of climate, was more than she could take. It's my fault that she's dead."

When things don't turn out as we would like them to, it is very tempting to assume that had we done things differently, the story would have had a happier ending. Clergymen know that any time there is a death, the survivors will feel guilty. Because the course of action they took turned out badly, they believe that the opposite course—keeping Mother at home, deferring the operation—would have turned out better. After all, how could it have turned out any worse?

There seem to be two elements involved in our readiness to feel guilt. The first is our strenuous need to believe that the world makes sense, that there is a cause for every effect and a reason for everything that happens. That leads us to find patterns and connections both where they really exist (smoking leads to lung cancer; people who wash their hands have fewer contagious diseases) and where they exist only in our minds (the Red Sox win every time I wear my lucky sweater; that boy I like talks to me on odd-numbered days, but not on even-numbered ones, except where there has been a holiday to throw the pattern off). How many public and personal superstitions are based on something good or bad having happened right after we did something, and our assuming that the same thing will follow the same pattern every time?

The second element is the notion that *we* are the cause of what happens, especially the bad things that happen. It seems to be a short step from believing that every event has a cause to believing that every disaster is our fault. The roots of this feeling may lie in our childhood. Psychologists speak of the infantile myth of omnipotence. A baby comes to think that the world exists to meet his needs, and that he makes everything happen in it. He wakes up in the morning and summons the rest of the world to its tasks. He cries, and someone comes to attend to him. When he is hungry, people feed him, and when he is wet, people change him. Very often, we do not completely outgrow that infantile notion that our wishes cause things to happen. A part of our mind continues to believe that people get sick because we hate them.

Our parents, in fact, often feed this notion. Not realizing how vulnerable our childhood egos are, they snap at us when they are tired or frustrated for reasons that have nothing to do with us. They bawl us out for being in the way, for leaving toys around or having the television set on too loud, and we in our childhood innocence assume that they are justified and we are the problem. Their anger may pass in a moment, but we continue to bear the scars of feeling at fault, thinking that whenever something goes wrong, we are to blame for it. Years later, should something bad happen to us or around us, feelings from our childhood re-emerge and we instinctively assume that we have messed things up again.

It is gratuitous, even cruel, to tell the person who has been hurt, whether by divorce or death or other disaster, "Maybe if you had acted differently, things would not have turned out so badly." When we say that, all we are really telling them is, "This is your fault for having chosen as you did." Sometimes marriages fail because people are immature, or because expectations are unrealistic on both sides. Sometimes people die because they have incurable diseases, not because their families turned to the wrong doctor or waited too long to go to the hospital. Sometimes businesses fail because economic conditions or powerful competition doom them, not because one person in charge made a wrong decision in a crucial moment. If we want to be able to pick up the pieces of our lives and go on living, we have to get over the irrational feeling that every misfortune is our fault, the direct result of our mistakes or misbehavior. We are really not that powerful. Not everything that happens in the world is our doing.

6. State the essay's main idea in your own words. Compare it to your prediction of the main idea. (*Note:* The main idea should sum up the smaller ideas of the essay.)

PREVIEW STEPS FOR "HEART ATTACK!"

1. a. Read the title of the second essay (page 89). Name the topic. (Who or what is this essay about?)

   b. Now predict the main idea. (What is the main point the author wants to make about this topic?)

   c. Read the first and last paragraphs of the essay. Revise your prediction if necessary. (*Note:* The main idea should sum up the smaller ideas of the essay.)

2. What in the author's background may have led him to the main idea? (See author's background, below title.)

3. Some words from the essay are listed below, accompanied by quotations. Mark any words you do not know and make an educated guess about their meanings using the context supplied by the quotations— and possibly Appendix A, Word Parts, on page 287. You may want to work with a small group of classmates.

   Note: This essay contains several medical words, but only a few are needed to understand the major ideas. Only key terms are listed here. If you see other words you don't know, just keep on reading.

   impending mortality "The patients were mostly men in their forties and fifties, and the meaning of this illness was clear to them—they were getting older; this was a reminder of their *impending mortality.*"

   data "All this information interested me enormously. . . . Now I was getting these *data* from the heart attack patients."

manifesting "How would medicine be different if we considered all these people . . . to be *manifesting* mental processes through their physical bodies?"

medieval ". . . at the farther reaches of this idea, you came uncomfortably close to *medieval* notions that a pregnant woman who suffered a fright would later produce a deformed child."

retrogressive "So this idea that mental processes caused disease seemed to have *retrogressive* aspects."

abdicate "Of course it isn't helpful to blame ourselves for an illness. . . . But that doesn't mean we should *abdicate* all responsibility as well."

ameliorate "We are better able to focus on what we can do now to *ameliorate* the illness."

4. At the end of the Preview, you may want to go over any new features of style that occur in the following reading selection. You will need to know the terms *jargon*, *metaphor*, *overstatement*, and *simile*. For help, see Appendix B, Guide to Literary Terms (page 291), with accompanying exercises on individual features.
5. Before reading "Heart Attack!" turn to pages 96–97 and skim the Reading Questions. Then read the essay to find answers to these questions. As you read, jot down any questions that occur to you.

Heart Attack!

Michael Crichton

Michael Crichton (1942–) began writing as a student at Harvard Medical School during the late 1960s. Some of his more popular works, such as Rising Sun *and* Jurassic Park, *have been made into major motion pictures.* Jurassic Park *is one of the top grossing films of all time. He is the creator and an executive producer of the NBC emergency room drama series* ER. *Crichton also writes under the pseudonyms Michael Douglas, Jeffrey Hudson, and John Lange.*

A major disaster befell the medical wards of the Beth Israel Hospital. 1
All the interns and residents went around shaking their heads. The disaster was that, by some quirk of fate or statistics, two-thirds of the patients on the ward had the same illness. Heart attack.

The residents acted as if all the theaters in town were playing 2
the same movie, and they'd seen it. Furthermore, most of these pa-
tients would be here for two weeks, so the movie wasn't going to change soon. The home staff was gloomy and bored, because, from a medical standpoint, heart attacks aren't terribly interesting. They are dangerous and life-threatening, and you worry about your patients, because they may die suddenly. But the diagnostic procedures were well worked out, and there were clear methods for following the progress of recovery.

By now I was in my final year of medical school, and I had de- 3
cided I would quit at the end of the year. So my three months at the Beth Israel were going to be all the internal medicine I would ever learn; I had to make the best of this time.

I decided to learn something about the feelings the patients 4
had about their disease. Because, although doctors were bored by myocardial infarcts, the patients certainly weren't. The patients were mostly men in their forties and fifties, and the meaning of this illness was clear to them—they were getting older; this was a reminder of their impending mortality and they would have to change their lives: work habits, diets, perhaps even their pattern of sexual relations.

So there was plenty of interest for me in these patients. But how 5
to approach them?

Some time earlier, I had read about the experiences of a Swiss 6
physician who, in the 1930s, had taken a medical post in the Alps be-
cause it allowed him to ski, which was his great passion. Naturally, this doctor ended up treating many skiing accidents. The cause of the accidents interested him, since he was himself a skier. He asked his patients why they had had their accidents, expecting to hear that they had taken a turn too quickly, or hit a patch of rock, or some other skiing explanation. To his surprise, everyone gave a psycho-

logical reason for the accident. They were upset about something, they were distracted, and so on. This doctor learned that the bald question "Why did you break your leg?" yielded interesting answers.

So I decided to try that. I went around and asked patients, 7 "Why did you have a heart attack?"

From a medical standpoint, the question was not so nonsensical 8 as it sounded. During the Korean War, post-mortems on young men had shown that the American diet produced advanced arteriosclerosis by the age of seventeen. You had to assume that all these patients had been walking around with severely clogged arteries since they were teenagers. A heart attack could happen any time. Why had they waited twenty or thirty years to develop a heart attack? Why had their heart attack happened this year and not next, this week and not last week?

But my question "Why did you have a heart attack?" also im- 9 plied that the patients had some choice in the matter, and therefore some control over their disease. I feared they might respond with anger. So I started with the most easygoing patient on the ward, a man in his forties who had had a mild attack.

"Why did you have a heart attack?" 10

"You really want to know?" 11

"Yes, I do." 12

"I got a promotion. The company wants me to move to Cincin- 13 nati. But my wife doesn't want to go. She has all her family here in Boston, and she doesn't want to go with me. That's why."

He reported this in a completely straightforward manner, with- 14 out a trace of anger. Encouraged, I asked other patients.

"My wife is talking about leaving me." 15

"My daughter wants to marry a Negro man." 16

"My son won't go to law school." 17

"I didn't get the raise." 18

"I want to get a divorce and feel guilty." 19

"My wife wants another baby, and I don't think we can afford 20 it."

No one was ever angry that I had asked the question. On the 21 contrary, most nodded and said, "You know, I've been thinking about that. . . ." And no one ever mentioned the standard medical causes of arteriosclerosis, such as smoking or diet or getting too little exercise.

Now, I hesitated to jump to conclusions. I knew all patients 22 tended to review their lives when they got really sick, and to draw some conclusion about why the illness had happened. Sometimes the explanations seemed pretty irrelevant. I'd seen a cancer patient who blamed her disease on a lifelong fondness for Boston cream pie, and an arthritis patient who blamed his mother-in-law.

On the other hand, it was accepted in a vague way that there   23
was a relationship between mental processes and disease. One clue came from timing of certain illnesses. For example, the traditional season for duodenal ulcers was mid-January, just after the Christmas holidays. No one knew why this should be, but a psychological factor in the timing of the disease seemed likely.

Another clue came from the association of some physical ill-   24
nesses with a characteristic personality. For example, a significant percentage of patients with ulcerative bowel disease had extremely irritating personalities. Since the disease itself was hard to live with, some doctors wondered if the disease caused the personality. But many suspected that it was the other way around: the personality caused the disease. Or at least whatever caused the bowel disease also caused the personality.

Third, there was a small group of physical diseases that could   25
be successfully treated with psychotherapy. Warts, goiter, and parathyroid disease responded to both surgery and psychotherapy, suggesting that these illnesses might have direct mental causes.

And, finally, it was everybody's ordinary experience that the   26
minor illnesses in our own lives—colds, sore throats—occurred at times of stress, times when we felt generally weak. This suggested that the ability of the body to resist infection varied with mental attitude.

All this information interested me enormously, but it was pretty   27
fringe stuff in the 1960s in Boston. Curious, yes. Worthy of note, yes. But nothing to pursue in a serious way. The great march of medicine was headed in another direction entirely.

Now, I was getting these data from the heart attack patients.   28
And what I was seeing was that their explanations made sense from the standpoint of the whole organism, as a kind of physical acting-out. These patients were telling me stories of events that had affected their hearts in a metaphorical sense. They were telling me love stories. Sad love stories, which had pained their hearts. Their wives and families and bosses didn't care for them. Their hearts were attacked.

And pretty soon their hearts were *literally* attacked. And they   29
experienced physical pain. And that pain, that attack, was going to

force a change in their lives, and the lives of those around them. These were men in late middle life, all undergoing a transformation that was signaled by this illness event.

It made almost too much sense. 30

Finally I brought it up with Herman Gardner. Dr. Gardner was 31 then chief of medicine at the hospital, and a remarkable, extremely thoughtful man. As it happened, he was the attending physician who made rounds with us each day. I said to him that I had been talking with the patients, and I told him their stories.

He listened carefully. 32

"Yes," he said. "You know, once I was admitted to the hospital 33 for a slipped disc, and sitting in bed I began to wonder why this had happened to me. And I realized that I had a paper from a colleague that I had to reject, and I didn't want to face up to it. To postpone it, I got a slipped disc. At the time, I thought it was as good an explanation as any for what had happened to me."

Here was the chief of medicine himself reporting the same kind of 34 experience. And it opened up all sorts of possibilities. Were psychological factors more important than we were acknowledging? Was it even possible that psychological factors were the most important causes of disease? If so, how far could you push that idea? Could you consider myocardial infarctions to be a brain disease? How would medicine be different if we considered all these people, in all these beds, to be manifesting mental processes through their physical bodies?

Because at the moment we were treating their physical bodies. 35 We acted as if the heart was sick and the brain had nothing to do with it. We treated the heart. Were all these people being treated for the wrong organs?

Such errors were known. For example, some patients with se- 36 vere abdominal pain actually had glaucoma, a disease of the eye. If you operated on their abdomens, you didn't cure the disease. But if you treated their eyes, the abdominal pains disappeared.

But to extend that idea more broadly to the brain suggested 37 something quite alarming. It suggested a new conception of medicine, a whole new view of patients and disease.

To take the simplest example, we all believed implicitly the 38 germ theory of disease. Pasteur proposed it one hundred years before, and it had stood the test of time. There were germs—microorganisms, viruses, parasites—that got into the body and caused infectious disease. That was how it worked.

We all knew that you were more likely to get infected at some 39
times than others, but the basic cause and effect—germs caused disease—was not questioned. To suggest that germs were always out
there, a constant factor in the environment, and that the disease
process therefore reflected our mental state, was to say something
else.

It was to say mental states caused disease. 40

And if you accepted that concept for infectious disease, where 41
did you draw the line? Did mental states also cause cancer? Did
mental states cause heart attacks? Did mental states cause arthritis?
What about diseases of old age? Did mental states cause
Alzheimer's? What about children? Did mental states cause leukemia
in young children? What about birth defects? Did mental states
cause mongolism at birth? If so, whose mental state—the mother's or
the child's? Or both?

It became clear that at the farther reaches of this idea, you came 42
uncomfortably close to medieval notions that a pregnant woman who
suffered a fright would later produce a deformed child. And any consideration of mental states automatically raised the idea of blame. If
you caused your illness, weren't you also to blame? Much medical attention had been devoted to removing ideas of blame from disease.
Only a few illnesses, such as alcoholism and other addictions, still
had notions of blame attached.

So this idea that mental processes caused disease seemed to 43
have retrogressive aspects. No wonder doctors hesitated to pursue it.
I myself backed away from it for many years.

It was Dr. Gardner's view that both the physical and the mental 44
aspects were important. Even if you imagined the heart attack had a
psychological origin, once the cardiac muscle was damaged it needed
to be treated as a physical injury. Thus the medical care we were giving was appropriate.

I wasn't so sure about this. Because, if you imagined that the 45
mental process had injured the heart, then couldn't the mental
process also heal the heart? Shouldn't we be encouraging people
to invoke their inner resources to deal with the injury? We certainly weren't doing that. We were doing the opposite: we were
constantly telling people to lie down, to take it easy, to give over
their treatment to us. We were reinforcing the idea that they were
helpless and weak, that there was nothing they could do, and
they'd better be careful even going to the bathroom because the

least strain and—poof!—you were dead. That was how weak you were.

This didn't seem like a good instruction from an authority fig-   46
ure to a patient's unconscious mental process. It seemed as if we might actually be delaying the cure by our behavior. But, on the other hand, some patients who refused to listen to their doctors, who jumped out of bed, would die suddenly while having a bowel move-ment. And who wanted to take responsibility for that?

Many years passed, and I had long since left medicine, before I   47
arrived at a view of disease that seemed to make sense to me. The view is this:

We cause our diseases. We are directly responsible for an illness   48
that happens to us.

In some cases, we understand this perfectly well. We knew we   49
should not have gotten run-down and caught a cold. In the case of more catastrophic illnesses, the mechanism is not so clear to us. But whether we can see a mechanism or not—whether there is a mecha-nism or not—it is healthier to assume responsibility for our lives and for everything that happens to us.

Of course it isn't helpful to blame ourselves for an illness. That   50
much is clear. (It's rarely helpful to blame anybody for anything.) But that doesn't mean we should abdicate all responsibility as well. To give up responsibility for our lives is not healthy.

In other words, given a choice of saying to ourselves, "I am sick   51
but it has nothing to do with me," or saying, " I am sick because I caused the sickness," we are better off behaving as if we did it to our-selves. I believe we are more likely to recover if we take that responsi-bility.

For one thing, when we take responsibility for a situation, we   52
also take control of it. We are less frightened and more practical. We are better able to focus on what we can do now to ameliorate the ill-ness, and to assist healing.

We also keep the true role of the doctor in better perspective.   53
The doctor is not a miracle worker who can magically save us but, rather, an expert adviser who can assist us in our own recovery. We are better off when we keep that distinction clear.

When I get sick, I go to my doctor like everyone else. A doc-   54
tor has powerful tools that may help me. Or those tools may hurt me, make me worse. I have to decide. It's my life. It's my responsi-bility.

READING QUESTIONS FOR "HEART ATTACK!"

Main Idea

1. State the essay's main idea in your own words. Compare it to your prediction of the main idea. (*Note:* The main idea should sum up the smaller ideas of the essay.)

   a. According to Crichton, what is the relationship between our mental state and our physical health?

   b. According to Crichton, how much responsibility are we supposed to take for our physical health?

Organization

2. a. Where in the essay is the main idea found?

   b. Why has the author placed the main idea there?

3. In what order are the paragraphs arranged? (Underline one.) Time / Least to most important / Most to least important / Simple listing / Logic: cause and effect / Other logic / Other

Style

4. How formal is the essay? (Circle your choice.)

   [Informal–1–2–3–4–5–6–7–8–9–10–Formal]

What indicators convinced you? (For a list of possible indicators and two benchmark essays, see Appendix F, The Formality Spectrum, on page 307.)

5. Where do you see the following features of style? List one or two examples of each with their paragraph numbers.

   Features (For definitions, see Appendix B, page 291.)

   a. jargon

   b. metaphor

   c. overstatement

   d. simile

   Content

6. Does the author propose any change? If so, what do you think would be the result of such change?

7. Do you agree with the author's main idea? Why or why not?

If you have not already read the essay and answered the Reading Questions, be sure to do so before you proceed.

COMPOSITION QUESTIONS

Listed below are the writing questions. Choose one and write an essay that answers it. Whichever question you choose, think of the person who will read your answer. The question may tell who your audience is. If not, think of a person you know and respect—preferably your instructor or a fellow student who will read your essay. Try to convince that person to believe you.

Bring in useful details from the selection(s) you have read and perhaps other incidents you know of. For ideas, review your answers to questions in the Preview and Reading Steps. When you first refer to a reading, give its title (in quotation marks) and the author's full name. Also, give the full name of anyone featured in the article the first time you mention that person.

Note: If you are assigned to write a one-paragraph essay, think of your answer to the question, and list several key points you could make to support your answer. Then choose just one of the points and explain it in detail.

1. Kushner points out that believing every event has a cause is different from believing that *we* are the cause of every disaster (paragraph 5). Kushner's final paragraph lists many causes of misfortune besides one person's making "a wrong decision in a crucial moment." How can Kushner's distinction help us take the right amount of responsibility for our lives? Would it make sense to take part of the responsibility for an illness or accident without following Crichton's suggestion to take it all (paragraph 51)? Consider an illness or accident and analyze the possible variables, including mental state and physical causes, that could have contributed to it.

2. Crichton says that, rather than feeling we have no control, "it is healthier to assume responsibility for our lives" (paragraph 49). Yet he also admits that "it isn't helpful to blame ourselves for an illness" (paragraph 50). Kushner, too, says people "make a bad situation worse by blaming themselves" (paragraphs 1 through 3). Research

has shown that women are especially prone to blame themselves. Does it make sense to take responsibility without taking blame?

3. Kushner says in paragraph 4 that we "need to believe that the world makes sense, that there is a cause" for our misfortunes. He suggests that this need leads us to superstitious behavior, as in Crichton's "arthritis patient who blamed his mother-in-law" and the cancer patient who blamed her "fondness for Boston cream pie" in paragraph 22. How can we look for cause and effect in our lives without creating superstitions?

4. When doctors ask people why they had a skiing accident (Crichton, paragraph 6) or a heart attack (paragraph 21), they almost always say the cause was their mental state. Kushner says people may even go so far as to believe their "wishes cause things to happen," seeing themselves as omnipotent (paragraph 5). To what extent is it reasonable to attribute misfortunes to our mental state?

5. According to Crichton, we feel better when we "assume responsibility for our lives" (paragraph 49). Yet Kushner's final paragraph suggests that overdoing this attitude makes us feel worse. Does it help to assume responsibility if we are looking backward at the causes of an illness or only if we are looking forward to possible cures?

6. Some systems of healing, including Christian Science and laughter therapy, suggest that our attitudes can lead to cures even without medical treatment. Choose one of the two systems and show how it advocates taking more responsibility for our fate, as Crichton proposes. To what extent do you agree with this system's attitude toward responsibility?

7. In "Heart Attack!" Michael Crichton suggests taking responsibility for our own misfortunes. Would this view apply to rape victims? To victims of a "hate crime"? Or would it be a way for the criminal and others to avoid facing their own responsibility?

8. Teachers, counselors, and medical personnel sometimes tell a crime victim, "There are steps you can take to prevent future problems." Does this advice help a victim develop a sense of control over the future? Or does the advice cause guilt about being a victim of the original crime?

9. In "Heart Attack!" Crichton says, "A doctor has powerful tools that may help me. Or these tools may hurt me. . . . I have to decide" (paragraph 54). How much responsibility should the patient take when dealing with an expert? Is a customer at a repair shop in the same position as a patient? You may want to consider the way Diane

made decisions in Quill's "Death and Dignity: A Case of Individualized Decision Making" (Unit 13, pp. 205–211).

REVISION QUESTIONS

Once you have finished writing your essay, ask yourself the following questions.

1. Is there any statement the reader might not understand?
2. Is there any statement that might offend the reader?
3. Is there anything that's not very convincing?
4. Have I changed the subject and then changed it back again?
5. Have I said the same thing twice?
6. Do I want to try using any feature of style I've seen in the reading selection?

EDITING QUESTIONS

Once you've made changes, ask someone else to read your essay. Change it again as needed. Then read your essay out loud and answer the following questions.

1. Does every sentence make sense?
2. Does every sentence use the kind of language that most people consider "good English" these days? (*Hint:* Imagine a TV announcer reading it.)
3. Do the periods, commas, and other punctuation show the rise and fall of my voice?
4. Are the words spelled right?

If your instructor asks you to copy your paper over, proofread for copying errors before you hand it in.

UNIT
SEVEN

◆

Equal Pay:
The Controversies

PREVIEW STEPS FOR UNIT SEVEN

1. Do you know women who earn less than men for doing the same work? Can you think of some reasons that would explain the difference in pay?

2. In the right-hand column below, check any reason(s) that apply. (Leave the columns under R and T blank for now.)

R. T.

☐ ☐ ☐ a. discrimination against women

☐ ☐ ☐ b. inborn differences

☐ ☐ ☐ c. learned differences

☐ ☐ ☐ d. different self-concept and goals

☐ ☐ ☐ e. difference in amount of job experience

☐ ☐ ☐ f. fewer years at any one job

☐ ☐ ☐ g. less investment by women employees in their own training/education

☐ ☐ ☐ h. less investment by employers in women's training/ education because employers expect women to stop working

☐ ☐ ☐ i. shorter work hours

☐ ☐ ☐ j. work in low-paying fields (education, etc.)

☐ ☐ ☐ k. employers' view that the woman is not the main breadwinner

☐ ☐ ☐ l. other: _____

3. a. Read the title of the first essay (page 104). Name the topic. (Who or what is this essay about?)

   b. Now predict the main idea. (What is the main point the author wants to make about this topic?)

   c. Read the first and last paragraphs. Revise your prediction if necessary. (*Note:* The main idea should sum up the smaller ideas of the essay.)

4. Some words from the essay are listed below, accompanied by quotations. Mark any words you do not know and make an educated guess about their meanings using the context supplied by the quotations—and possibly Appendix A, Word Parts, on page 287 You may want to work with a small group of classmates.

median "Women still earn only 70 cents for every dollar earned by men, according to 1991 *median* annual wage data from the Census Bureau."

amalgams "Those figures are just averages, *amalgams* of jobs ranging from door-to-door sales to deal making."

parity "... it is often the hourly workers who come closest to *parity*, while the white-collar crowd earns as little as half."

fiscal year "... the government's last *fiscal year* ... ended October 1. ..."

statute "... that act has no *statute* of limitations, while the Equal Pay Act has a two-year limit."

colleagues "Most women can't address the pay gap because they don't know what their *colleagues* earn."

deprecating "... they make self-*deprecating* remarks. ... For instance, a woman might remark that she is fat. ..."

negates " 'Asking for a raise requires a kind of self-promotion' that *negates* this training. ..."

alleges "She *alleges* that . . . the firm had paid more to a male coworker who brought in no revenue."

generated "... a unit of General Electric Company says ... several people helped bring in the fees that she says she *generated*."

headhunter " 'Since I filed my lawsuit,' she says, 'one *headhunter* told me probably no major firm on Wall Street would touch me.' "

5. Now read the following article. As you read, jot down any questions that occur to you.

(*Note:* Question 6 appears after the essay.)

Three Decades After the Equal Pay Act, Women's Wages Remain Far from Parity

Joan E. Rigdon

Women have little to celebrate tomorrow on the 30th anniversary of the Equal Pay Act.   1

Women still earn only 70 cents for every dollar earned by men, according to 1991 median annual wage data from the Census Bureau. That is up a dime from 1963—which means women's earnings have gained on men's by a ratio of one-third of one percent a year over the past three decades.   2

Minority women fare worse. In 1991, black and Hispanic women earned 62 cents and 54 cents, respectively, for every dollar earned by white men, according to median annual wage data from the Census Bureau.   3

Those figures are just averages, amalgams of jobs ranging from door-to-door sales to deal making. Numbers for individual professions show that it is often the hourly workers who come closest to parity, while the white-collar crowd earns as little as half.   4

Female cashiers, for instance, made 95 cents on the male dollar last year, while female securities brokers earned only 52 cents, according to weekly wage figures from the Bureau of Labor Statistics.   5

Female financial managers—including those who close multimillion-dollar deals—earned only 62 cents on the male dollar.

Is the Equal Employment Opportunity Commission doing   6
much to help? Critics think not. In the government's last fiscal year, which ended Oct. 1, 1992, the EEOC filed only two lawsuits under the act, down from six the year before and from a high of 79 in fiscal 1980. "That sends a message to employers," says Helen Norton, deputy director for work and family programs at the nonprofit Women's Legal Defense Fund in Washington.

Don Livingston, general counsel for the EEOC, says the com-   7
mission files most sex-discrimination cases under the Civil Rights Act of 1964 because that act has no statute of limitations, while the Equal Pay Act has a two-year limit. In fiscal 1991, the EEOC filed 24 sex-discrimination pay-gap cases under both acts, he says.

A Question of Credentials

Companies have long argued that women get paid less because their   8
credentials don't stack up to men's. But research from Peter Hammer-schmidt pokes holes in that theory. An economics professor at Eckerd College in St. Petersburg, Fla., he analyzed the pay and credentials of 194 corporate managers randomly chosen from 800 who took a leadership course at Eckerd in recent years. His findings: If women were men with the same credentials, they would earn about 18% more.

Most women can't address the pay gap because they don't   9
know what their colleagues earn. And finding out is difficult—pay is a topic more taboo than sex. When they do find out, it is often because they have a friend in payroll, or they have pieced together years of clues about colleagues' spending habits.

That's how Marcia Rafter says she found out. During her eight   10
years at Citibank, Ms. Rafter watched as many of her male colleagues, who brought in fewer profits, purchased boats and expensive homes—things she says she couldn't afford. When she asked for raises, she says she was told that as a single woman she didn't need as much money as a man.

"I was No. 1 or No. 2 in terms of profits, but my compensation   11
never reflected that," Ms. Rafter alleges. She says she was fired in 1988 as a vice president of positioning and arbitrage. Citibank, a unit of Citicorp, declines to comment, noting that Ms. Rafter has filed a suit against it.

Clues from Gossip

One geologist, who declines to be named, says she got a hint that she   12
was being paid less than less-experienced male co-workers by chatting with drillers on her field site. Then a friend told her that one of
her male co-workers, who had only one year on the job, was getting
paid about the same as she was, even though she had five years experience.

    To see if the gossip was true, she called a former boss who filled   13
her in on average salaries for workers with her credentials and experience: about $40,000 compared with the $26,000 she was earning at
the time. "It really steamed me," she says. She quit this year, and is
now looking for a new job.

    In running and not fighting, the geologist wasn't alone. Experts   14
say women are less savvy at negotiating pay than men, and several
women who have bargained for raises agree. Among them is Debo-
rah Tannen, the Georgetown University linguistics professor who has
coached members of Congress on the different communication patterns of men and women.

    Ms. Tannen, author of "You Just Don't Understand," says that   15
girls are taught at an early age not to stand out and that as women
they make self-deprecating remarks, waiting for friends to build them
up. For instance, a woman might remark that she is fat, expecting a
reply that she isn't. "Asking for a raise requires a kind of self-promotion" that negates this training, Ms. Tannen says.

    That distaste for confrontation applies even to Wall Street women   16
who may thrive on confrontation on the job. Consider Liz Sobol, who re-
signed as Kidder, Peabody & Co.'s director of corporate finance in 1991.
Shortly thereafter she sued the company in U.S. District Court in New
York. She alleges that in 1988, Kidder paid her $655,000 for bringing in
about $9 million in fees but that the year before the firm had paid more
to a male co-worker who brought in no revenue.

    Kidder, a unit of General Electric Company, says that Ms.   17
Sobol was paid in the top one-third of her peer group and that several people helped bring in the fees that she says she generated. A
spokeswoman says compensation at Kidder is based only partly on
fees, but declines to elaborate.

    Ms. Sobol's first reaction to the pay flap: "I just wanted to hide   18
under the covers and hope the world would go away." It was her
husband who encouraged her to sue. And the cost may be great.

"Since I filed my lawsuit," she says, "one headhunter told me probably no major firm on Wall Street would touch me."

6. State the essay's main idea in your own words. Compare it to your prediction of the main idea. (*Note:* The main idea should sum up the smaller ideas of the essay.)

7. Rigdon discusses several possible reasons for unequal pay. Return to the Unit Preview, question 2, on page 102. For each reason Rigdon considers, list (in the R column) the paragraph number where that reason appears.

PREVIEW STEPS FOR "WHY WOMEN ARE PAID LESS THAN MEN"

1. a. Read the title of the second essay (page 108). Name the topic. (Who or what is this essay about?)

   b. Now predict the main idea. (What is the main point the author wants to make about this topic?)

   c. Read the first and last paragraphs of the essay. Revise your prediction if necessary. (*Note:* The main idea should sum up the smaller ideas of the essay.)

2. What in the author's background may have led him to the main idea? (See author's background, below title.)

3. Some words from the essay are listed below, accompanied by quotations. Mark any words you do not know and make an educated guess about their meanings using the context supplied by the quotations—and possibly Appendix A, Word Parts, on page 287. You may want to work with a small group of classmates.

attribute "... it was possible to *attribute* the earnings gap to large differences in educational *attainments*."

attainments See above quotation.

decade "The *decade* between 25 and 35 ..."

tenure "It is the decade when lawyers become partners in the good firms, when business managers make it onto the 'fast track,' when academics get *tenure* at good universities. ..."

acquisition "... promotion and skill *acquisition* ..."

4. At the end of the Preview, you may want to go over any new features of style that occur in the following reading selection. You will need to know the term *metaphor*. For help, see Appendix B, Guide to Literary Terms (page 291), with accompanying exercises on individual features.

5. Before reading "Why Women Are Paid Less Than Men," turn to pages 111–114 and skim the Reading Questions. Then read the essay to find answers to these questions. As you read, jot down any questions that occur to you.

Why Women Are Paid Less Than Men

Lester C. Thurow

Lester C. Thurow (1938–) has taught economics at Harvard and at the Massachusetts Institute of Technology. He has also served as a staff member on the President's Council of Economic Advisors. His writings, focusing on economics, politics, and manage-

ment, have been featured in Fortune, Los Angeles Times, Nation, *and* USA Today.

In the 40 years from 1939 to 1979 white women who work full time have with monotonous regularity made slightly less than 60 percent as much as white men. Why?   1

Over the same time period, minorities have made substantial progress in catching up with whites, with minority women making even more progress than minority men.   2

Black men now earn 72 percent as much as white men (up 16 percentage points since the mid-1950s), but black women earn 92 percent as much as white women. Hispanic men make 71 percent of what their white counterparts do, but Hispanic women make 82 percent as much as white women. As a result of their faster progress, fully employed black women make 75 percent as much as fully employed black men while Hispanic women earn 68 percent as much as Hispanic men.   3

This faster progress may, however, end when minority women finally catch up with white women. In the bible of the New Right, George Gilder's "Wealth and Poverty," the 60 percent is just one of Mother Nature's constants like the speed of light or the force of gravity.   4

Men are programmed to provide for their families economically while women are programmed to take care of their families emotionally and physically. As a result men put more effort into their jobs than women. The net result is a difference in work intensity that leads to that 40 percent gap in earnings. But there is no discrimination against women—only the biological facts of life.   5

The problem with this assertion is just that. It is an assertion with no evidence for it other than the fact that white women have made 60 percent as much as men for a long period of time.   6

"Discrimination against women" is an easy answer but it also has its problems as an adequate explanation. Why is discrimination against women not declining under the same social forces that are leading to a lessening of discrimination against minorities? In recent years women have made more use of the enforcement provisions of the Equal Employment Opportunities Commission and the courts than minorities. Why do the laws that prohibit discrimination against women and minorities work for minorities but not for women?   7

When men discriminate against women, they run into a prob- 8
lem. To discriminate against women is to discriminate against your
own wife and to lower your own family income. To prevent women
from working is to force men to work more.

When whites discriminate against blacks, they can at least think 9
that they are raising their own incomes. When men discriminate
against women they have to know that they are lowering their own
family income and increasing their own work effort.

While discrimination undoubtedly explains part of the male- 10
female earnings differential, one has to believe that men are monu-
mentally stupid or irrational to explain all of the earnings gap in
terms of discrimination. There must be something else going on.

Back in 1939 it was possible to attribute the earnings gap to 11
large differences in educational attainments. But the educational gap
between men and women has been eliminated since World War II. It
is no longer possible to use education as an explanation for the lower
earnings of women.

Some observers have argued that women earn less money since 12
they are less reliable workers who are more apt to leave the labor
force. But it is difficult to maintain this position since women are less
apt to quit one job to take another and as a result they tend to work
as long, or longer, for any one employer. From any employer's perspective they are more reliable, not less reliable, than men.

Part of the answer is visible if you look at the lifetime earnings 13
profile of men. Suppose that you were asked to predict which men in
a group of 25-year-olds would become economically successful. At
age 25 it is difficult to tell who will be economically successful, and
your predictions are apt to be highly inaccurate.

But suppose that you were asked to predict which men in a 14
group of 35-year-olds would become economically successful. If you
are successful at age 35, you are very likely to remain successful for
the rest of your life. If you have not become economically successful
by age 35, you are very unlikely to do so later.

The decade between 25 and 35 is when men either succeed or 15
fail. It is the decade when lawyers become partners in the good firms,
when business managers make it onto the "fast track," when academics get tenure at good universities, and when blue-collar workers
find the job opportunities that will lead to training opportunities and
the skills that will generate high earnings.

If there is any one decade when it pays to work hard and to be consistently in the labor force, it is the decade between 25 and 35. For those who succeed, earnings will rise rapidly. For those who fail, earnings will remain flat for the rest of their lives. 16

But the decade between 25 and 35 is precisely the decade when women are most apt to leave the labor force or become part-time workers to have children. When they do, the current system of promotion and skill acquisition will extract an enormous lifetime price. 17

This leaves essentially two avenues for equalizing male and female earnings. 18

Families where women who wish to have successful careers, compete with men, and achieve the same earnings should alter their family plans and have their children either before 25 or after 35. Or society can attempt to alter the existing promotion and skill acquisition system so that there is a longer time period in which both men and women can attempt to successfully enter the labor force. 19

Without some combination of these two factors, a substantial fraction of the male-female earnings differentials are apt to persist for the next 40 years, even if discrimination against women is eliminated. 20

READING QUESTIONS FOR "WHY WOMEN ARE PAID LESS THAN MEN"

Main Idea

1. State the essay's main idea in your own words. Compare it to your prediction of the main idea. (*Note:* The main idea should sum up the smaller ideas of the essay.)

Organization

2. a. Where in the essay is the main idea found?

b. Why has the author placed the main idea there?

3. In what order are the paragraphs arranged? (Underline one.) Time /
Least to most important / Most to least important / Simple listing /
Logic: cause and effect / Other logic / Other

Style

4. How formal is the essay? (Circle your choice.)

[Informal—1—2—3—4—5—6—7—8—9—10—Formal]

What indicators convinced you? (For a list of possible indicators and
two benchmark essays, see Appendix F, The Formality Spectrum, on
page 307.)

5. Where do you see the following feature of style? List one or two examples of it with its paragraph numbers.

Features (For definitions, see Appendix B, page 291.)

a. metaphor

Content

6. Thurow discusses several possible reasons for unequal pay. Return to
the Unit Preview, question 2, on page 107). For each reason Thurow
considers, list (in the T column) the paragraph number where that
reason appears.
7. Would Thurow say that married women's lack of experience explains their low salaries compared to men's?

8. a. In paragraphs 4 and 5, Thurow mentions an idea of George Gilder's that men and women are programmed differently. Here, does the word "programmed" mean "taught from infancy" or "pre-wired at birth"?

   b. Does Thurow agree with Gilder's idea?

9. a. How much anti-female discrimination does Thurow see? (Note paragraphs 8, 9, and 10.)

   b. Thurow says, "When men discriminate against women they have to know that they are lowering their own family income. . . ." If a man underpays his secretary, can this keep down women's salaries in general and, therefore, his own wife's?

   c. Would this effect depend on whether his wife is employed and what her field is?

   d. Does an employer sit down and think about such an effect when he is deciding what to pay?

10. In paragraphs 15–17, the decade between 25 and 35 is said to be important. Why is it so special?

11. a. Thurow gives two possible solutions to the problem. What is the first?

    b. Do you think Thurow's first solution is practical?

12. a. What is Thurow's second solution?

    b. Do you think this second solution is practical?

If you have not already read the essay and answered the Reading Questions, be sure to do so before you proceed.

COMPOSITION QUESTIONS

Listed below are the writing questions. Choose one and write an essay that answers it. Whichever question you choose, think of the person who will read your answer. The question may tell who your audience is. If not, think of a person you know and respect—preferably your instructor or a fellow student who will read your essay. Try to convince that person to believe you.

Bring in useful details from the selection(s) you have read and perhaps other incidents you know of. For ideas, review your answers to questions in the Preview and Reading Steps. When you first refer to a reading, give its title (in quotation marks) and the author's full name. Also, give the full name of anyone featured in the article the first time you mention that person.

Note: If you are assigned to write a one-paragraph essay, think of your answer to the question, and list several key points you could make to support your answer. Then choose just one of the points and explain it in detail.

1. According to Thurow, the crucial variable in explaining unequal pay is the age at which a woman takes time away from work, not the amount of training or experience she has. Agree or disagree.

2. Thurow's first solution (paragraph 19) is that families "have their children either before 25 or after 35." Consider the practical implications of each alternative. Would either alternative be a realistic one in the United States today? Why or why not?

3. Thurow's second solution (paragraph 19) is that society can allow a longer time period in which women can become successful. Would that solution work in the United States today? Why or why not?

4. If you plan to have children, do you think either of Thurow's two solutions would be likely to fit the career plans of you and your life partner? Why or why not?

5. Compare two explanations of the unequal pay situation. You may want to compare Rigdon's and Thurow's. Or compare either to another author you have read. Argue that one view is more believable than the other.

6. From an employer's point of view, would you rather spend money to train a man or a woman? Consider quality of work, total number of years each is apt to stay with the company, and the number of hours per week each is apt to work.

7. Is either Rigdon's or Thurow's essay dated in its explanations of the pay differential? Explain your reasoning.

8. Using facts from the reading selections, argue that a merit pay system would or would not be fairer to women than the present seniority system.

9. Thurow assumes that it is the woman who will work part-time or leave the labor force. Would it be possible to shift the responsibility for child care? If so, would this shift result in higher pay for women?

10. Thurow downplays discrimination as a reason for the pay gap between men and women (see paragraphs 7–10). Argue that his reasoning is weak.

11. Rigdon calls attention to two problems women have in gaining higher salaries: They lack knowledge about how their pay compares to that of other workers (paragraph 9), and they have difficulty marketing themselves (paragraphs 14 and 15). Propose a solution to either or both of these problems.

12. According to Rigdon, women who are paid by the hour come closer than salaried workers to receiving equal pay (see paragraphs 4 and 5). Paragraph 9 suggests one possible reason: that salaried workers often have trouble finding out how much their co-workers earn. Another possibility is that if the salaried workers were paid by the hour, their pay would be equal to men's (that is, they simply do not work as many hours as men). How would you explain the difference?

REVISION QUESTIONS

Once you have finished writing your essay, ask yourself the following questions.

1. Is there any statement the reader might not understand?
2. Is there any statement that might offend the reader?
3. Is there anything that's not very convincing?
4. Have I changed the subject and then changed it back again?
5. Have I said the same thing twice?
6. Do I want to try using any feature of style I've seen in the reading selection?

EDITING QUESTIONS

Once you've made changes, ask someone else to read your essay. Change it again as needed. Then read your essay out loud and answer the following questions.

1. Does every sentence make sense?
2. Does every sentence use the kind of language that most people consider "good English" these days? (*Hint:* Imagine a TV announcer reading it.)
3. Do the periods, commas, and other punctuation show the rise and fall of my voice?
4. Are the words spelled right?

If your instructor asks you to copy your paper over, proofread for copying errors before you hand it in.

Obedience:
A Good Quality?

PREVIEW STEPS FOR UNIT EIGHT

1. Think back to your early days (ten years old or younger) and your relationship then with your parent(s) or guardian(s). How did you view them? (Indicate by a check in the appropriate blanks.)

   guardian 1   **guardian 2**
   ☐   ☐   a. authority figure
   ☐   ☐   b. teacher
   ☐   ☐   c. role model
   ☐   ☐   d. other or combination of above: _____

2. Consider the alternatives in question 1. What type of role would you take with your future children? Why?

3. a. Read the title of the first essay (page 119). Name the topic. (Who or what is this essay about?)

   b. Now predict the main idea. (What is the main point the author wants to make about this topic?)

   c. Read the first and last paragraphs. Revise your prediction if necessary. (*Note:* The main idea should sum up the smaller ideas of the essay.)

4. Some words from the essay are listed below, accompanied by quotations. Mark any words you do not know and make an educated guess about their meanings using the context supplied by the quotations— and possibly Appendix A, Word Parts, on page 287. You may want to work with a small group of classmates.

contemporaries "The last thought that would have entered my parents' minds was to ask their children what was good or bad for children. We were not their *contemporaries*, nor their equals, and they were not concerned with our ideas on how to raise a family."

Bar Mitzvah "When I got to thirteen (*Bar Mitzvah* and manhood), I took a chance."

token "Most of the time we got only *token* punishments—small pinches, twists and pokes."

5. Now read the following essay. As you read, jot down any questions that occur to you.

(*Note:* Question 6 appears after the essay.)

"When I Need Your Opinion I'll Give It to You"

Sam Levenson

Although there were eight of us children, we were outnumbered by two parents. Ours was a decidedly parent-centered home. Since respect for age was a cornerstone of our tradition, it followed that Mama and Papa had the right to lead, and we had the right to be led by them. We had very few other rights. We had lots of wrongs which were going to be corrected by any methods our parents saw fit. The last thought that would have entered my parents' minds was to ask their children what was good or bad for children. We were not their contemporaries, nor their equals, and they were not concerned with our ideas on how to raise a family. "When I need your opinion I'll give it to you."

1

We had to wait our turn to speak our minds. It was not clear to   2
us when that turn would come, but I knew that I would have to become a little older and a little wiser before I would be called in as a
consultant by my parents. If I offered a suggestion, Mama would say,
"Wait, Papa is talking." When I got to be thirteen (Bar Mitzvah and
manhood), I took a chance. "Now, Ma?"

"Not yet."   3

Most things were "none of my business"—even when they were   4
talking about having my tonsils out. I got the idea finally that my
mind was to be used to mind: to mind Papa, mind your teacher,
mind your manners, mind your shoes. My shoes were my brother's,
my hat was my father's, my bed was anybody's, so I didn't really feel
entitled to a mind of my own.

They did not have to explain the basis for their actions, nor did   5
they say, "This hurts me more than it hurts you." If you pressed them
for a reason they quoted some authority known as "Because!" If
Mama said No to something I wanted to do, and I used the argument
that "Louie is doing it, and Georgie is doing it, and Benny . . ." she
would cut in with "When I tell you No, don't tell me Who."

It is not as difficult as it seems to explain the common use of   6
corporal punishment in those days. Anything, animate or inanimate,
that did not respond to reason was hit with the palm of the hand: gas
burners, radio, drawers, windows, or children. With the latter a combination of couch therapy and corporal punishment worked best.
The kid was told to stretch out on the lounge. He then pulled down
his pants and "voluntarily" exposed his psyche for the shock treatment. Most of the time we got only token punishments—small
pinches, twists and pokes.

Did we end up hating our parents? No. Why? Because we un-   7
derstood the dogma involved. It was the dogma of parental responsibility, of preventive therapy, of virtue being its own reward and evil
bringing punishment. Did we enjoy the practice? Of course not. We
understood that a world as tough as ours required tough parents and
tough teachers. They had to fight fire with fire. The fight against individual corruption was part of the fight against the environment.
The moral standard of the home had to be higher than that of the
street. "You are not on the street; you are in our home. This is not a
cellar nor a poolroom. Here we act like human beings, not like animals." I remember the speech well. Like royalty, Mama said "we."
"We have been put to shame by what you did." Did it make me feel

guilty? It sure did. Did I feel I had let the family down? I sure did. Was it worth a quick sharp pain in the rear end to be reminded of my obligations? It sure was. Better one stabbing moment of truth at home than a stabbing in the street.

6. State the essay's main idea in your own words. Compare it to your prediction of the main idea. (*Note:* The main idea should sum up the smaller ideas of the essay.)

PREVIEW STEPS FOR "WOULD YOU OBEY A HITLER?"

1. a. Read the title of the second essay (page 123). Name the topic. (Who or what is this essay about?)

b. Now predict the main idea. (What is the main point the author wants to make about this topic?)

c. Read the first and last paragraphs of the essay. Revise your prediction if necessary. (*Note:* The main idea should sum up the smaller ideas of the essay.)

2. What in the author's background may have led her to the main idea? (See author's background, below title.)

3. Some words from the essay are listed below, accompanied by quotations. Mark any words you do not know and make an educated guess about their meanings using the context supplied by the quotations—

and possibly Appendix A, Word Parts, on page 287. You may want to work with a small group of classmates.

qualms "The drama of the clearcut choice between obeying orders or *qualms* of conscience seems clearest for the man in uniform. He must *decide* to pull the trigger."

subject "Imagine yourself as a *subject* in Dr. Milgram's setup. You walk into a laboratory on the Yale campus . . ."

negative reinforcement "Jack Williams . . . explains that if punishment makes you learn faster, that's *negative reinforcement*—as opposed to learning faster when rewarded (*positive reinforcement*)."

positive reinforcement See above quotation.

electrode " 'This *electrode* . . . is connected to the shock generator in the next room. . . .' "

hoaxed "The learner is not being shocked: in fact, he is in cahoots with the experimenter. He is part of a play, and you are the only person *hoaxed* in the setup."

blithely "Dr. Milgram had thought that the labels [such as 'intense shock' and 'danger: severe shock'] and voltage designations would stop the teachers [from pulling switches on a board to give electric shocks to someone]. But instead virtually everyone 'went *blithely* to the end of the board, seemingly indifferent to the verbal designations.' "

appalled "Dr. Milgram was *appalled* that many subjects . . . went to the end of the board, giving the harshest punishment."

dubious "There a modest suite of offices was rented in a run-down section. The sign on the door said, 'Research Associates of Bridgeport,' a deliberately vague title. . . . Yet, even with this *dubious* authority, the levels of obedience were high, although not as high as on the Yale campus."

callous " 'With numbing regularity good people were seen to knuckle under the demands of authority and perform actions that were *callous* and severe.' "

4. At the end of the Preview, you may wish to go over any new features of style that occur in the following reading selection. You will need to know the terms *cliché, jargon,* and *metaphor.* For help, see Appendix B, Guide to Literary Terms (page 291), with accompanying exercises on individual features.

5. Before reading "Would You Obey a Hitler?" turn to pages 128–129 and skim the Reading Questions. Then read the essay to find answers to these questions. As you read, jot down any questions that occur to you.

Would You Obey a Hitler?

Jeanne Reinert

Jeanne Reinert (1941–) earned her bachelor's degree in journalism from the University of Texas. After working briefly as a newspaper editor, she spent nine years as a writer and editor at Science Digest. *Reinert served as an officer of the League of Women Voters for six years and has been active in other civic and professional organizations.*

Who looks in the mirror and sees a person ready and willing to inflict   1
pain and suffering on another in his mercy? Even if commanded? All
of our senses revolt against the idea.

The drama of a clearcut choice between obeying orders or   2
qualms of conscience seems clearest for a man in uniform. He must
decide to pull the trigger.

Being behind the trigger is very dramatic, but obeying orders is   3
an everyday event for all of us. Seldom do we have a chance to test
our actions when confronted with a clearcut choice between hurting
a person and obeying orders.

In the early 1960s, Stanley Milgram, a psychologist at Yale Uni-   4
versity, devised an experimental setup to give that choice to subjects.
He wanted to measure obedience. He had been taken with the histo-

rian's thesis that the Germans shared an extreme trait—a willingness to obey orders. This character flaw was, the theory goes, responsible for the Germans' carrying out Hitler's mad plan against the Jews. Dr. Milgram wanted to test this theory by comparing obedience in America and in Germany. He disguised his obedience tests as experiments in learning.

Imagine yourself as a subject in Dr. Milgram's setup. You walk into a laboratory on the Yale campus after answering an ad that asked for paid volunteers ($4.50 per hour) for an educational experiment.   5

At your appointment, you and another volunteer, a nervous man in his 50s, are told that the experiment in which you will participate is set up to test the effect of negative reinforcement on the human learning process. Jack Williams, the experimenter conducting the tests, explains that if punishment makes you learn faster, that's negative reinforcement—as opposed to learning faster when rewarded (positive reinforcement). In this experiment the punishment is an electric shock.   6

Williams also states, "The money is yours for coming to the laboratory. It's yours no matter what happens."   7

Then Williams takes two pieces of paper, shakes them together in a hat and each of you draw one to see who will be the teacher and who the learner. The nervous volunteer announces he is the learner; your slip of paper says "teacher."   8

The experimenter seats the learner in a chair and explains the procedure. "We have to strap down your arms to avoid excessive movement during the experiment.   9

"This electrode," he continues, "is connected to the shock generator in the next room. Do either of you have any questions before we go into the next room?"   10

"Are these shocks strong, are they dangerous?" asks the learner.   11

"No," replies Williams, "although they may be extremely painful, they cause no permanent tissue damage."   12

The experiment involves word pairing (e.g., nice–day, fat–pig, etc.). You, the teacher, read a word to the learner and ask him to match it with one of four other words. The learner pushes one of four switches to indicate which of the four answers he believes is correct. If he is right, you go on to the next set of words. If he is wrong, you push a switch that buzzes and gives him an electric shock. Then you go to the next group of words.   13

Your position is before the electric shock generator, 30 levers in   14
a row across the instrument panel. Each lever is clearly labelled in 15-volt jumps from 15 to 450 volts. When a lever is pushed down, a pilot light turns bright red, a buzzer sounds, a blue light flashes under the label "voltage energizer," the dial on the meter swings about and mechanical clicks are heard.

To be sure you know what is going on, you are given a sample   15
shock, activated by the third switch, on the wrist. This 45-volt shock lets you know how the shock feels.

You are instructed to call out the voltage level before pressing   16
the lever each time the learner merits a shock. You note that the levers are marked from left to right in broad categories, "slight shock, moderate shock, strong shock, very strong shock, intensity shock, danger: severe shock," and the two switches on the far right are simply marked "XXX."

When the lesson begins, the learner makes a lot of mistakes. In   17
fact, he answers about three wrong answers to one right one. As the shocks get stronger, you are, of course, unhappy about their level. It quickly is apparent that the learner is going to give a lot more wrong answers. So you appeal to Williams, who responds, "Please go on." You protest and he says, "The experiment requires that you continue."

The learner is strapped in, he cannot get free. You have already   18
been assured that the money is yours regardless. The experimenter has no actual authority over you. But he is requesting you to obey his commands. Would you do it? Would you injure the learner just because someone told you to do so? You know from your own experience that the shocks are painful. What you do not know is that the experiment is rigged. The learner is not being shocked: in fact, he is in cahoots with the experimenter. He is part of a play, and you are the only person hoaxed in the setup.

Before the pilot study, Dr. Milgram took the idea to a class of   19
senior Yale psychology students and asked them to predict the distribution of behavior among 100 subjects. The entire class predicted that only a very small number of people would go to the extreme 450-volt shock. They predicted from none to three percent of any 100 people. Dr. Milgram's colleagues also thought few, if any, subjects would go beyond the shock labeled "very strong shock."

But they did go beyond. In fact, Dr. Milgram got such complete   20
obedience that there was nothing to measure. He was, after all, interested in getting people to disobey. His first 40 people went beyond

the expected breakoff point. Not one stopped before 300 volts. Only 14 persons stopped shocking the strapped-in learner before going to the very end of the shocks.

In the pilot studies, no noise was heard from the strapped-in learner. Dr. Milgram had thought that the labels and voltage designations would stop the teachers. But instead virtually everyone "went blithely to the end of the board, seemingly indifferent to the verbal designations." 21

Dr. Milgram never expected such obedience. So he began to vary the props and scripts in his private play to see what changes would encourage the teacher to rebel. 22

The first change was to add protests from the victim. Mild protests did no good. Then the victim began to put up a vigorous fight. Dr. Milgram was appalled that many subjects, nonetheless, went to the end of the board, giving the harshest punishment. But at least some subjects did break off and give the experimenters something to measure. It also proved that obedience was much, much stronger than suspected. The victim's cries were tape-recorded so all subjects heard the same protests. 23

Finding in pilot studies that the teacher turned his eyes away from the victim who could be seen dimly behind a silvered glass, Dr. Milgram devised various ways to make it more difficult for the teacher to ignore his victim. 24

Voice protests were heard. The victim was in another room, but the door was left ajar. At 75 volts, the learner grunted when shocked, also at 90 and 105 volts. At 120 volts, he shouted that the shocks were painful. At 135 volts he groaned, and at 150 he screamed, "Get me out of here! I won't be in the experiment anymore! I refuse to go on!" At 180 volts, he screamed, "I can't stand the pain." Still, 37.5 percent of the teachers went to 450 volts. 25

Each successive scheme brought the teacher and learner into more personal contact until in the final scheme the victim received a shock only when his hand rested on the shockplate. The experimenter then ordered the teacher to push the subject's hand down on the plate. The teacher actually had to physically subdue the victim against his will to give him the shock. No one was more surprised than Milgram that the very first person so commanded reached over and fell upon the victim's arm. Thirty out of every 100 were still willing to go all the way with the shock level when commanded. 26

Dumbfounded by this high compliance, Dr. Milgram then decided the prestige of Yale was causing his subjects to be especially obedient. So the experiment was moved to Bridgeport, 20 miles away. There a modest suite of offices was rented in a run-down section. The sign on the door said, "Research Associates of Bridgeport," a deliberately vague title. If anyone asked what the work was for, they were told, "for industry." 27

Yet, even with this dubious authority, the levels of obedience were high, although not as high as on the Yale campus. Forty-eight percent of the people were totally obedient to the commands versus 65 percent under the same conditions at Yale. 28

What these scores do not show is the torment that accompanied the teacher's task. Subjects would sweat, tremble, stutter, bite their lips, and groan as they were caught up in the web of conflict—to obey the calm experimenter's commands or the call of the poor man being shocked. The teachers often broke out in hysterical laughter. 29

Persons would argue with the experimenter, asking if he would take the responsibility. They wondered aloud if the victim had a heart condition. Some would exclaim, "You keep the money," but many times they kept on pulling the levers, despite all of their words to the contrary. They would complain that the other guy was suffering, that it was a hell of an experiment. Some got angry. Some just stood up and proceeded to leave the laboratory. 30

No teacher was kept at the controls once they had reached 450 volts. People either stopped before 350 volts, or carried on to the end, proving there was no limit to their obedience. Hateful as they found it to obey, it must have seemed better for them than to break off. 31

When those who pressed the levers to the end finished their task, the experimenter called a halt. The obedient teachers were relieved. They would mop their brows. Some fumbled for cigarettes. 32

Then Mr. Williams rushed to assure the teachers that it wasn't as bad as it seemed. Most important, the teachers met their screaming victim and had a reconciliation. The real purposes of the experiment were explained, and the participants were promised that the full results of the experiment would be sent to them when it was complete. They were asked to describe how they felt and how painful they believed the shocks to be. Also they were to rate on a scale how tense they were during the experiment. Dr. Milgram wanted to be sure that the persons understood that they had been hoaxed and that the man was only acting as he screamed in agony. 33

Dr. Milgram never imagined that it would be so hard to get   34
people to defy the commands. As he explains, "With numbing regularity good people were seen to knuckle under the demands of authority and perform actions that were callous and severe. Men who in
everyday life are responsible and decent were seduced by the trap-
pings of authority. . . ."

To date, Dr. Milgram has tested 1,000 people with the steady   35
results—very, very obedient. Of course, if people were not willing to
conform to the many rules that link us in a broader society, chaos
would prevail. But Milgram's results suggest quite the opposite, that
perhaps we have forgotten the formula for saying no. It looks as
though few outrages are so grand as to force us to be defiant. "I was
only following orders" is going to be with us for a long time.

READING QUESTIONS FOR "WOULD YOU OBEY A HITLER?"

Main Idea

1. State the essay's main idea in your own words. Compare it to your
   prediction of the main idea. (*Note:* The main idea should sum up the
   smaller ideas of the essay.)

Organization

2. a. Where in the essay is the main idea found?

   b. Why has the author placed the main idea there?

3. In what order are the paragraphs arranged? (Underline one.) Time /
   Least to most important / Most to least important / Simple listing /
   Logic: cause and effect / Other logic / Other

Style

4. How formal is the essay? (Circle your choice.)

   [Informal—1—2—3—4—5—6—7—8—9—10—Formal]

   What indicators convinced you? (For a list of possible indicators and two benchmark essays, see Appendix F, The Formality Spectrum, on page 307.)

5. Where do you see the following features of style? List one or two examples of each with their paragraph numbers.

   Features (For definitions, see Appendix B, page 291.)

   a. cliché

   b. jargon

   c. metaphor

Content

6. Does the author propose any change? If so, what do you think would be the result of such a change?

7. Do you agree with the author's main idea? Why or why not?

If you have not already read the essay and answered the Reading Questions, be sure to do so before you proceed.

COMPOSITION QUESTIONS

Listed below are the writing questions. Choose one and write an essay that answers it. Whichever question you choose, think of the person who will read your answer. The question may tell who your audience is. If not, think of a person you know and respect—preferably your instructor or a fellow student who will read your essay. Try to convince that person to believe you.

Bring in useful details from the selection(s) you have read and perhaps other incidents you know of. For ideas, review your answers to questions in the Preview and Reading Steps. When you first refer to a reading, give its title (in quotation marks) and the author's full name. Also, give the full name of anyone featured in the article the first time you mention that person.

Note: If you are assigned to write a one-paragraph essay, think of your answer to the question, and list several key points you could make to support your answer. Then choose just one of the points and explain it in detail.

1. No one really knows why people react the way those in the Milgram study did. Offer some possible explanations for such behavior. In developing your hypotheses, consider how your parents related to you—as authority figures, teachers, role models—and how you want to relate to your children. (Since these hypotheses need to be proven through investigation, be certain not to state them as facts.)

2. Can one expect absolute obedience in rearing children and then, when they are adults, expect them to be selective about obeying? If so, how do they make the transition? (For insights, you might research the developmental stages outlined by psychologist Erik Erikson.)

3. Compare and/or contrast the way your parents reared you with the way Sam Levenson was reared. Evaluate these approaches, indicating what you feel are their pros and cons. Consider Milgram's findings in making your evaluation.

4. What do children need to learn about authority and about various situations they may find themselves in? Do children need to learn principles or assertiveness or both in order to avoid obeying blindly as the Milgram subjects did? In answering this question, you may find it useful to imagine that you are a parent or a high-school principal.

5. Do you think a typical nurse would disobey a doctor's order if it seemed morally wrong? (For example, the order might be to stop or to continue life support.) Why? Consider some of the pressures mentioned by Reinert and any other pressures you can think of. (For insights, you might research the stages of moral development outlined by psychologist Lawrence Kohlberg.)

6. Milgram observed that his subjects acted remarkably alike regardless of the experimental conditions he created. Yet the article does reveal important differences. What situational factors appear to affect people's levels of obedience?

7. Both Milgram's study and the story of Kitty Genovese, recounted in "37 Who Saw Murder Didn't Call the Police" (Unit 3), are analyzed in a collection entitled *Doing Unto Others: Joining, Molding, Conforming, Helping, Loving* (edited by Z. Rubin, Prentice Hall, 1974). Consider why both events might appear in the same text.

REVISION QUESTIONS

Once you have finished writing your essay, ask yourself the following questions.

1. Is there any statement the reader might not understand?
2. Is there any statement that might offend the reader?
3. Is there anything that's not very convincing?
4. Have I changed the subject and then changed it back again?
5. Have I said the same thing twice?
6. Do I want to try using any feature of style I've seen in the reading selection?

EDITING QUESTIONS

Once you've made changes, ask someone else to read your essay. Change it again as needed. Then read your essay out loud and answer the following questions.

1. Does every sentence make sense?
2. Does every sentence use the kind of language that most people consider "good English" these days? (*Hint:* Imagine a TV announcer reading it.)
3. Do the periods, commas, and other punctuation show the rise and fall of my voice?
4. Are the words spelled right?

If your instructor asks you to copy your paper over, proofread for copying errors before you hand it in.

UNIT
NINE

❖

Resisting Civil Authority

PREVIEW STEPS FOR UNIT NINE

In response to questions 1 and 2, try these steps: Write your answers, talk them over with three or four classmates, and then discuss them with the whole class.

1. a. What is civil disobedience?

   b. Can you name a few acts of civil disobedience during the last 75 years?

2. What is pacifism?

3. a. Read the title of the first essay (page 135). Name the topic. (Who or what is this essay about?)

   b. Now predict the main idea. (What is the main point the author wants to make about this topic?)

   c. Read the first and last paragraphs. Revise your prediction if necessary. (*Note:* The main idea should sum up the smaller ideas of the essay.)

4. Some words from the essay are listed below, accompanied by quotations. Mark any words you do not know and make an educated guess about their meanings using the context supplied by the quotations—and possibly Appendix A, Word Parts, on page 287. You may want to work with a small group of classmates.

dispensation "A forced worship is plainly a contradiction in terms, under that *dispensation* in which the worship of the Father must be in spirit and in truth."

ordinance "Civil government is a divine *ordinance*, (Rom. 13:1, I Pet. 2:13–16) instituted to promote the best welfare of man. . . ."

magistrates ". . . hence *magistrates* are to be regarded as God's ministers who should be terror to evildoers and a praise to them that do well."

5. Now read the following essay. As you read, jot down any questions that occur to you.

(*Note:* Question 6 appears after the essay.)

Liberty of Conscience in Its Relation to Civil Government

by Orthodox Friends

Explanatory note: This short document was part of a Declaration of Faith made by the Orthodox branch of Friends (Quakers) in a conference convened in Richmond, Indiana, in September 1887. The Declaration has been widely used by Quakers ever since. Its ideas, however, were expressed well back into the previous century and even in the 1600s. The excerpt below deals with the relationship between Friends and the government.

That conscience should be free, and that in matters of religious doctrine and worship man is accountable only to God, are truths which are plainly declared in the New Testament; and which are confirmed by the whole scope of the Gospel, and by the example of our Lord and His disciples. To rule over the conscience, and to command the spiritual allegiance of his creature man, is the high and sacred prerogative of God alone. In religion every act ought to be free. A forced worship is plainly

1

Source: Online. Available http://cpcug.org/user/wsamuel/rdf.html

a contradiction in terms, under that dispensation in which the worship of the Father must be in spirit and in truth. (John 4:24)

We have ever maintained that it is the duty of Christians to obey   2 the enactments of civil government, except those which interfere with our allegiance to God. We owe much to its blessings. Through it we enjoy liberty and protection, in connection with law and order. Civil government is a divine ordinance, (Rom. 13:1 [*Note: This Bible passage appears below the essay.*], I Pet. 2:13–16) instituted to promote the best welfare of man, hence magistrates are to be regarded as God's ministers who should be a terror to evildoers and a praise to them that do well. Therefore, it is with us a matter of conscience to render them respect and obedience in the exercise of their proper functions.

Romans 13:1-7: "Let every person be subject to the governing authorities; for there is no authority except from God, and those authorities that exist have been instituted by God. Therefore whoever resists authority resists what God has appointed, and those who resist will incur judgment. For rulers are not a terror to good conduct, but to bad. Do you wish to have no fear of the authority? Then do what is good, and you will receive its approval; for it is God's servant for your good. But if you do what is wrong, you should be afraid, for the authority does not bear the sword in vain! It is the servant of God to execute wrath on the wrongdoer. Therefore one must be subject, not only because of wrath but also because of conscience. For the same reason you also pay taxes, for the authorities are God's servants, busy with this very thing. Pay to all what is due them—taxes to whom taxes are due, revenue to whom revenue is due, respect to whom respect is due, honor to whom honor is due." (New Revised Standard Version)

---

6. State the essay's main idea in your own words. Compare it to your prediction of the main idea. (*Note:* The main idea should sum up the smaller ideas of the essay.)

PREVIEW STEPS FOR "THE BOSTON TEA PARTY"

1. a. Read the title of the second essay (page 138). Name the topic. (Who or what is this essay about?)

b. Now predict the main idea. (What is the main point the author wants to make about this topic?)

c. Read the first and last paragraphs of the essay. Revise your prediction if necessary. (*Note:* The main idea should sum up the smaller ideas of the essay.)

2. What in the author's background may have led him to the main idea? (See author's background, below title.)

3. Some words from the essay are listed below, accompanied by quotations. Mark any words you do not know and make an educated guess about their meanings using the context supplied by the quotations— and possibly Appendix A, Word Parts, on page 287. You may want to work with a small group of classmates.

conspicuous "Charles Townshend, as Chancellor of the Exchequer, . . . a brilliant young man, without any political principles worth mentioning, was the most *conspicuous* among a group of wire-pullers who were coming to be known as 'the king's friends.' "

unscrupulous "Serious illness soon kept [the Earl of] Chatham at home, and left Townshend all-powerful in the cabinet, because he was bold and utterly *unscrupulous* and had the king to back him."

audacity "His *audacity* knew no limits, and he made up his mind that the time had come for gathering all the disputed American questions, as far as possible, into one bundle, and disposing of them once for all."

ingenious "A truly *ingenious* scheme was devised."

consignees "Ships laden with tea were accordingly sent in the autumn of 1773 to Boston, New York, Philadelphia, and Charleston; and *consignees* were appointed to receive the tea in each of these towns."

jurisdiction "At Philadelphia the tea-ship was met and sent back to England before it had come within the *jurisdiction* of the custom-house."

decorum "The excitement was intense, but the proceedings were characterized from first to last by perfect quiet and *decorum*."

preconcerted "The only way to prevent this was to rip open the tea-chests and spill their contents into the sea, and this was done, according to a *preconcerted* plan and without the slightest uproar or disorder, by a small party of men disguised as Indians."

4. At the end of the Preview, you may want to go over any new features of style that occur in the following reading selection. You will need to know the terms *cliché* and *metaphor*. For help, see Appendix B, Guide to Literary Terms (page 291), with accompanying exercises on individual features.

5. Before reading "The Boston Tea Party," turn to pages 141–142 and skim the Reading Questions. Then read the essay to find answers to these questions. As you read, jot down any questions that occur to you.

Boston Tea Party

John Fiske

John Fiske was a famous nineteenth-century American historian, specializing in the American Revolution. He also published two volumes of essays on important American figures in history, American historical events, and a few world-renowned authors. His religious concerns were revealed in The Idea of God as Affected by Modern Knowledge *and* Through Nature to God. *He lectured at Harvard University.*

Condensed from *The War of Independence*. Published by Houghton, Mifflin and Company. Copyrighted © by John Fiske in 1889 (expired).

Charles Townshend, as Chancellor of the Exchequer,... a brilliant   1
young man, without any political principles worth mentioning, was the
most conspicuous among a group of wire-pullers who were coming to be
known as "the king's friends." Serious illness soon kept [the Earl of]
Chatham at home, and left Townshend all-powerful in the cabinet, because he was bold and utterly unscrupulous and had the king to back
him. His audacity knew no limits, and he made up his mind that the time
had come for gathering all the disputed American questions, as far as
possible, into one bundle, and disposing of them once for all. So in May,
1767, he brought forward in Parliament a series of acts for raising and applying a revenue in America. The colonists, he said, had objected to a direct tax, but they had often submitted to port duties, and could not reasonably refuse to do so again. Duties were accordingly to be laid on glass,
paper, lead, and painter's colours; on wine, oil, and fruits, if carried directly to America from Spain and Portugal; and especially on tea. ...

The Americans had [for six years] successfully resisted the   2
Townshend acts and secured the repeal of all the duties except on
tea. As for tea they had plenty, but not from England; they smuggled
it from Holland in spite of custom-houses and search-warrants.
Clearly, unless the Americans could be made to buy tea from England
and pay the duty on it, the king must own himself defeated. Since it
appeared that they could not be forced into doing this, it remained to
be seen if they could be tricked into doing it. A truly ingenious
scheme was devised. Tea sent by the East India Company to America
had formerly paid a duty in some British port on the way. This duty
was now taken off, so that the price of tea for America might be lowered. The company's tea thus became so cheap that the American
merchant could buy a pound of it and pay the threepence duty beside for less than it cost him to smuggle a pound of tea from Holland.
It was supposed that the Americans would of course buy the tea
which they could get most cheaply, and would thus be beguiled into
submission to that principle of taxation which they had hitherto resisted. Ships laden with tea were accordingly sent in the autumn of
1773 to Boston, New York, Philadelphia, and Charleston; and consignees were appointed to receive the tea in each of these towns.

Under the guise of a commercial operation, this was purely a po-   3
litical trick. It was an insulting challenge to the American people, and
merited the reception which they gave it. They would have shown
themselves unworthy of their rich political heritage had they given it
any other. In New York, Philadelphia, and Charleston, mass-meetings

of the people voted that the consignees should be ordered to resign their offices, and they did so. At Philadelphia the tea-ship was met and sent back to England before it had come within the jurisdiction of the custom-house. At Charleston the tea was landed, and as there was no one to receive it or pay the duty, it was thrown into a damp cellar and left there to spoil.

In Boston things took a different turn. The stubborn courage of Governor Hutchinson prevented the consignees, two of whom were his own sons, from resigning; the ships arrived and were anchored under guard of a committee of citizens; if they were not unloaded within twenty days, the custom-house officers were empowered by law to seize them and unload them by force; and having once come within the jurisdiction of the custom-house, they could not go out to sea without a clearance from the collector or a pass from the governor. The situation was a difficult one, but it was most nobly met by the men of Massachusetts. The excitement was intense, but the proceedings were characterized from first to last by perfect quiet and decorum. In an earnest and solemn, almost prayerful spirit, the advice of all the towns in the commonwealth was sought, and the response was unanimous that the tea must on no account whatever be landed. Similar expressions of opinion came from other colonies, and the action of Massachusetts was awaited with breathless interest. Many town-meetings were held in Boston, and the owner of the ships was ordered to take them away without unloading; but the collector contrived to fritter away the time until the nineteenth day, and then refused a clearance. On the next day, the 16th of December, 1773, seven thousand people were assembled in town-meeting in and around the Old South Meeting-House, while the owner of the ships was sent out to the governor's house at Milton to ask for a pass. It was nightfall when he returned without it, and there was then but one thing to be done. By sunrise the next morning the revenue officers would board the ships and unload their cargoes, the consignees would go to the custom-house and pay the duty, and the king's scheme would have been crowned with success. The only way to prevent this was to rip open the tea-chests and spill their contents into the sea, and this was done, according to a preconcerted plan and without the slightest uproar or disorder, by a small party of men disguised as Indians. Among them were some of the best of the townsfolk, and the chief manager of the proceedings was Samuel Adams. The destruction of the tea has often been spoken of, especially by British historians, as a "riot," but nothing could have been less like a riot. It was really the deliberate action of the commonwealth of Mass-achusetts, and the only fitting reply to the king's insulting trick. It was hailed with delight throughout the thirteen colonies, and there is nothing in our whole history of which an educated American should feel more proud.

READING QUESTIONS FOR "THE BOSTON TEA PARTY"

Main Idea

1. State the essay's main idea in your own words. Compare it to your prediction of the main idea. (*Note:* The main idea should sum up the smaller ideas of the essay.)

Organization

2. a. Where in the essay is the main idea found?

   b. Why has the author placed the main idea there?

3. In what order are the paragraphs arranged? (Underline one.) Time / Least to most important / Most to least important / Simple listing / Logic: cause and effect / Other logic / Other

Style

4. How formal is the essay? (Circle your choice.)

   [Informal—1—2—3—4—5—6—7—8—9—10—Formal]

   What indicators convinced you? (For a list of possible indicators and two benchmark essays, see Appendix F, The Formality Spectrum, on page 307.)

5. Where do you see the following features of style? List one or two examples of each with their paragraph numbers.

   Features (For definitions, see Appendix B, page 291.)

   a. cliché

   b. metaphor

   Content

6. Does the author propose any change? If so, what do you think would be the result of such change?

7. Do you agree with the author's main idea? Why or why not?

8. When Jesus overturned the money tables in the Jewish temple (Mark 11:15–17), was he committing an act of civil disobedience according to the quotation from Romans on p. 136?

If you have not already read the essay and answered the Reading Questions, be sure to do so before you proceed.

COMPOSITION QUESTIONS

Listed below are the writing questions. Choose one and write an essay that answers it. Whichever question you choose, think of the person who will read your answer. The question may tell who your audience is. If not, think of a person you know and respect—preferably your instructor or a fellow student who will read your essay. Try to convince that person to believe you.

Bring in useful details from the selection(s) you have read and perhaps other incidents you know of. For ideas, review your answers to questions in the Preview and Reading Steps. When you first refer to a reading, give its title (in quotation marks) and the author's full name. Also, give the full name of anyone featured in the article the first time you mention that person.

Note: If you are assigned to write a one-paragraph essay, think of your answer to the question, and list several key points you could make to support your answer. Then choose just one of the points and explain it in detail.

1. Do you favor the pacifism of the Quakers or the civil disobedience of Samuel Adams? Why?

2. Think of some act or program of civil disobedience during the last 50 years. Was it justified? Why or why not?

3. Explain the difference between planned civil disobedience, spontaneous rioting, and terrorism. Which, if any, do you think can be justified?

4. Reread the quotation from Romans in the Preview (page 136). In your opinion, were the acts of Samuel Adams and the other colonists (who held to no taxation without representation) morally wrong? Why or why not?

5. Reread the quotation from Romans in the Preview (page 136). In your opinion, were the civil disobedience acts of Rev. Martin Luther King unchristian? Consider your own standards, the Quakers' standards (in the preview article), and King's own standards (explained in his essay "Letter from Birmingham Jail—April 16, 1963," from *Why We Can't Wait*).

6. Nazi law required Germans to turn Jews over to the civil authorities. Were the Christians who hid Jews acting unchristian? Consider the Quaker standards and the quotation from Romans (in the Preview) as well as your own standards.

7. Do you agree with the Quakers that civil disobedience should occur only if the civil governments "interfere with our allegiance to God"? Why? If not, explain what other factors you would consider also.

8. Usually adults can leave a church, but children cannot, and some religious groups require children to accept conditions or activities that civil law labels as child abuse. If civil authorities interfere, thus disrupting the religious practices of these groups, do these groups have the moral right to exert nonviolent acts of civil disobedience?

9. Writing about the Boston Tea Party, Fiske says that "there is nothing in our whole history of which an educated American should feel more proud." Do you agree with Fiske? Why or why not?

10. In your locality, state, region, or nation, is there any particular issue or situation that you think deserves the civil disobedience of collective citizens?

REVISION QUESTIONS

Once you have finished writing your essay, ask yourself the following questions.

1. Is there any statement the reader might not understand?
2. Is there any statement that might offend the reader?
3. Is there anything that's not very convincing?
4. Have I changed the subject and then changed it back again?
5. Have I said the same thing twice?
6. Do I want to try using any feature of style I've seen in the reading selection?

EDITING QUESTIONS

Once you've made changes, ask someone else to read your essay. Change it again as needed. Then read your essay out loud and answer the following questions.

1. Does every sentence make sense?
2. Does every sentence use the kind of language that most people consider "good English" these days? (*Hint:* Imagine a TV announcer reading it.)

3. Do the periods, commas, and other punctuation show the rise and fall of my voice?

4. Are the words spelled right?

If your instructor asks you to copy your paper over, proofread for copying errors before you hand it in.

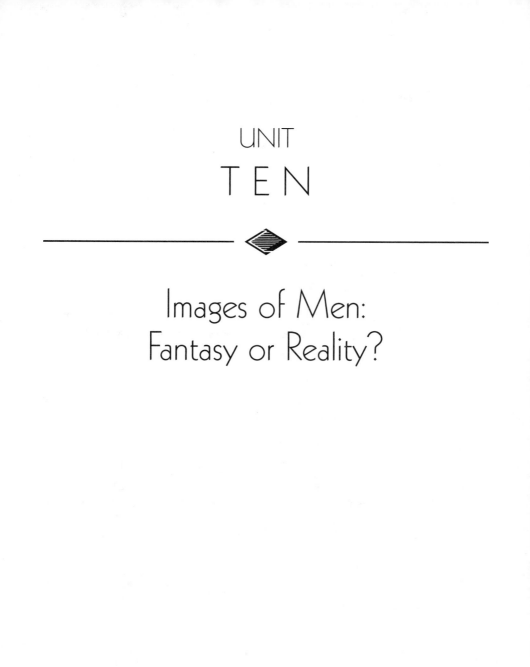

UNIT

T E N

Images of Men:
Fantasy or Reality?

PREVIEW STEPS FOR UNIT TEN

In response to questions 1 and 2, try these steps: Write your answers, talk them over with three or four classmates, and then discuss them with the whole class.

1. a. Take two minutes to list the words that come to mind when you hear the word *men*.

   b. Do the same for the word *women*.

   c. Now mark each word with a plus or minus sign to show whether it is a "good" word (something a person of that sex would like to be called) or a "bad" word.

   d. Check to see which list—*men* or *women*—had more positive words. Are you biased in favor of your own sex?

2. Consider which sex differences are learned and which are inborn. Mark each word on the lists above with "L" (learned) or "I" (inborn). Then compare notes with someone else to see whether you agree.

3. a. Read the title of the first essay (page 149). Name the topic. (Who or what is this essay about?)

   b. Now predict the main idea. (What is the main point the author wants to make about this topic?)

   c. Read the first and last paragraphs. Revise your prediction if necessary. (*Note:* The main idea should sum up the smaller ideas of the essay.)

4. Some words from the essay are listed below, accompanied by quotations. Mark any words you do not know and make an educated guess about their meanings using the context supplied by the quotations—and possibly Appendix A, Word Parts, on page 287. You may want to work with a small group of classmates.

nurturant "I want a wife who is a good *nurturant* attendant to my children. . . ."

adherence ". . . my sexual needs may entail more than strict *adherence* to *monogamy*."

monogamy See above quotation.

5. Now read the following essay. As you read, jot down any questions that occur to you.

(*Note:* Question 6 appears after the essay.)

I Want a Wife

Judy Brady

I belong to that classification of people known as wives. I am A Wife.   1
And, not altogether incidentally, I am a mother.

   Not too long ago a male friend of mine appeared on the scene   2
fresh from a recent divorce. He had one child, who is, of course, with
his ex-wife. He is obviously looking for another wife. As I thought
about him while I was ironing one evening, it suddenly occurred to
me that I, too, would like to have a wife. Why do I want a wife?

I would like to go back to school so that I can become economi-   3
cally independent, support myself, and, if need be, support those dependent upon me. I want a wife who will work and send me to
school. And while I am going to school I want a wife to keep track of
the children's doctor and dentist appointments. And to keep track of
mine, too. I want a wife to make sure my children eat properly and
are kept clean. I want a wife who will wash the children's clothes and
keep them mended. I want a wife who is a good nurturant attendant
to my children, who arranges for their schooling, makes sure that
they have an adequate social life with their peers, takes them to the
park, the zoo, etc. I want a wife who takes care of the children when
they are sick, a wife who arranges to be around when the children
need special care, because, of course, I cannot miss classes at school.
My wife must arrange to lose time at work and not lose the job. It
may mean a small cut in my wife's income from time to time, but I
guess I can tolerate that. Needless to say, my wife will arrange and
pay for the care of the children while my wife is working.

I want a wife who will take care of my physical needs. I want a   4
wife who will keep my house clean. A wife who will pick up after me.
I want a wife who will keep my clothes clean, ironed, mended, replaced when need be, and who will see to it that my personal things
are kept in their proper place so that I can find what I need the
minute I need it. I want a wife who cooks the meals, a wife who is a
good cook. I want a wife who will plan the menus, do the necessary
grocery shopping, prepare the meals, serve them pleasantly, and then
do the cleaning up while I do my studying. I want a wife who will
care for me when I am sick and sympathize with my pain and loss of
time from school. I want a wife to go along when our family takes a
vacation so that someone can continue to care for me and my children when I need a rest and change of scene.

I want a wife who will not bother me with rambling complaints   5
about a wife's duties. But I want a wife who will listen to me when I
feel the need to explain a rather difficult point I have come across in
my course of studies. And I want a wife who will type my papers for
me when I have written them.

I want a wife who will take care of the details of my social life.   6
When my wife and I are invited out by my friends, I want a wife who
will take care of the babysitting arrangements. When I meet people at
school that I like and want to entertain, I want a wife who will have the
house clean, will prepare a special meal, serve it to me and my friends,

and not interrupt when I talk about the things that interest me and my friends. I want a wife who will have arranged that the children are fed and ready for bed before my guests arrive so that the children do not bother us. I want a wife who takes care of the needs of my guests so that they feel comfortable, who makes sure that they have an ashtray, that they are passed the hors d'oeuvres, that they are offered a second helping of the food, that their wine glasses are replenished when necessary, that their coffee is served to them as they like it.

And I want a wife who knows that sometimes I need a night out   7
by myself.

I want a wife who is sensitive to my sexual needs, a wife who   8
makes love passionately and eagerly when I feel like it, a wife who makes sure that I am satisfied. And, of course, I want a wife who will not demand sexual attention when I am not in the mood for it. I want a wife who assumes the complete responsibility for birth control, because I do not want more children. I want a wife who will remain sexually faithful to me so that I do not have to clutter up my intellectual life with jealousies. And I want a wife who understands that my sexual needs may entail more than strict adherence to monogamy. I must, after all, be able to relate to people as fully as possible.

If, by chance, I find another person more suitable as a wife than   9
the wife I already have, I want the liberty to replace my present wife with another one. Naturally, I will expect a fresh, new life; my wife will take the children and be solely responsible for them so that I am left free.

When I am through with school and have a job, I want my wife   10
to quit working and remain at home so that my wife can more fully and completely take care of a wife's duties.

My God, who wouldn't want a wife?   11

6. State the essay's main idea in your own words. Compare it to your prediction of the main idea. (*Note:* The main idea should sum up the smaller ideas of the essay.)

7. In describing why she wants a wife, Brady constantly uses the words *I, me, my,* and *mine.* Why does she do this?

8. How does Brady picture husbands? How can you tell?

9. Are there any sentences where Brady is unfair to men, either exaggerating or failing to show both sides of the story?

PREVIEW STEPS FOR "CONFESSIONS OF A FEMALE CHAUVINIST SOW"

1. a. Read the title of the second essay (page 154). Name the topic. (Who or what is this essay about?)

    b. Now predict the main idea. (What is the main point the author wants to make about this topic?)

    c. Read the first and last paragraphs of the essay. Revise your prediction if necessary. (*Note:* The main idea should sum up the smaller ideas of the essay.)

2. What in the author's background may have led her to the main idea? (See author's background, below title.)

3. Some words from the essay are listed below, accompanied by quotations. Mark any words you do not know and make an educated guess about their meanings using the context supplied by the quotations—and possibly Appendix A, Word Parts, on page 287. You may want to work with a small group of classmates.

marionette ". . . like *marionette* strings, pulling us this way or that."

lexicon "They have a *lexicon* with which they tease the enemy: ofay, goy, honky, gringo."

hypocritical ". . . they tried to make you do things in the dark they wouldn't respect you for afterwards. . . . They appeared to be *hypocritical*, self-seeking, *exploitative*. . . ."

exploitative See above quotation.

empathetic "Women are just people-oriented; they learn to be *empathetic* at an early age."

flaccid "Images of . . . *flaccid* penises rising and falling with the Dow Jones average . . ."

chauvinism "The prejudices of childhood are hard to outgrow. . . . There it is, *chauvinism* waving its cancerous tentacles from the depths of my *psyche*."

psyche See above quotation.

masochistic ". . . brutality is masculine. . . . Women . . . are indeed more *masochistic* than men."

coevals ". . . I thought all boys around my age and grade were creeps and bores. . . . I had a certain contempt for my *coevals* . . ."

solace "Some women never lose that contempt for men of their own age. That . . . may be one reason why some sensible men of middle years find *solace* in young women."

vignette "I remember coming home from school one day. . . . [The author goes on to tell a story about what happened that day.] The point of this *vignette* is the nature of the laughter . . ."

cacophony "Boys are messy, boys are mean, boys are rough, boys are stupid and have sloppy handwriting. A *cacophony* of childhood memories rushes through my head . . ."

5. At the end of the Preview, you may want to go over any new features of style that occur in the following reading selection. You will need to know the terms *allusion, cliché, irony of situation, irony of wording, jargon, metaphor, overstatement,* and *simile.* For help, see Appendix B, Guide to Literary Terms (page 291), with accompanying exercises on individual features.

6. Before reading "Confessions of a Female Chauvinist Sow," turn to pages 159–162 and skim the Reading Questions. Then read the essay to find answers to these questions. As you read, jot down any questions that occur to you.

Confessions of a Female Chauvinist Sow

Anne Roiphe

Born in 1935, Anne Roiphe grew up in New York City, graduated from Sarah Lawrence College, and later studied in Munich, Germany. She has written several novels concerned largely with women's search for identity, including Digging Out, Up the Sandbox, Long Division, *and* Torch Song, *as well as articles for* The New York Times Magazine, New York *magazine, and* Vogue.

I once married a man I thought was totally unlike my father and I imag-   1
ined a whole new world of freedom emerging. Five years later it was clear even to me—floating face down in a wash of despair—that I had simply chosen a replica of my handsome daddy-true. The updated version spoke English like an angel but—good God!—underneath he was my father exactly: wonderful, but not the right man for me.

Most people I know have at one time or another been fouled up   2
by their childhood experiences. Patterns tend to sink into the unconscious only to reappear, disguised, unseen, like marionette strings, pulling us this way or that. Whatever ails people—keeps them up at night, tossing and turning—also ails movements no matter how historically huge or politically important. The women's movement can-

not remake consciousness, or reshape the future, without acknowl-edging and shedding all the unnecessary and ugly baggage of the past. It's easy enough now to see where men have kept us out of clubs, baseball games, graduate schools; it's easy enough to recognize the hidden directions that limit Sis to cake-baking and Junior to bridge-building; it's now possible for even Miss America herself to identify what they have done to us, and, of course, they have and they did and they are. . . . But along the way we also developed our own hidden prejudices, class assumptions, and an anti-male humor and collection of expectations that gave us, like all oppressed groups, a secret sense of superiority (co-existing with a poor self-image—it's not news that people can believe two contradictory things at once).

Listen to any group that suffers materially and socially. They have a lexicon with which they tease the enemy: ofay, goy, honky, gringo. "Poor pale devils," said Malcolm X loud enough for us to hear, although blacks had joked about that to each other for years. Behind some of the women's liberation thinking lurk the rumors, the prejudices, the defense systems of generations of oppressed women whispering in the kitchen together, presenting one face to their men-folk and another to their card clubs, their mothers and sisters. All this is natural enough but potentially dangerous in a revolutionary situation in which you hope to create a future that does not mirror the past. The hidden anti-male feelings, a result of the old system, will foul us up if they are allowed to persist.

During my teen years I never left the house on my Saturday night dates without my mother slipping me a few extra dollars—mad money, it was called. I'll explain what it was for the benefit of the new generation in which people just sleep with each other: the fellow was supposed to bring me home, lead me safely through the asphalt jungle, protect me from slithering snakes, rapists, and the like. But my mother and I knew young men were apt to drink too much, to slosh down so many rye-and-gingers that some hero might well lead me in front of an oncoming bus, smash his daddy's car into Tiffany's window or, less gallantly, throw up on my new dress. Mad money was for getting home on your own, no matter what form of insanity your date happened to evidence. Mad money was also a wallflower's rope ladder; if the guy you came with suddenly fancied someone else, well, you didn't have to stay there and suffer, you could go home. Boys were fickle and likely to be unkind; my mother and I knew that, as surely as we knew they tried to make you do things in the dark they wouldn't respect you for afterwards, and in fact would spread the word and spoil your rep. Boys liked to be flattered; if you made them feel important they would eat out of your hand. So talk to them about their interests, don't alarm them with displays of intelligence— we all knew that, we groups of girls talking into the wee hours of the night in a kind of easy companionship we thought impossible with boys. Boys were prone to have a good time, get you pregnant, and then pretend they didn't know your name when you came knocking on their door for finances or comfort. In short, we believed boys were less moral than we were. They appeared to be hypocritical, self-seeking, exploitative, untrustworthy, and very likely to be showing off their precious masculinity. I never had a girl friend I thought would be unkind or embarrass me in public. I never expected a girl to lie to me about her marks or sports skill or how good she was in bed. Altogether—without anyone's directly coming out and saying so—I gathered that men were sexy, powerful, very interesting, but not very nice, not very moral, humane, and tender, like us. Girls played fairly while men, unfortunately, reserved their honor for the battlefield.

Why are there laws insisting on alimony and child support? Well,   5
everyone knows that men don't have an instinct to protect their young and, given half a chance, with the moon in the right phase, they will run off and disappear. Everyone assumes a mother will not let her child starve, yet it is necessary to legislate that a father must not do so. We are taught to accept the idea that men are less than decent; their charms may be manifold but their characters are riddled with faults. To this day I never blink if I hear that a man has gone to find his fortune in South America, having left his pregnant wife, his blind mother, and taken the family car. I still gasp in horror when I hear of a woman leaving her asthmatic infant for a rock group in Taos because I can't seem to avoid the assumption that men are naturally heels and women the ordained carriers of what little is moral in our dubious civilization.

My mother never gave me mad money thinking I would ditch a   6
fellow for some other guy or that I would pass out drunk on the floor. She knew I would be considerate of my companion because, after all, I was more mature than the boys that gathered about. Why was I more mature? Women just are people-oriented; they learn to be empathetic at an early age. Most English students (students interested in humanity, not artifacts) are women. Men and boys—so the myth goes—conceal their feelings and lose interest in anybody else's.

Everyone knows that even little boys can tell the difference between one kind of a car and another—proof that their souls are mechanical, their attention directed to the non-human.

I remember shivering in the cold vestibule of a famous men's 7
athletic club. Women and girls are not permitted inside the club's door. What are they doing in there, I asked? They're naked, said my mother, they're sweating, jumping up and down a lot, telling each other dirty jokes, and bragging about their stock market exploits. Why can't we go in? I asked. Well, my mother told me, they're afraid we'd laugh at them.

The prejudices of childhood are hard to outgrow. I confess that 8
every time my business takes me past that club, I shudder. Images of large bellies resting on massage tables and flaccid penises rising and falling with the Dow Jones average flash through my head. There it is, chauvinism waving its cancerous tentacles from the depths of my psyche.

Minorities automatically feel superior to the oppressor because, 9
after all, they are not hurting anybody. In fact, they feel they are morally better. The old canard that women need love, men need sex—believed for too long by both sexes—attributes moral and spiritual superiority to women and makes of men beasts whose urges send them prowling into the night. This false division of good and bad, placing deforming pressures on everyone, doesn't have to contaminate the future. We know that the assumptions we make about each other become a part of the cultural air we breathe and, in fact, become social truths. Women who want equality must be prepared to give it and to believe in it, and in order to do that it is not enough to state that you are as good as any man, but also it must be stated that he is as good as you and both will be humans together. If we want men to share in the care of the family in a new way, we must assume them as capable of consistent loving tenderness as we.

I rummage about and find in my thinking all kinds of anti-male 10
prejudices. Some are just jokes and others I will have a hard time abandoning. First, I share an emotional conviction with many sisters that women given power would not create wars. Intellectually I know that's ridiculous; great queens have waged war before; the likes of Lurleen Wallace, Pat Nixon, and Mrs. General Lavelle can be depended upon in the future to guiltlessly condemn to death other people's children in the name of some ideal of their own. Little girls, of course, don't take toy guns out of their hip pockets and say "Pow,

pow" to all their neighbors and friends like the average well-adjusted little boy. However, if we gave little girls the six-shooters, we would soon have double the pretend body count.

Aggression is not, as I secretly think, a male-sex-linked charac- 11 teristic: brutality is masculine only by virtue of opportunity. True, there are 1,000 Jack the Rippers for every Lizzie Borden, but that surely is the result of social forms. Women as a group are indeed more masochistic than men. The practical result of this division is that women seem nicer and kinder, but when the world changes, women will have a fuller opportunity to be just as rotten as men and there will be fewer claims of female moral superiority.

Now that I am entering early middle age, I heard many women 12 complaining of husbands and ex-husbands who are attracted to younger females. This strikes the older woman as unfair, of course. But I remember a time when I thought all boys around my age and grade were creeps and bores. I wanted to go out with an older man: a senior or, miraculously, a college man. I had a certain contempt for my co-evals, not realizing that the freshman in college I thought so desirable, was some older girl's creep. Some women never lose that contempt for men of their own age. That isn't fair either and may be one reason why some sensible men of middle years find solace in young women.

I remember coming home from school one day to find my 13 mother's card game dissolved in hysterical laughter. The cards were floating in black rivers of running mascara. What was so funny? A woman named Helen was lying on a couch pretending to be her husband with a cold. She was issuing demands for orange juice, aspirin, suggesting a call to a specialist, complaining of neglect, of fate's cruel finger, of heat, of cold, of sharp pains on the bridge of the nose that might indicate brain involvement. What was so funny? The ladies explained to me that all men behave just like that with colds, they are reduced to temper tantrums by simple nasal congestion, men cannot stand any little physical discomfort—on and on the laughter went.

The point of this vignette is the nature of the laughter—us 14 laughing at them, us feeling superior to them, us ridiculing them behind their backs. If they were doing it to us we'd call it male chauvinist pigness; if we do it to them, it is inescapably female chauvinist sowness and, whatever its roots, it leads to the same isolation. Boys are messy, boys are mean, boys are rough, boys are stupid and have sloppy handwriting. A cacophony of childhood memories rushes through my head, balanced, of course, by all the well-documented feelings of inferiority and envy. But the important thing, the hard thing, is to wipe the slate clean, to start again without the meanness of the past. That's why it's so important that the women's movement not become anti-male and allow its most prejudiced spokesmen total leadership. The much-chewed-over abortion issue illustrates this. The women's-liberation position, insisting on a woman's right to determine her own body's destiny, leads in fanatical extreme to a kind of emotional immaculate conception in which the father is not judged even half-responsible—he has no rights, and no consideration is to be given to his concern for either the woman or the fetus.

Woman, who once was abandoned and disgraced by an un- 15 wanted pregnancy, has recently arrived at a new pride of ownership or disposal. She has traveled in a straight line that still excludes her sexual partner from an equal share in the wanted or unwanted pregnancy. A better style of life may develop from an assumption that men are as human as we. Why not ask the child's father if he would like to bring up the child? Why not share decisions, when possible, with the male? If we cut them out, assuming an old-style indifference on their part, we perpetuate the ugly divisiveness that has characterized relations between the sexes so far.

Hard as it is for many of us to believe, women are not really su- 16 perior to men in intelligence or humanity—they are only equal.

READING QUESTIONS FOR "CONFESSIONS OF A FEMALE CHAUVINIST SOW"

Main Idea

1. State the essay's main idea in your own words. Compare it to your prediction of the main idea. (*Note:* The main idea should sum up the smaller ideas of the essay.)

Organization

2. a. Where in the essay is the main idea found?

b. Why has the author placed the main idea there?

3. In what order are the paragraphs arranged? (Underline one.) Time /
    Least to most important / Most to least important / Simple listing /
    Logic: cause and effect / Other logic / Other

Style

4. How formal is the essay? (Circle your choice.)

    [Informal—1—2—3—4—5—6—7—8—9—10—Formal]

    What indicators convinced you? (For a list of possible indicators and
    two benchmark essays, see Appendix F, The Formality Spectrum, on
    page 307.)

5. Where do you see the following features of style? List one or two ex-
    amples of each with their paragraph numbers.

    Features (For definitions, see Appendix B, page 291.)

    a. allusion

    b. cliché

    c. irony of situation

   d. irony of wording

   e. jargon

   f. metaphor

   g. overstatement

   h. simile

Content

6. a. When saying women are at fault, how does the author include herself?

   b. What is the effect of her including herself?

   c. Would you say this essay is directed mainly to women or to men?

7. Would Roiphe say there is any prejudice on the part of Brady (the author of "I Want a Wife")?

8. a. According to Roiphe, women say men have many bad qualities. Consult paragraph 4 and list the qualities. (You might want to compare this list to your list under Preview Questions 1 and 2.)

   b. Underline any of these bad qualities you think are true of men—at least in part.
   c. For each underlined quality, mark "L" (learned) or "I" (inborn). (Why does this matter?)
   d. Judging from your list, do you think women are entitled to some feelings of superiority or not?

9. Does the author propose any change? If so, what do you think would be the result of that change?

If you have not already read the essay and answered the Reading Questions, be sure to do so before you proceed.

COMPOSITION QUESTIONS

Listed below are the writing questions. Choose one and write an essay that answers it. Whichever question you choose, think of the person who will read your answer. The question may tell who your audience is. If not, think of a person you know and respect—preferably your instructor or a fellow student who will read your essay. Try to convince that person to believe you.

Bring in useful details from the selection(s) you have read and perhaps other incidents you know of. For ideas, review your answers to questions in the Preview and Reading Steps. When you first refer to a reading, give its title (in quotation marks) and the author's full name. Also, give the full name of anyone featured in the article the first time you mention that person.

Note: If you are assigned to write a one-paragraph essay, think of your answer to the question, and list several key points you could make to support your answer. Then choose just one of the points and explain it in detail.

1. In "I Want a Wife," Brady lists various responsibilities of a wife. Choose one from her list. Is it fair for the wife to have that responsibility? If so, under what circumstances?

2. What does Brady see as a problem, and what do you think her solutions might be? For any solution suggested by her essay, evaluate its chances of working.

3. According to Roiphe, women say men have many bad qualities. Choose one from her list. In general, do men actually have more of that quality than women? If so, is the difference inborn or learned? (Your notes from Reading Question 8 may help here.)

4. How does Roiphe suggest improving relationships between men and women? Do you think her solution is realistic? That is, can women do as Roiphe suggests, and if they do, how will men respond?

5. Compare the solutions suggested by Brady and Roiphe. Which seems more workable?

6. From the point of view of a man, write an essay called "I Want a Husband." Convince your reader that women treat men unfairly.

REVISION QUESTIONS

Once you have finished writing your essay, ask yourself the following questions.

1. Is there any statement the reader might not understand?
2. Is there any statement that might offend the reader?
3. Is there anything that's not very convincing?
4. Have I changed the subject and then changed it back again?
5. Have I said the same thing twice?
6. Do I want to try using any feature of style I've seen in the reading selection?

EDITING QUESTIONS

Once you've made changes, ask someone else to read your essay. Change it again as needed. Then read your essay out loud and answer the following questions.

1. Does every sentence make sense?
2. Does every sentence use the kind of language that most people consider "good English" these days? (*Hint:* Imagine a TV announcer reading it.)
3. Do the periods, commas, and other punctuation show the rise and fall of my voice?
4. Are the words spelled right?

If your instructor asks you to copy your paper over, proofread for copying errors before you hand it in.

UNIT

ELEVEN

The Right to Bear Arms

PREVIEW STEPS FOR UNIT ELEVEN

In response to questions 1 and 2, try these steps: Write your answers, talk them over with three or four classmates, and then discuss them with the whole class.

1. a. Think of the word *gun*. Jot down whatever comes to your mind for two minutes. (This is private writing—for your eyes only.)

   b. Reread your ideas and put a plus sign by anything that sounds good or appealing about guns. Put a minus sign by anything that sounds negative.
   c. Judging from your own reactions, what do you think most people like about guns?

   What do they dislike?

2. Under what circumstances would you carry a firearm? Check any that apply.
   ☐ to safeguard your family
   ☐ for hunting
   ☐ live/work in a dangerous area
   ☐ have a dangerous occupation such as police work
   ☐ live under a dictatorship
   ☐ in war (*Note:* "Conscientious objectors" can opt out of fighting.)
   ☐ never (would rather die than take a life)
   ☐ other: _____

3. a. Read the title of the first essay (page 168). Name the topic. (Who or what is this essay about?)

b. Now predict the main idea. (What is the main point the author wants to make about this topic?)

c. Read the first and last paragraphs. Revise your prediction if necessary. (*Note:* The main idea should sum up the smaller ideas of the essay.)

4. Some words from the essay are listed below, accompanied by quotations. Mark any words you do not know and make an educated guess about their meanings using the context supplied by the quotations—and possibly Appendix A, Word Parts, on page 287. You may want to work with a small group of classmates.

militia "*Militia*s, such as the Minutemen, were composed of private citizens who supplied their own weapons. . . ."

construed "The Constitution shall never be *construed* to prevent the people from keeping arms."

infringed "A well-regulated militia, being necessary to preserve the security of the Free State, the right of the people to bear arms shall not be *infringed*."

ordnance (not **ordinance**) "Many anti-gun activists believe that . . . the rights of private citizens to maintain their own *ordnance* does not exist."

tyranny "Our founding fathers used their own privately held military weapons . . . to overthrow *tyranny* in government. . . ."

revocation "We, the people, retain the right to . . . protect ourselves from illegal *revocation* of our constitutional rights. . . ."

usurped "If any of these rights is ever *usurped*, it is the duty of the armed citizen to . . . defend the Constitution—by force. . . ."

concur "The Bureau of Alcohol, Tobacco, and Firearms now says only 'sporting purpose' firearms are legal. Congress, the President, and the Supreme Court *concur*."

viable ". . . even after the Civil War, militarily *viable* weapons have remained in citizens' hands."

5. Now read the following essay. As you read, jot down any questions that occur to you.

(*Note:* Question 6 appears after the essay.)

American Revolutionary

Matthew Edwards

"Firearms stand next in importance to the Constitution itself.   1
They are the American people's liberty, teeth, and keystone
under independence. The rifle and pistol are equally indispens-
able and they deserve a place of honor with all that's good.
When firearms go, all goes. We need them every hour."
                                                   —George Washington

The Constitution preserves "the advantage of being armed,   2
which Americans possess over the people of almost every other
nation . . . [where] the governments are afraid to trust the people with arms."
                            —James Madison, *The Federalist Papers*, #46.

"I ask, sir, what is the militia? It is the whole people. . . . To dis-   3
arm the people is the best and most effectual way to enslave
them. . . ."
                                                        —George Mason

"The Constitution shall never be construed to prevent the peo-   4
ple from keeping arms."

—Samuel Adams

The Second Amendment of the U.S. Constitution reads, "A   5
well-regulated militia, being necessary to preserve the security of the
Free State, the right of the people to bear arms shall not be infringed." Many anti-gun activists believe that the Second Amendment allows only state police and national guard units. In their view,
the rights of private citizens to maintain their own ordnance does not
exist. History shows this view to be false.

Militias, such as the Minutemen, were composed of private citi-   6
zens who supplied their own weapons and kept them in their own
homes. The British marched on Lexington and Concord to seize private arms stockpiles from the citizens of those towns. That march
was the spark that brought on a Revolutionary War. Our founding
fathers used their own privately-held military weapons to overthrow
tyranny in government, and out of this came a new nation. The Second Amendment was written to ensure the people the means to
throw off government again should it become necessary.

The Second Amendment recognized the rights of citizens to   7
defend their rights, lives, and property from anyone who threat-
ened them, including their own government. The Federal Government has no authority to revoke citizen militia privileges unless the
people amend the Constitution so as to grant the government this
power. We, the people, retain the right to bear arms in order to
protect ourselves from illegal revocation of our constitutional
rights, including the Second Amendment. If any of these rights is
ever usurped, it is the duty of the armed citizen to preserve, protect, and defend the Constitution—by force, as a means of last
resort.

In fact, the Second Amendment has been illegally usurped by   8
government. The 1968 Gun Control Act, a direct translation of
Hitler's own gun-control legislation, declares that only sporting-
purpose arms may be lawfully owned by civilians. But the Second
Amendment is not about duck-hunting: the Second Amendment was
created to afford citizens the protection of ordnance for military purpose. Changing our Constitution requires an amendment in itself,
not just a law. The Bureau of Alcohol, Tobacco, and Firearms now

says only "sporting purpose" firearms are legal. Congress, the President, and the Supreme Court concur. Thus, the Second Amendment has been unconstitutionally abridged.

Some say that street crime justifies our government's illegal ban   9
on semi-automatic "assault rifles." First of all, even if street crime is considered just cause to change our Constitution, we must uphold the Constitution until it is changed. Second, assault rifles are rarely used in crime. Pistols and shotguns are much more effective at the close ranges at which crimes generally occur. Criminals realize this: fewer than 1% of all firearms crimes involve assault rifles, according to the Bureau of Alcohol, Tobacco, and Firearms. A third point: even after the Civil War, militarily viable weapons have remained in citizens' hands. Street crime is, by comparison, a small problem—a small excuse for taking away the freedom of law-abiding citizens to arm themselves.

The government has illegally done away with an important con-   10
stitutional liberty. It is your duty as a citizen to defend the Constitution of the United States against all enemies, foreign and domestic. Prepare now to defend liberty.

> "The strongest reason for the people to retain the right to keep   11
> and bear arms is, as a last resort, to protect themselves against
> tyranny in government."
>
> —Thomas Jefferson

6. State the essay's main idea in your own words. Compare it to your prediction of the main idea. (*Note:* the main idea should sum up the smaller ideas of the essay.)

PREVIEW STEPS FOR "THE HYDROGEN BOMB LOBBY"

1. a. Read the title of the second essay (page 172). Name the topic. (Who or what is this essay about?)

b. Now predict the main idea. (What is the main point the author wants to make about this topic?)

c. Read the first and last paragraphs of the essay. Revise your prediction if necessary. (*Note:* The main idea should sum up the smaller ideas of the essay.)

2. What in the author's background may have led him to the main idea? (See author's background, below title.)

3. Some words from the essay are listed below, accompanied by quotations. Mark any words you do not know and make an educated guess about their meanings using the context supplied by the quotations— and possibly Appendix A, Word Parts, on page 287. You may want to work with a small group of classmates.

   zealot ". . . a group of firearm *zealots* formed the National Hydrogen Bomb Assn. . . ."

   deterrent "The bomb . . . has a *deterrent* effect. If somebody knows you have a nuclear weapon in your house, they're going to think twice about breaking in."

4. At the end of the Preview, you may want to go over any new features of style that occur in the following reading selection. You will need to know the terms *cliché, irony of wording,* and *understatement.* For help, see Appendix B, Guide to Literary Terms (page 291), with accompanying exercises on individual features.

5. Before reading "The Hydrogen Bomb Lobby," note that an actual hydrogen bomb would sicken or kill people for hundreds of square miles. Would a lobbying group really want to demand private ownership of hydrogen bombs? Or could this essay be satire—humor used to make a serious point? Now turn to pages 174–175 and skim the Reading Questions. Then read the essay to find answers to these questions. As you read, jot down any questions that occur to you.

The Hydrogen Bomb Lobby

Art Buchwald

Art Buchwald (1925–) joined the Marines at 17 and spent over three years in the Pacific during World War II. After college, where he edited the campus humor magazine, Buchwald began writing newspaper columns, first in Paris and, since 1952, in Washington, DC. In 1982, he won a Pulitzer Prize for outstanding commentary. He has also written a Broadway play and 30 books, including two memoirs.

As soon as it was revealed that a reporter for *Progressive* magazine   1
had discovered how to make a hydrogen bomb, a group of firearm zealots formed the National Hydrogen Bomb Assn., and they are now lobbying against any legislation to stop Americans from owning one.

"The Constitution," said the association's spokesman, "gives   2
everyone the right to own and bear arms. It doesn't spell out what kind of arms. But since anyone can now make a hydrogen bomb, the public should be able to buy it to protect themselves."

"Don't you think it's dangerous to have one in the house, par-   3
ticularly where there are children around?"

"The National Hydrogen Bomb Assn. hopes to spend a good   4
portion of its dues on educating people in the safe handling of this type of weapon. We are instructing owners to keep the bomb in a locked closet and the fuse separately in a drawer. We also will hold classes in how to fire the bomb. We believe that if a person knows how to take care of his bomb there is no danger to himself or his family."

"Some people consider the hydrogen bomb a very lethal   5
weapon which could kill somebody."

The spokesman said, "Hydrogen bombs don't kill people— 6 people kill people. The bomb is for self-protection and it also has a deterrent effect. If somebody knows you have a nuclear weapon in your house, they're going to think twice about breaking in."

"But those who want to ban the bomb for American citizens 7 claim that if you have one locked in the closet, with the fuse in a drawer, you would never be able to assemble it in time to repulse an intruder."

"That's garbage put out by the anti-nuclear weapon people. We 8 are only advocating ownership of hydrogen weapons by law-abiding citizens. If someone commits a crime with one, he should get a stiff jail sentence."

"Another argument against allowing people to own a bomb is 9 that at the moment it is very expensive to build one. So what your association is backing is a program which would allow the middle and upper classes to acquire a bomb while poor people will be left defenseless with just handguns."

"That's pure propaganda put out by the bleeding hearts. In a 10 year or two there will be Saturday Night Hydrogen Bomb Specials costing less than a hundred dollars. It's worth that to protect your family."

"Would your association be willing to permit the registration 11 of bombs by their owners?"

"Absolutely not. If we ever go to war the Communists will have 12 a list of everybody in this country who owns the bomb. They could disarm us overnight. The strength of this nation is still in a citizens' army, and our members are pledged to fight to the last man."

"Do you plan to use the bomb for hunting?" 13

"Only for big game. We're not going to use it on a rabbit or a 14 duck because that would be overkill. But it's a perfect weapon for knocking down an elk or a bear."

"A recent Gallup survey has indicated that 78 percent of the 15 people polled said they were in favor of banning the hydrogen bomb in private hands. What is your response to that?"

"Our recent survey indicates just the opposite," he replied. 16 "People favor keeping the bomb out of the hands of criminal elements, and believe that if you carry one around in your pocket you should have a license. But it's nobody's damn business what you do with one at home."

READING QUESTIONS FOR "THE HYDROGEN BOMB LOBBY"

Main Idea

1. State the essay's main idea in your own words. Compare it to your prediction of the main idea. (*Note:* The main idea should sum up the smaller ideas of the essay.)

Organization

2. a. Where in the essay is the main idea found?

   b. Why has the author placed the main idea there?

3. In what order are the paragraphs arranged? (Underline one.) Time / Least to most important / Most to least important / Simple listing / Logic: cause and effect / Other logic / Other

Style

4. How formal is the essay? (Circle your choice.)

   [Informal–1–2–3–4–5–6–7–8–9–10–Formal]

   What indicators convinced you? (For a list of possible indicators and two benchmark essays, see Appendix F, The Formality Spectrum, on page 307.)

5. Where do you see the following features of style? List one or two examples of each with their paragraph numbers.

Features (For definitions, see Appendix B, page 291.)

a. cliché

b. irony of wording

c. understatement

Content

6. Does the author propose any change? If so, what do you think would be the result of such change?

7. Do you agree with the author's main idea? Why or why not?

8. Complete the following chart of pro-gun and anti-gun arguments. Fill in paragraph numbers for each quotation in the chart. The first argument is labeled for you.
   • Of the pro-gun arguments, Edwards gives points a, b, and c. Buchwald states point a and points d through h (in place of gun, he substitutes the word "bomb" for the purpose of satire).
   • Fill in as many anti-gun arguments as you can, using inference or your own logic.

Pro-Gun Arguments (Edwards/Buchwald)	Anti-Gun Arguments (Supply your own)
a. The Constitution gives the "right to bear arms" (Edwards, par. 5) and doesn't say what kind (Buchwald, par. 2).	Our forefathers could not foresee hydrogen bombs or even semi-automatic (rapid-fire) guns.
b. Without guns, we can be controlled by tyrants (Edwards, par.).	
c. To change the Constitution legally, we must use the process of constitutional amendment [approval by convention/or by legislature of 3/4 of the states] (Edwards, par.).	
d. Guns are safe if people learn to use them safely (Buchwald, par.).	
e. Guns don't kill people—people kill people (Buchwald, par.).	
f. Guns deter crime (Buchwald, par.).	
g. Anyone can afford an inexpensive gun (Buchwald, par.).	
h. Guns are useful for hunting (Buchwald, par.).	

If you have not already read the essay and answered the Reading Questions, be sure to do so before you proceed.

COMPOSITION QUESTIONS

Listed below are the writing questions. Choose one and write an essay that answers it. Whichever question you choose, think of the person who will read your answer. The question may tell who your audience is. If not, think of a person you know and respect—preferably your instructor or a fellow student who will read your essay. Try to convince that person to believe you.

Bring in useful details from the selection(s) you have read and perhaps other incidents you know of. For ideas, review your answers to questions in the Preview and Reading Steps. When you first refer to a reading, give its title (in quotation marks) and the author's full name. Also, give the full name of anyone featured in the article the first time you mention that person.

Note: If you are assigned to write a one-paragraph essay, think of your answer to the question, and list several key points you could make to support your answer. Then choose just one of the points and explain it in detail.

1. The second amendment gives people the right to bear arms but does not say what kind—so Buchwald's fictional "Bomb Lobby" claims that people have the right to carry any arms, including hydrogen bombs. Would you go that far? If not, where would you draw the line? Consider the characteristics and uses of bombs, knives, and various types of guns (Edwards mentions three types in paragraph 9).

2. If the Constitution needs to be changed, is it better to amend it (seek approval by convention/legislature of three-fourths of the states) or to interpret it to fit current trends, beliefs, and situations? Compare amending to interpreting: Who has the power to do each, and how much time would each process take?

3. Explosives, machine guns and military-purpose semiautomatics are all capable of rapid multiple killings. Use of these weapons is highly restricted for private citizens but is permitted for the military. Under such circumstances, will the people be able to resist government tyranny?

4. In the United States, are we in more danger from tyrants if we don't have guns—or from criminals and mentally ill killers if guns are widely available? In considering the danger of tyranny, you might compare the World War II experiences of Switzerland, where all adult males had to own guns, and the Jewish ghettoes of Germany and Poland, where no one could own guns.

5. Argue that the United States has no rational, comprehensive policy toward weapons control. What evidence can you find that politicians use this issue to divert attention from the really difficult issues involved in crime?

6. Consider that women are often easy targets for crimes of violence. (See "37 Who Saw Murder Didn't Call Police" in Unit 3.) Consider

also that the poor and minorities do not get the same police protection as middle-class whites. Argue for or against the idea that law-abiding citizens need to carry guns for self-protection.

7. The National Rifle Association sponsors gun safety classes. However, home accidents with guns are still alarmingly common. Argue for or against the position that guns can be kept safely in the home.

REVISION QUESTIONS

Once you have finished writing your essay, ask yourself the following questions.

1. Is there any statement the reader might not understand?
2. Is there any statement that might offend the reader?
3. Is there anything that's not very convincing?
4. Have I changed the subject and then changed it back again?
5. Have I said the same thing twice?
6. Do I want to try using any feature of style I've seen in the reading selection?

EDITING QUESTIONS

Once you've made changes, ask someone else to read your essay. Change it again as needed. Then read your essay out loud and answer the following questions.

1. Does every sentence make sense?
2. Does every sentence use the kind of language that most people consider "good English" these days? (*Hint:* Imagine a TV announcer reading it.)
3. Do the periods, commas, and other punctuation show the rise and fall of my voice?
4. Are the words spelled right?

If your instructor asks you to copy your paper over, proofread for copying errors before you hand it in.

UNIT
TWELVE

Pornography:
Free Speech?

PREVIEW STEPS FOR UNIT TWELVE

In response to questions 1 and 2, try these steps: Write your answers, talk them over with three or four classmates, and then discuss them with the whole class.

1. For the next three or four minutes, list as many reasons as you can for legally allowing pornography.

2. For the next three or four minutes, list as many reasons as you can for NOT legally allowing pornography.

3. a. Read the title of the first essay (page 182). Name the topic. (Who or what is this essay about?)

   b. Now predict the main idea. (What is the main point the author wants to make about this topic?)

   c. Read the first and last paragraphs. Revise your prediction if necessary. (*Note:* The main idea should sum up the smaller ideas of the essay.)

4. Some words from the essay are listed below, accompanied by quotations. Mark any words you do not know and make an educated guess about their meanings using the context supplied by the quotations—

and possibly Appendix A, Word Parts, on page 287. You may want to work with a small group of classmates.

entrenchment "Canada's new constitution, the Charter of Rights and Freedoms, includes an expansive equality guarantee and a serious *entrenchment* of freedom of expression."

anti-Semite "The first case to confront expressive guarantees with equality requirements under the new constitution came in the case of James Keegstra, an *anti-Semite* who taught *Holocaust revisionism* to schoolchildren in Alberta."

Holocaust revisionism See above quotation.

concededly "We argued that group libel, most of it *concededly* expression, promotes the disadvantage of unequal groups. . . ."

defamation "We argued that group *defamation* in this sense is not a mere expression of opinion but a practice of discrimination in verbal form. . . ."

enmity ". . . group-based *enmity*, ill will, intolerance, and prejudice are the attitudinal engines of the exclusion, *denigration*, and subordination that make up and propel social inequality. . . ."

denigration See above quotation.

bigotry ". . . without *bigotry*, social systems of enforced separation, *ghettoization,* and *apartheid* would be unnecessary, impossible, and unthinkable. . . ."

ghettoization See above quotation.

apartheid See above quotation.

stigmatization ". . . stereotyping and *stigmatization* of historically disadvantaged groups through group hate propaganda shape their social image and reputation. . . ."

degradation ". . . systemic discrimination . . . keeps target groups in subordinated positions through the promotion of terror, intolerance, *degradation*, segregation, exclusion, *vilification*, violence, and *genocide*."

vilification See above quotation.

genocide See above quotation.

antiegalitarian "The Court recognized the provision as a content restriction—content that had to be stopped because of its *antiegalitarian* meaning and devastating consequences."

5. Now read the following essay. As you read, jot down any questions that occur to you.

(*Note:* Question 6 appears after the essay.)

Equality and Speech

Catharine A. MacKinnon

Canada's new constitution, the Charter of Rights and Freedoms, in-   1
cludes an expansive equality guarantee and a serious entrenchment
of freedom of expression. The Supreme Court of Canada's first move
was to define equality in a meaningful way—one more substantive
than formal, directed toward changing unequal social relations rather
than monitoring their equal positioning before the law. The positive
spin of the Canadian interpretation holds the law to promoting
equality, projecting the law into a more equal future, rather than remaining rigidly neutral in ways that either reinforce existing social inequality or prohibit changing it, as the American constitutional perspective has increasingly done in recent years.

The first case to confront expressive guarantees with equality re- 2
quirements under the new constitution came in the case of James
Keegstra, an anti-Semite who taught Holocaust revisionism to schoolchildren in Alberta. Prosecuted and convicted under Canada's hate
propaganda provision, Keegstra challenged the statute as a violation of
the new freedom of expression guarantee. [The Women's Legal Education and Action Fund (LEAF)] intervened to argue that the hate propaganda law promoted equality. We argued that group libel, most of it
concededly expression, promotes the disadvantage of unequal groups;
that group-based enmity, ill will, intolerance, and prejudice are the attitudinal engines of the exclusion, denigration, and subordination that
make up and propel social inequality; that without bigotry, social systems of enforced separation, ghettoization, and apartheid would be unnecessary, impossible, and unthinkable; that stereotyping and stigmatization of historically disadvantaged groups through group hate
propaganda shape their social image and reputation, which controls
their access to opportunities more powerfully than their individual abil-
ities ever do; and that it is impossible for an individual to receive equality of opportunity when surrounded by an atmosphere of group hate.

We argued that group defamation in this sense is not a mere ex- 3
pression of opinion but a practice of discrimination in verbal form, a
link in systemic discrimination that keeps target groups in subordinated positions through the promotion of terror, intolerance, degradation, segregation, exclusion, vilification, violence, and genocide.
We said that the nature of the practice can be understood and its impact measured from the damage it causes, from immediate psychic
wounding to consequent physical aggression.

The Supreme Court of Canada agreed with this approach, a 4
majority upholding the hate propaganda provision, substantially on
equality grounds. The Court recognized the provision as a content
restriction—content that had to be stopped because of its antiegalitarian meaning and devastating consequences.

Subsequently, the Winnipeg authorities arrested a whole 5
pornography store and prosecuted the owner, Donald Victor Butler,
for obscenity. Butler was convicted but said the obscenity law was an
unconstitutional restriction on his Charter-based right of freedom of
expression. LEAF argued that if Canada's obscenity statute, prohibiting "undue exploitation of sex, or sex and violence, cruelty, horror, or crime," was interpreted to institutionalize some people's
views about women and sex over others, it would be unconstitu-

tional. But if the community standards applied were interpreted to prohibit harm to women as harm to the community, it was constitutional because it promoted sex equality.

The Supreme Court of Canada essentially agreed, upholding   6
the obscenity provision on sex equality grounds. It said that harm to women—which the Court was careful to make "contextually sensitive" and found could include humiliation, degradation, and subordination—was harm to society as a whole.

6. State the essay's main idea in your own words. Compare it to your prediction of the main idea. (*Note:* The main idea should sum up the smaller ideas of the essay.)

PREVIEW STEPS FOR "WHY WE MUST PUT UP WITH PORN"

1. a. Read the title of the second essay (page 185). Name the topic. (Who or what is this essay about?)

   b. Now predict the main idea. (What is the main point the author wants to make about this topic?)

   c. Read the first and last paragraphs of the essay. Revise your prediction if necessary. (*Note:* The main idea should sum up the smaller ideas of the essay.)

2. What in the author's background may have led her to the main idea? (See author's background, below title.)

3. Some words from the essay are listed below, accompanied by quotations. Mark any words you do not know and make an educated guess

about their meanings using the context supplied by the quotations—
and possibly Appendix A, Word Parts, on page 287. You may want
to work with a small group of classmates.

misogynistic "It's about a doctor so obsessed with keeping a young
woman all to himself that he amputates her legs and arms and keeps
what's left of her in a box. Maybe it's art, maybe it's a disgusting
misogynistic piece of *claptrap*."

claptrap See above quotation.

legacy "All of us, women and men, have to salute our Founding Fathers and say: Thanks for the *legacy* of freedom you gave us."

4. At the end of the Preview, you may want to go over any new features
   of style that occur in the following reading selection. You will need
   to know the terms *cliché* and *metaphor*. For help, see Appendix B,
   Guide to Literary Terms (page 291), with accompanying exercises on
   individual features.

5. Before reading "Why We Must Put Up with Porn" turn to pages
   188–189 and skim the Reading Questions. Then read the essay to
   find answers to these questions. As you read, jot down any questions
   that occur to you.

Why We Must Put Up with Porn

Susan Isaacs

*Susan Isaacs has written seven best-selling novels, two of which
have been made into movies (*Compromising Positions, *starring
Susan Sarandon and Raul Julia;* Shining Through, *starring
Michael Douglas and Melanie Griffith) and another of which the
movie rights have been sold to Disney (*Lily White *for Whoopi
Goldberg). She is a screenwriter and a book reviewer for five
major newspapers. She is a member of the National Book Critics*

Circle, The Creative Coalition, Poets and Writers, and Mystery Writers of America. For the last of these, she serves as chair of the Committee on Free Expression. Ms. Isaacs has also worked on several anti-censorship campaigns and is a member of the National Coalition Against Censorship.

If you and I were sitting together, listening to a little Vivaldi, sipping   1
herbal tea, chatting about men and women, arguing about politics
and art, we might get around to what to do about the porn problem—at which point you'd slam down your cup and demand, How
can you of all people defend smut-peddling slimeballs who portray
women being beaten and raped?

Well . . .   2

You're the one (you'd be sure to remind me) who hates any   3
kind of violence against women. You're the one who even gets upset
when James Cagney, in *The Public Enemy*, the 1931 classic, smashes
a grapefruit into Mae Clarke's face, for heaven's sake!

That's right, I'd say.   4

So? Don't you want to protect women? Why not ban books   5
and films that degrade women?

Let's have another cup of tea and I'll tell you.   6

The problem is, who is going to decide what is degrading to   7
women? If there were to be a blue-ribbon panel, who would select its
members? Jerry Falwell of the religious right? Andrea Dworkin, who
has written that all sexual intercourse is an expression of men's contempt for women? They certainly do not speak for me. Okay, what
about a blue-ribbon panel of, say, Hillary Rodham Clinton, Sandra
Day O'Connor, Jackie Joyner-Kersee, Katie Couric, Wendy Wasser-
stein, and Anne Tyler? A dream team, right?

Sure. But I'll be damned if I'd hand over my right to determine   8
what I see and read to America's best and brightest any more than I
would to my husband, my editor, my best friend, or my mother. And
you, my tea-sipping companion, and you, out there in Salt Lake City,
Sioux City, Jersey City: You also should decide for yourself.

But, you might say next, this sexually explicit garbage eggs peo-   9
ple on to vicious criminal behavior.

The truth is, this remains unproven. While research has pointed   10
to a correlation between both alcohol abuse and dysfunctional families and violent behavior, it has *not* established the same link between

pornography and violence. When serial killer Ted Bundy was trying to get his death sentence commuted in 1989, he claimed that a lifetime of reading pornography made him the monster he was. And why shouldn't he? It was an easy out: It would clear him of responsibility for his evil deeds.

But, you say, proof or no proof, there is so much trash out there and I don't like it! Well, neither do I, but censorship is not the answer. The First Amendment gives you the right to picket a theater or start a letter-writing campaign against any work you consider loathsome. You do not have the right, however, to prevent others from seeing it.   11

Look, it's rarely easy being a defender of the First Amendment. More often than not, we wind up fighting for the right to burn the flag or burn a cross or say awful racist and sexist things. Or consider a movie like the upcoming *Boxing Helena*. It's about a doctor so obsessed with keeping a young woman all to himself that he amputates her legs and arms and keeps what's left of her in a box. Maybe it's art, maybe it's a disgusting, misogynistic piece of claptrap.   12

But if we want our great and beloved Constitution to work, we cannot abandon its principles when they don't suit us. To have speech we love, we have to defend speech we hate. Besides, most controversial material is open to more than one interpretation. To some, Robert Mapplethorpe's black-and-white photographs of nude men are breathtaking art; others think them immoral filth. In my own novel, *Almost Paradise*, the heroine, as a child, is sexually abused by her father. This criminal betrayal colors her life. It was a nightmare for my character, and painful, even sickening, for me to write. Had some zealot been able to ban all references to incest—regardless of context or purpose—my novel would never have gotten written.   13

We can't hand over to anyone the power to decide what's appropriate for all. Because a year or a decade from now, someone might want to ban all depictions of career women or day-care centers, using the argument that they undermine family unity. Think that sounds extreme? Don't—historically, censorship has often been the first step toward dictatorship.   14

That's why we have to stand up for the First Amendment and not be moved, no matter how tempting it is to succumb to a just-this-once mentality. All of us, women and men, have to salute our Founding Fathers and say: Thanks for the legacy of freedom you gave us. And don't worry. We have the strength, the will, and yes, the guts to defend it.   15

READING QUESTIONS FOR "WHY WE MUST PUT UP WITH PORN"

Main Idea

1. State the essay's main idea in your own words. Compare it to your prediction of the main idea. (*Note:* The main idea should sum up the smaller ideas of the essay.)

Organization

2. a. Where in the essay is the main idea found?

   b. Why has the author placed the main idea there?

3. In what order are the paragraphs arranged? (Underline one.) Time / Least to most important / Most to least important / Simple listing / Logic: cause and effect / Other logic / Other

Style

4. How formal is the essay? (Circle your choice.)

   [Informal—1—2—3—4—5—6—7—8—9—10—Formal]

   What indicators convinced you? (For a list of possible indicators and two benchmark essays, see Appendix F, The Formality Spectrum, on page 307.)

5. Where do you see the following features of style? List one or two examples of each with their paragraph numbers.

   Features (For definitions, see Appendix B, page 291.)

   a. metaphor

   b. cliché

   Content

6. Does the author propose any change? If so, what do you think would be the result of such change?

7. Do you agree with the author's main idea? Why or why not?

If you have not already read the essay and answered the Reading Questions, be sure to do so before you proceed.

COMPOSITION QUESTIONS

Listed below are the writing questions. Choose one and write an essay that answers it. Whichever question you choose, think of the person who will read your answer. The question may tell who your audience is. If not, think of a person you know and respect—preferably your instructor or a fellow student who will read your essay. Try to convince that person to believe you.

Bring in useful details from the selection(s) you have read and perhaps other incidents you know of. For ideas, review your answers to questions in the Preview and Reading Steps. When you first refer to a reading, give its title (in quotation marks) and the author's full name. Also, give the full name of anyone featured in the article the first time you mention that person.

Note: If you are assigned to write a one-paragraph essay, think of your answer to the question, and list several key points you could make to support your answer. Then choose just one of the points and explain it in detail.

1. When it comes to defending pornography, do you agree more with the United States' First Amendment or the equality guarantee of Canada's new constitution? Explain your position.
2. In the view of some, the new Canadian constitution expands the guarantee of equality at the expense of freedom of expression. Explain why this change in power is either good or bad.
3. When it comes to defending pornography, do you agree more with Susan Isaacs, Jerry Falwell, or Andrea Dworkin? (See paragraph 7.) Explain how your views are different from those of the other two. (*Note:* If you choose this question you will need to find examples of their writing or speeches elsewhere.)
4. Do you see any relationship between the positions MacKinnon and Isaacs take and their levels of formality, as well as any other features of style you care to comment on? Explain.
5. If you believe in censoring pornography, how would you answer Isaacs' concern that "historically, censorship has often been the first step toward dictatorship"?
6. Isaacs argues, "We can't hand over to anyone the power to decide what's appropriate for all." She writes that you "should decide for yourself" what is degrading to women. Explain why you agree or don't agree with her reasoning, and whether a law should be based on what you decide or not.
7. If the United States Supreme Court were to rule that a five-person panel had to be set up to determine what is or is not pornographic, who would you select to serve on this commission? Explain why each is qualified to deliver the best judgment according to your standards or protective position.

REVISION QUESTIONS

Once you have finished writing your essay, ask yourself the following questions.

1. Is there any statement the reader might not understand?
2. Is there any statement that might offend the reader?
3. Is there anything that's not very convincing?
4. Have I changed the subject and then changed it back again?
5. Have I said the same thing twice?
6. Do I want to try using any feature of style I've seen in the reading selection?

EDITING QUESTIONS

Once you've made changes, ask someone else to read your essay. Change it again as needed. Then read your essay out loud and answer the following questions.

1. Does every sentence make sense?
2. Does every sentence use the kind of language that most people consider "good English" these days? (*Hint:* Imagine a TV announcer reading it.)
3. Do the periods, commas, and other punctuation show the rise and fall of my voice?
4. Are the words spelled right?

If your instructor asks you to copy your paper over, proofread for copying errors before you hand it in.

Physician-Assisted Suicide

PREVIEW STEPS FOR UNIT THIRTEEN

1. Recall a time when someone you knew was dying slowly and painfully. This might have been a friend, a relative, or even a pet. (If this is not part of your experience, recall such a time in a movie, short story, or book.) Did you ever wish that person or animal could die a quick death? Jot down some notes about the situation and your reactions to it. You may or may not want to discuss these notes with a classmate.

   For questions 2 and 3, you may want to write your answers, talk them over with three or four classmates, and then discuss them with the whole class.

2. a. If you were in great pain, or if you were becoming "nonhuman" in body or mind, would you want to live?

   b. Should you have the right to choose physician-assisted suicide (PAS)?

3. a. Read the title of the first essay (page 195). Name the topic. (Who or what is this essay about?)

   b. Now predict the main idea. (What is the main point the author wants to make about this topic?)

   c. Read the first and last paragraphs. Revise your prediction if necessary. (*Note:* The main idea should sum up the smaller ideas of the essay.)

4. Some words from the essay are listed below, accompanied by quotations. Mark any words you do not know and make an educated guess about their meanings using the context supplied by the quotations—and possibly Appendix A, Word Parts, on page 287. You may want to work with a small group of classmates.

euthanasia " '. . . to end a patient's life by lethal injection, mercy killing, or active *euthanasia.*' " (*Note:* This quotation is from Meisel's article, the second reading.)

ethicist "Daniel Callahan, an *ethicist* . . . , [says,] 'People who assist suicides ought to have a problem; that they don't and cast themselves as heroic—that's the problem.' "

5. Now read the following essay. As you read, jot down any questions that occur to you.

(*Note:* Question 6 appears after the essay.)

Threat of Assisted Suicide

Maggie Gallagher

This is a tale of two doctors, and two dying men.   1

One Washington, DC, doctor received a phone call from a 33-   2
year-old AIDS patient who had, according to *The Washington Post*, "talked of suicide for weeks." He asked for his doctor's help. So the doctor went that evening to his patient's home and showed the man's lover how to kill with morphine. Six hours later, the patient was dead.

About the same time, Dr. Carlos Gomez of the University of   3
Virginia Medical Center received a very similar request from a young man with AIDS. But Dr. Gomez's response was 180 degrees opposite: He told his patient he always interpreted a suicide request as a

cry for help. He changed the patient's medical routine, started morphine, and gave the sick man the private phone numbers for both his beeper and home so he wouldn't feel alone.

Two cries for help; two responses: Which was the caring one?   4
That's the question we all face in the newly energized debate over "assisted suicide." Two lower courts have ruled that a lethal injection is a constitutional right. The American Medical Association, by contrast, recently reaffirmed its opposition to physician-assisted suicide. The question seems headed for the Supreme Court. In the court of public opinion, the battle already rages.

Efforts to slow our rush to euthanasia are producing—as last   5
week's cover story of the Sunday *New York Times* magazine put it— "an odd coalition" of agnostics and believers, pro-lifers and pro-choicers, "AIDS activists and Orthodox rabbis, the American Medical Association and Pope John Paul II."

Listen to these diverse voices. They include people such as Herbert   6
Hendin, a psychiatrist and co-founder of the American Suicide Foundation, who traveled to the Netherlands (where assisted suicide is legal) and brought back horror stories: a depressed 50-year-old woman, otherwise healthy, who asked to be (and was) put to death two months after she lost a son to cancer; a chronically ill man who requested death after his wife offered him the options of a nursing home or euthanasia. Hendin is particularly troubled by the effect of legalized killing on doctors: "The first assisted suicide may give them a moment's pause. The second is easier. It eventually turns into a kind of compulsion."

Or Yale Kamisar, a University of Michigan law school professor   7
and ACLU member, who notes—"flabbergasted": "If assisted suicide went through, we'd be providing more safeguards for criminals picked up on the street than we would for the terminally ill."

Or Kathleen Foley, a pain specialist for New York's Memorial   8
Sloan-Kettering Cancer Center, who notes, "It's a well-documented fact that those asking for assisted suicide almost always change their minds once we have their pain under control."

Or Linda Emanuel, who just left Harvard Medical School to   9
become director of the AMA's Institute for Ethics: The suicide debate, she says, "is a defining moment in medicine. If doctors are allowed to kill patients, the doctor-patient relationship will never be the same again."

Or Daniel Callahan, an ethicist at the Hastings Center, who 10
puts the self-glorifying stance of the Dr. Kevorkians in perspective:
"The Nazi doctors felt they were doing something patriotic. People
who assist suicides ought to have a problem; that they don't and cast
themselves as heroic—that's the problem."

Caring for the ill, as Dr. Gomez does, is so much more difficult, 11
time-consuming and expensive than just killing them off. If suicide is
permissible, it will soon become morally, if not legally, mandatory. It
already is in the Netherlands, notes Dr. Hendin: "It was almost as if
you were a poor sport for not choosing it."

Mercy or murder? The stakes are high: What kind of people 12
are we? And what kind of people will we soon become?

6. State the essay's main idea in your own words. Compare it to your
   prediction of the main idea. (*Note:* The main idea should sum up the
   smaller ideas of the essay.)

PREVIEW STEPS FOR "REFLECTIONS ON 'DEATH WITH DIGNITY ACT'"

1. a. Read the title of the second essay (page 199). Name the topic.
      (Who or what is this essay about?)

   b. Now predict the main idea. (What is the main point the author
      wants to make about this topic?)

   c. Read the first and last paragraphs of the essay. Revise your predic-
      tion if necessary. (*Note:* The main idea should sum up the smaller
      ideas of the essay.)

2. What in the author's background may have led him to the main idea? (See author's background, below title.)

3. Some words from the essay are listed below, accompanied by quotations. Mark any words you do not know and make an educated guess about their meanings using the context supplied by the quotations—and possibly Appendix A, Word Parts, on page 287. You may want to work with a small group of classmates.

referendum The "Oregon electorate approved a *referendum* legalizing physician-assisted suicide."

arbitrary "It was *arbitrary*. . . . it favored those who were just plain lucky to have a doctor who was willing."

paternalism ". . . more than a few must have been dispatched by doctors on their own initiative . . . in part because the tradition of medical *paternalism* applied to all medical practices. . . ."

fortitude It "may well demand more energy and *fortitude* to comply with [the law] than some terminally ill people . . . are likely to have."

stringent There are "*stringent* qualifications as to who may act as a witness."

hospice The attending physician is "obligated to provide the patient with information about . . . the alternatives, 'including but not limited to comfort care, *hospice* care, and pain control.'"

active euthanasia "The act does not 'authorize a physician . . . to end a patient's life by lethal injection, mercy killing, or *active euthanasia*.'"

passive euthanasia Doctors "still anguish over *passive euthanasia* . . . even with the sanitized name of 'forgoing life-sustaining treatment. . . .'"

totalitarian "These practices must be viewed in context, and the American context is a democratic one. The Nazi euthanasia program did not make the Nazis *totalitarian*; it was their totalitarian political system that made the euthanasia program acceptable."

4. At the end of the Preview of the second article, you may want to go over any new features of style that occur in the following reading selection. You will need to know the terms *allusion*, *metaphor*, and *simile*. For help, see Appendix B, Guide to Literary Terms (page 291), with accompanying exercises on individual features.

5. Before reading "Reflections on 'Death with Dignity Act,'" turn to pages 202–204 and skim the Reading Questions. Then read the essay to find answers to these questions. As you read, jot down any questions that occur to you.

Reflections on "Death with Dignity Act"

Alan Meisel

Alan Meisel directs the University of Pittsburgh Center for Medical Ethics. A lawyer, he is an authority on legal aspects of decision-making in the physician-patient relationship. His work has included two books on informed consent and one on the right to refuse medical treatment.

The barrier between assisted suicide and forgoing life-sustaining treatment cracked like the Liberty Bell on the second Tuesday of November when the Oregon electorate approved a referendum legalizing physician-assisted suicide. Like the Liberty Bell, the barrier was cast with this flaw, and like the Liberty Bell, it turned out to be fatal. 1

The line that the courts and legislatures have tried to draw between act and omission has never been a particularly bright one, and it has been increasingly under assault in a variety of ways. . . . Ever 2

Excerpts reprinted with the permission of the American Society of Law, Medicine & Ethics, from its newsletter, *ASLME Briefings*, 12 (Winter 1995): 1, 4–5.

since Dr. Kevorkian opened up operations in 1990—with Dr. Quill and "It's Over, Debbie" playing important supporting roles—it's been clear that the line would be breached; the only question was when. My own guess—10 or 15 years—was very wide of the mark.

Assisted suicide and its close cousin, mercy killing, have been   3
an open secret in the medical profession for a long time. For instance, on November 28, 1986, a front page story in *The New York Times*, titled "1936 Secret Is Out: Doctor Sped George V's Death," revealed that the king of England, suffering from terminal cancer, had been given more than enough morphine to ease his pain. In . . . [*Law, Medicine & Health Care*, 1987–88], Leonard Glantz concluded that although judging from news accounts mercy killing occurs with some frequency, there are few reported prosecutions for performing it. . . . Many preferred it that way; it allowed us to maintain the all-life-is-sacred myth while at the same time administering compassion when needed. It allowed us to temper law with justice.

There were at least two serious problems with this approach,   4
however. The first was that it was arbitrary and discriminatory, and the second that it was subject to potentially grave abuse. While not limited exclusively to royalty, it was discriminatory because it favored those who had the sophistication, the financial resources, the connections, and the time and energy to find a cooperative doctor, but sometimes it favored those who were just plain lucky to have a doctor who was willing. The other problem was that there was no guarantee that such a doctor would necessarily await the request of the dying patient. How many people (possibly including King George V) would rather have suffered to the end rather than going swiftly into the night will never be known, but we can surmise that more than a few must have been dispatched by doctors on their own initiative, in part because of doctors' fears of opening up the topic for discussion and in part because the tradition of medical paternalism applied to all medical practices. . . .

Legalizing assisted suicide and placing it in the hands of physi-   5
cians under legal supervision will bring an end to these problems. But will it cause other, perhaps more serious, ones? Are we, as some would have it, headed down the slippery slope toward Nazidom?

The Oregon "Death with Dignity Act" will have no such result.   6
In fact, it is so carefully crafted, so narrowly-drawn, and so laden with procedural safeguards that it may well demand more energy and fortitude to comply with it than some terminally ill people who nominally qualify are likely to have. A person must be an Oregon resident, over age 18, "capable" (i.e., in possession of decision-making capac-

ity), and suffering from a terminal disease which will lead to death within six months. The person must make a written and two oral requests for medication to end his or her life, the written one "substantially in the form" provided in the act, signed, dated, witnessed by two persons in the presence of the patient who attest that the patient is "capable, acting voluntarily, and not being coerced to sign the request," and there are stringent qualifications as to who may act as a witness. The patient's decision must be an "informed" one, and the attending physician is therefore obligated to provide the patient with information about the diagnosis, prognosis, potential risks, and probable consequences of taking the medication to be prescribed, and the alternatives, "including but not limited to comfort care, hospice care, and pain control." There must be a confirmation of the diagnosis, the patient's decision-making capacity, and the patient's voluntariness by another physician. There are requirements for counseling if the patient is thought to be suffering from a mental disorder, for documentation, for a waiting period, for notification of the patient's next-of-kin, and reporting to state authorities.

But the real hooker is that having complied with all of this, the person requesting to die is only entitled to a prescription for medication to end his or her life. The act does not "authorize a physician or any other person to end a patient's life by lethal injection, mercy killing, or active euthanasia." What this means is that there are likely to be some—possibly many—situations in which patients are not able to administer the medication to themselves by the time they meet all the statutory requirements, or there are likely to be aesthetically unpleasant instances in which patients are able to take some but not all of the medication and wind up merely taking a long deep snooze or making themselves nauseous. I would venture to guess that many patients who are able to comply with the act are also capable of hoarding enough pills to end their lives without a doctor's help, and for them the act will provide no advantage.

7

The Oregon "Death with Dignity Act" does not herald the rebirth of Nazidom. Almost 20 years after the Quinlan case, doctors still anguish over passive euthanasia; even with the sanitized name of "forgoing life-sustaining treatment" or "termination of life support," some anguish so much that they manage to avoid doing it [as reported by] Solomon [in the] *American Journal of Public Health*, 1993. . . . It's not likely that they're going to embrace assisted suicide with open arms, let alone abuse it. But more important, we are not the Nazis. We can even progress further down the slippery slope and

8

still not become the Nazis. These practices must be viewed in context, and the American context is a democratic one. The Nazi euthanasia program did not make the Nazis totalitarian; it was their totalitarian political system that made the euthanasia program acceptable. Democratic political systems provide ample opportunities for establishing toeholds on the slippery slope and contain requirements that make me confident that we can compassionately practice assisted suicide and prevent its abuse.

READING QUESTIONS FOR "REFLECTIONS ON 'DEATH WITH DIGNITY ACT'"

Main Idea

1. State the essay's main idea in your own words. Compare it to your prediction of the main idea. (*Note:* The main idea should sum up the smaller ideas of the essay.)

Organization

2. a. Where in the essay is the main idea found?

   b. Why has the author placed the main idea there?

3. In what order are the paragraphs arranged? (Underline one.) Time / Least to most important / Most to least important / Simple listing / Logic: cause and effect / Other logic / Other

Style

4. How formal is the essay? (Circle your choice.)

   [Informal—1—2—3—4—5—6—7—8—9—10—Formal]

What indicators convinced you? (For a list of possible indicators and two benchmark essays, see Appendix F, The Formality Spectrum, on page 307.)

5. Where do you see the following features of style? List one or two examples with their page numbers.

   Features (For definitions, see Appendix B, page 291.)

   a. allusion

   b. metaphor

   c. simile

Note also that paragraph 3 contains an oxymoron, "open secret." An oxymoron is an apparent contradiction.

Content

6. According to Meisel, how far down the slippery slope toward Nazidom is American society likely to go—not at all, a little way, or all the way?

7. According to Meisel, does the Oregon Act contain not enough procedural safeguards, just enough, or too many?

8. Does the author propose any change? If so, what do you think would be the result of such change?

9. Do you agree with the author's main idea? Why or why not?

If you have not already read the essay and answered the Reading Questions, be sure to do so before you proceed. Composition Questions for this essay are found on pages 214–217.

PREVIEW STEPS FOR "DEATH AND DIGNITY: A CASE OF INDIVIDUALIZED DECISION MAKING"

1. a. Read the title of the second essay (page 205). Name the topic. (Who or what is this essay about?)

   b. Now predict the main idea. (What is the main point the author wants to make about this topic?)

   c. Read the first and last paragraphs of the essay. Revise your prediction if necessary. (*Note:* The main idea should sum up the smaller ideas of the essay.)

2. What in the author's background may have led him to the main idea? (See author's background, below title.)

3. This essay contains several medical words, but no new ones are needed to understand the major ideas. If you see words you don't know, just keep on reading.

4. At the end of the Preview, you may want to go over any new features of style that occur in the following reading selection. You will need to know the term *metaphor*. For help, see Appendix B, Guide to Literary Terms (page 291), with accompanying exercises on individual features.

5. Before reading "Death and Dignity: A Case of Individualized Decision Making" turn to pages 212–214 and skim the Reading Questions. Then read the essay to find answers to these questions. As you read, jot down any questions that occur to you.

Death and Dignity: A Case of Individualized Decision Making

Timothy E. Quill

Timothy E. Quill, M.D., has written multiple articles based on physician-assisted suicide found in The New England Journal of Medicine *and other journals. As a former hospice director, Dr. Quill has experience using medication to control pain for dying patients. He currently works at the University of Rochester School of Medicine in New York.*

Diane was feeling tired and had a rash. A common scenario, though there was something subliminally worrisome that prompted me to check her blood count. Her hematocrit was 22, and the white-cell count was 4.3 with some metamyelocytes and unusual white cells. I wanted it to be viral, trying to deny what was staring me in the face. Perhaps in a repeated count it would disappear. I called Diane and   1 told her it might be more serious than I had initially thought—that the test needed to be repeated and that if she felt worse, we might have to move quickly. When she pressed for the possibilities, I reluctantly opened the door to leukemia. Hearing the word seemed to make it exist. "Oh, shit!" she said. "Don't tell me that." Oh, shit! I thought, I wish I didn't have to.

Diane was no ordinary person (although no one I have ever come to know has been really ordinary). She was raised in an alcoholic family and had felt alone for much of her life. She had vaginal cancer as a young woman. Through much of her adult life, she had struggled with depression and her own alcoholism. I had come to know, respect, and admire her over the previous eight years as she confronted these problems and gradually overcame them. She was an incredibly clear, at times brutally honest, thinker and communicator. As she took control of her life, she developed a strong sense of independence and confidence. In the previous 3 1/2 years, her hard work had paid off. She was completely abstinent from alcohol, she had established much deeper connections with her husband, college-age son, and several friends, and her business and her artistic work were blossoming. She felt she was really living fully for the first time.

Not surprisingly, the repeated blood count was abnormal, and detailed examination of the peripheral-blood smear showed myelocytes. I advised her to come into the hospital, explaining that we needed to do a bone marrow biopsy and make some decisions relatively rapidly. She came to the hospital knowing what we would find. She was terrified, angry, and sad. Although we knew the odds, we both clung to the thread of possibly that it might be something else.

The bone marrow confirmed the worst: acute myelomonocytic leukemia. In the face of this tragedy, we looked for signs of hope. This is an area of medicine in which technological intervention has been successful, with cures 25 percent of the time—long-term cures. As I probed the costs of these cures, I heard about induction chemotherapy (three weeks in the hospital, prolonged neutropenia, probable infectious complications, and hair loss; 75 percent of patients respond, 25 percent do not). For the survivors, this is followed by consolidation chemotherapy (with similar side effects; another 25 percent die, for a net survival of 50 percent). Those still alive, to have a reasonable chance of long-term survival, then need bone marrow transplantation (hospitalization for two months and whole-body irradiation, with complete killing of the bone marrow, infectious complications, and the possibility for graft-versus-host disease—with a survival of approximately 50 percent, or 25 percent of the original group). Though hematologists may argue over the exact percentages, they don't argue about the outcome of no treatment—certain death in days, weeks, or at most a few months.

Believing that delay was dangerous, our oncologist broke the news to Diane and began making plans to insert a Hickman catheter and begin induction chemotherapy that afternoon. When I saw her shortly thereafter, she was enraged at his presumption that she would want treatment, and devastated by the finality of the diagnosis. All she wanted to do was go home and be with her family. She had no further questions about treatment and in fact had decided that she wanted none. Together we lamented her tragedy and the unfairness of life. Before she left, I felt the need to be sure that she and her husband understood that there was some risk in delay, that the problem was not going to go away, and that we needed to keep considering the options over the next several days. We agreed to meet in two days.

She returned in two days with her husband and son. They had talked extensively about the problem and the options. She remained very clear about her wish not to undergo chemotherapy and to live whatever time she had left outside the hospital. As we explored her thinking further, it became clear that she was convinced she would die during the period of treatment and would suffer unspeakably in the process (from hospitalization, from lack of control over her body, from the side effects of chemotherapy, and from pain and anguish). Although I could offer support and my best effort to minimize her suffering if she chose treatment, there was no way I could say any of this would not occur. In fact, the last four patients with acute leukemia at our hospital had died very painful deaths in the hospital during various stages of treatment (a fact I did not share with her). Her family wished she would choose treatment but sadly accepted her decision. She articulated very clearly that it was she who would be experiencing all the side effects of treatment and that odds of 25 percent were not good enough for her to undergo so toxic a course of therapy, given her expectations of chemotherapy and hospitalization and the absence of a closely matched bone marrow donor. I had her repeat her understanding of the treatment, the odds, and what to expect if there were no treatment. I clarified a few misunderstandings, but she had a remarkable grasp of the options and the implications.

    I have been a longtime advocate of active, informed patient 7
choice of treatment or nontreatment, and of a patient's right to die with as much control and dignity as possible. Yet there was something about her giving up a 25 percent chance of long-term survival in favor of almost certain death that disturbed me. I had seen Diane fight and use her considerable inner resources to overcome alcoholism and depression, and I half expected her to change her mind over the next week. Since the window of time in which effective treatment can be initiated is rather narrow, we met several times that week. We obtained a second hematology consultation and talked at length about the meaning and implications of treatment and nontreatment. She talked to a psychologist she had seen in the past. I gradually understood the decision from her perspective and became convinced that it was the right decision for her. We arranged for home hospice care (although at that time Diane felt reasonably well, was active, and looked healthy), left the door open for her to change her mind, and tried to anticipate how to keep her comfortable in the time she had left.

    Just as I was adjusting to her decision, she opened up another 8
area that would stretch me profoundly. It was extraordinarily important to Diane to maintain control of herself and her own dignity during the time remaining to her. When this was no longer possible, she clearly wanted to die. As a former director of a hospice program, I know how to use pain medicines to keep patients comfortable and lessen suffering. I explained the philosophy of comfort care, which I strongly believe in. Although Diane understood and appreciated this, she had known of people lingering in what was called relative comfort, and she wanted no part of it. When the time came, she wanted to take her life in the least painful way possible. Knowing of her desire for independence and her decision to stay in control, I thought this request made perfect sense. I acknowledged and explored this wish but also thought it was out of the realm of currently accepted medical practice and that it was more than I could offer or promise. In our discussion, it became clear that preoccupation with her fear of a lingering death would interfere with Diane's getting the most out of the time she had left until she found

a safe way to ensure her death. I feared the effects of a violent death on her family, the consequences of an ineffective suicide that would leave her lingering in precisely the state she dreaded so much, and the possibility that a family member would be forced to assist her, with all the legal and personal repercussions that would follow. She discussed this at length with her family. They believed that they should respect her choice. With this in mind, I told Diane that information was available from the Hemlock Society that might be helpful to her.

A week later she phoned me with a request for barbiturates for   9 sleep. Since I knew that this was an essential ingredient in a Hemlock Society suicide, I asked her to come to the office to talk things over. She was more than willing to protect me by participating in a superficial conversation about her insomnia, but it was important to me to know how she planned to use the drugs and to be sure that she was not in despair or overwhelmed in a way that might color her judgment. In our discussion, it was apparent that she was having trouble sleeping, but it was also evident that the security of having enough barbiturates available to commit suicide when and if the time came would leave her secure enough to live fully and concentrate on the present. It was clear that she was not despondent and that in fact she was making deep, personal connections with her family and close friends. I made sure that she knew how to use the barbiturates for sleep, and also that she knew the amount needed to commit suicide. We agreed to meet regularly, and she promised to meet with me before taking her life, to ensure that all other avenues had been exhausted. I wrote the prescription with an uneasy feeling about the boundaries I was exploring—spiritual, legal, professional, and personal. Yet I also felt strongly that I was setting her free to get the most out of the time she had left and to maintain dignity and control on her own terms until her death.

The next several months were very intense and important for   10 Diane. Her son stayed home from college, and they were able to be with one another and say much that had not been said earlier. Her husband did his work at home so that he and Diane could spend more time together. She spent time with her closest friends. I had her come into the hospital for a conference with our residents, at which she illustrated in a most profound and personal way the importance of informed decision making, the right to refuse treatment, and the extraordinarily personal effects of illness and interaction with the medical system. There were emotional and physical hardships as well. She had periods of intense sadness and anger. Several times she became very weak, but she received transfusions as an outpatient and responded with marked improvement of symptoms. She had two serious infections that responded surprisingly well to empirical courses of oral antibiotics. After three tumultuous months, there were two weeks of relative calm and well-being, and fantasies of a miracle began to surface.

Unfortunately, we had no miracle. Bone pain, weakness, fatigue, and fevers began to dominate her life. Although the hospice workers, family members, and I tried our best to minimize the suffering and promote comfort, it was clear that the end was approaching. Diane's immediate future held what she feared the most—increasing discomfort, dependence, and hard choices between pain and sedation. She called up her closest friends and asked them to come over to say goodbye, telling them that she would be leaving soon. As we had agreed, she let me know as well. When we met, it was clear that she knew what she was doing, that she was sad and frightened to be leaving, but that she would be even more terrified to stay and suffer. In our tearful goodbye, she promised a reunion in the future at her favorite spot on the edge of Lake Geneva, with dragons swimming in the sunset. 11

Two days later her husband called to say that Diane had died. She had said her final goodbyes to her husband and son that morning, and asked them to leave her alone for an hour. After an hour, which must have seemed an eternity, they found her on the couch, lying very still and covered by her favorite shawl. There was no sign of struggle. She seemed to be at peace. They called me for advice about how to proceed. When I arrived at their house, Diane indeed seemed peaceful. Her husband and son were quiet. We talked about what a remarkable person she had been. They seemed to have no doubts about the course she had chosen or about their cooperation, although the unfairness of the illness and the finality of her death were overwhelming to us all. 12

I called the medical examiner to inform him that a hospice patient had died. When asked about the cause of death, I said, "acute leukemia." He said that was fine and that we should call a funeral director. Although acute leukemia was the truth, it was not the whole story. Yet any mention of suicide would have given rise to a 13 police investigation and probably brought the arrival of an ambu-lance crew for resuscitation. Diane would have become a "coroner's case," and the decision to perform an autopsy would have been made at the discretion of the medical examiner. The family or I could have been subject to criminal prosecution, and I to profes-sional review, for our roles in support of Diane's choices. Although I truly believe that the family and I gave her the best care possible, allowing her to define her limits and directions as much as possible, I am not sure the law, society, or the medical profession would agree. So I said "acute leukemia" to protect all of us, to protect Diane from an invasion into her past and her body, and to continue to shield society from the knowledge of the degree of suffering that people often undergo in the process of dying. Suffering can be less-ened to some extent, but in no way eliminated or made benign, by the careful intervention of a competent, caring physician, given cur-rent social constraints.

Diane taught me about the range of help I can provide if I know 14 people well and if I allow them to say what they really want. She taught me about life, death, and honesty and about taking charge and facing tragedy squarely when it strikes. She taught me that I can take small risks for people that I really know and care about. Although I did not assist in her suicide directly, I helped indirectly to make it possible, suc-cessful, and relatively painless. Although I know we have measures to help control pain and lessen suffering, to think that people do not suf-fer in the process of dying is an illusion. Prolonged dying can occasion-ally be peaceful, but more often the role of the physician and family is limited to lessening but not eliminating severe suffering.

I wonder how many families and physicians secretly help pa- 15 tients over the edge into death in the face of such severe suffering. I wonder how many severely ill or dying patients secretly take their lives, dying alone in despair. I wonder whether the image of Diane's final aloneness will persist in the minds of her family, or if they will remember more the intense, meaningful months they had together before she died. I wonder whether Diane struggled in that last hour, and whether the Hemlock Society's way of death by suicide is the most benign. I wonder why Diane, who gave so much to so many of us, had to be alone for the last hour of her life. I wonder whether I will see Diane again, on the shore of Lake Geneva at sunset, with dragons swimming on the horizon.

READING QUESTIONS FOR "DEATH AND DIGNITY: A CASE OF INDIVIDUALIZED DECISION MAKING"

Main Idea

1. State the essay's main idea in your own words. Compare it to your prediction of the main idea. (*Note:* The main idea should sum up the smaller ideas of the essay.)

Organization

2. a. Where in the essay is the main idea found?

   b. Why has the author placed the main idea there?

3. In what order are the paragraphs arranged? (Underline one.) Time / Least to most important / Most to least important / Simple listing / Logic: cause and effect / Other logic / Other

Style

4. How formal is the essay? (Circle your choice.)

   [Informal—1—2—3—4—5—6—7—8—9—10—Formal]

   What indicators convinced you? (For a list of possible indicators and two benchmark essays, see Appendix F, The Formality Spectrum, on page 307.)

5. Where do you see the following feature of style? List one or two examples with their paragraph numbers.

Feature (For a definition, see Appendix B, page 291.)

metaphor

Content

6. What were the two major decisions Diane made that affected the length of her remaining life?

7. What were the purposes of Dr. Quill's frequent contacts with Diane?

8. Does the author propose any change? If so, what do you think would be the result of such change?

9. Do you agree with the author's main idea? Why or why not?

10. Listed below are some major steps on the slippery slope. At the right, show which author(s) discussed each step: give the initials "G," "M," or "Q" and the number of the paragraph where it appears. The first one is done for you.

Steps on the Slippery Slope*

A person:

a. has death delayed by "life support" (oxygen, feeding tube, etc.).	M1
b. dies naturally; life support is not possible.	
c. dies naturally; life support is possible but the doctor stops it or does not start it (passive euthanasia).	
d. commits suicide with or without someone else's knowledge or advice.	
e. commits suicide with someone else's help.	
f. is killed by someone who knew he/she wanted to die.	
g. is killed without being able to state his or her wishes (is unconscious, unable to speak, or unable to understand the process).	
h. is killed without anyone's asking his/her wishes.	
i. is killed against his/her known wishes—out of concern for the person, for selfish reasons, or to get rid of "undesirables."	

*Steps a, b, and c refer to terminally ill patients. All other steps could also apply to people who are chronically ill, depressed, or merely seen as a nuisance by others.

If you have not already read the essay and answered the Reading Questions, be sure to do so before you proceed.

COMPOSITION QUESTIONS

Listed below are the writing questions. Choose one and write an essay that answers it. Whichever question you choose, think of the person who will read your answer. The question may tell who your audience is. If not, think of a person you know and respect—preferably your instructor or a fellow student who will read your essay. Try to convince that person to believe you.

Bring in useful details from the selection(s) you have read and perhaps other incidents you know of. For ideas, review your answers to questions in the Preview and Reading Steps. When you first refer to a reading, give its title (in quotation marks) and the author's full name. Also, give the full name of anyone featured in the article the first time you mention that person.

Note: If you are assigned to write a one-paragraph essay, think of your answer to the question, and list several key points you could make to support your answer. Then choose just one of the points and explain it in detail.

1. Gallagher and Quill disagree on the issue of pain control. Gallagher and Meisel disagree on the slippery slope issue—whether allowing some acceptable form of physician-assisted suicide (PAS) could lead to wholesale killing of unwanted people. For one of these issues, sort the evidence and the statements by authorities. Then compare these details and suggest why the details don't match. For example, is one author exaggerating or dealing with a different situation than the other author?

2. Some doctors quote the Hippocratic Oath they have sworn to uphold: "Above all, do no harm." Does PAS harm patients, as Gallagher says, or help patients, as Quill says?

3. Gallagher and other opponents of PAS point to a possible conflict of interest among patients, families, and doctors. Any of these three may have their judgment clouded by guilt, anger, lack of information, or concern about money. Some supporters of PAS suggest a committee decision. Would this solution resolve the problem? In case of a conflict of values, whose values would win out? Quill suggests that patients would decide; Meisel notes that doctors have acted on their own initiative in the past.

4. Is it wrong, as Gallagher suggests, to consider the cost of expensive long-term care for dying patients? Should cost be disregarded in an effort to prolong life or, instead, should society spend limited resources on patients who can be cured? Would consideration of cost be one case of the abuse Meisel mentions?

5. Meisel disagrees with Gallagher on the "slippery slope" argument—that allowing some acceptable form of PAS could lead to wholesale killing of unwanted people. List some kinds of assisted

death and arrange them from most to least acceptable. Where would a doctor's "do not resuscitate" order fit? Where would Quill's Diane fit?

6. Do you believe Gallagher's argument that PAS could lead to other kinds of assisted death? If so, predict the point(s) where Americans might "slip," or begin to accept one more category. What types, if any, should become more acceptable? Meisel mentions some possibilities: ending (or not starting) life support and ending patients' lives on their behalf if they are not able to pull the plug or do not understand the process.

7. Meisel lists several "procedural safeguards" built into the Oregon law and objects to one of them. What additions, subtractions, or changes would improve this law? Consider the dangers that Gallagher mentions or the procedures that Quill was careful to use.

8. The Oregon law, as explained by Meisel, clearly gives the choice of PAS to terminally-ill patients. Its underlying view is that dying patients own their own lives and have the right to die. Should society take this attitude toward other rational suicides—for example, by the chronically ill? (Gallagher disagrees: see her "tale of two doctors, and two dying men.")

9. Gallagher asks, "Mercy or murder?" Is PAS a form of murder, or is it voluntary manslaughter (killing without malice), or—as the name suggests—is it merely helping patients to do the deed? Are any of these actions more morally acceptable than the others?

10. Some doctors and nurses are purposely killing patients (or helping patients do the deed) by giving more than enough medication to stop the pain. Others are willing to give enough medication to stop the pain, knowing that this large a dose will also end their patients' lives. This is called the "double effect." Is there a moral difference between the two? Review Gallagher and Meisel to infer the position of each, and then give your views.

11. Meisel says that legalizing PAS would give the poor a privilege the rich already have. Gallagher and others say that PAS would be a convenient way to discard people who cannot afford expensive treatment—or other people who are not valued by society (for example, minority group members, the disabled, or the elderly). Will PAS benefit or harm these "second-class citizens"?

12. According to Meisel, some people say PAS is necessary in rare cases but is best limited through prohibition. That is, if the procedure is

against the law, doctors will use it secretly and sparingly. Meisel says openness is needed in order to have clear guidelines and equal access. Quill says openness will protect all concerned. Predict the effect of prohibition. You may want to consider the effects of prohibiting abortion, alcohol, other drugs, and gays in the military.

REVISION QUESTIONS

Once you have finished writing your essay, ask yourself the following questions.

1. Is there any statement the reader might not understand?
2. Is there any statement that might offend the reader?
3. Is there anything that's not very convincing?
4. Have I changed the subject and then changed it back again?
5. Have I said the same thing twice?
6. Do I want to try using any feature of style I've seen in the reading selection?

EDITING QUESTIONS

Once you've made changes, ask someone else to read your essay. Change it again as needed. Then read your essay out loud and answer the following questions.

1. Does every sentence make sense?
2. Does every sentence use the kind of language that most people consider "good English" these days? (*Hint:* Imagine a TV announcer reading it.)
3. Do the periods, commas, and other punctuation show the rise and fall of my voice?
4. Are the words spelled right?

If your instructor asks you to copy your paper over, proofread for copying errors before you hand it in.

UNIT
FOURTEEN

◆

Reactions to Crowded Cities

PREVIEW QUESTIONS FOR UNIT FOURTEEN

1. a. Under each of two headings, city and country, list the first five-
      words or phrases that come to your mind.

      City   **Country**

   b. Underline the words that deal with people's lifestyles.
   c. Mark each underlined word with a "+" or "−" sign to show
      whether the word has pleasant or unpleasant associations for you.
   d. Count the positive words on each list (city and country). Which
      list contains more positives?

2. Have you ever studied another culture or lived in another country? If
   so, what do you notice about modern American cities that is different
   from cities of other times or places?

3. Below are three short preview essays: "Everyone Belonged," "Sex
   Morals on the Lower East Side," and "The Poets Were Paid." For
   each, note the title, as well as the first and last sentences. Then predict the main idea that all three essays share.

4. Some words from the essays are listed below, accompanied by quotations. Mark any words you don't know and make an educated guess
   about their meanings using the context supplied by the quotations—
   and possibly Appendix A, Word Parts, on page 287.
   conjecture "'When is your sister getting married?' was commonly
   heard. There was no *conjecture* and no one made up any stories."

radius ". . . nearly three-quarters of a million people lived within the *radius* of some twenty city blocks. . . ."

attributed "Perhaps this higher standard of boy-and-girl relationship could be *attributed* to the more clearly defined separation between 'good girls' and 'bad girls,' and the existence of a definite '*line of demarcation*' like the red-light district."

line of demarcation See above quotation.

synagogue "My early morning impression of the East Side . . . was of young boys streaming out of tenements to go to the *synagogue* to say *kaddish* for a departed parent. . . ."

kaddish See above quotation.

Marshall Plan "We had the *Marshall Plan* down there a half century ago . . . the poorest of the poor helping still poorer ones across the Atlantic somewhere."

settlement houses "Hundreds of sweatshop employees . . . came home, washed up, had supper, and went to the . . . *settlement houses* to learn English. . . ."

Note: Question 5 appears after the essays.

Everyone Belonged

Harry Golden

Nowadays we say, "He's a good neighbor, he minds his own business." It was just the opposite on the Lower East Side of New York among the Jews, and in Little Italy among the Italians, and in Hell's Kitchen among the Irish. Everybody knew when someone lost a job or someone got another or someone was promoted.   1

Reprinted by permission of The Putnam Publishing Group from *Ess, Ess, Mein Kindt*, by Harry Golden. Copyright © 1966 by Harry Golden.

"No baby yet?" was quite a natural question to ask of a young   2
woman who had been married a year. "When is your sister getting
married?" was commonly heard. There was no conjecture and no
one made up any stories. They asked, and they always got an honest
answer.

The grocery man Mr. Solomon was blind. My mother would say   3
"go to the blind one." She meant no insult. The blind were called
blind and the lame were called lame; they were all part of the community because of this directness. The afflicted felt a deep sense of
belonging. There were no outsiders.

Sex Morals on the Lower East Side

Harry Golden

When I recall that nearly three-quarters of a million people lived   1
within the radius of some twenty city blocks, on New York's East
Side, it is interesting that the sex morals were of such a comparatively
high standard. I do not remember ever hearing the term "rape," although it is possible that some of those things went on under cover.
Basically, however, when you saw an unmarried girl walking down
the street with a fellow, you immediately thought of them in terms of
marriage. In fact it was a terrible disgrace among Jewish people if a
daughter "went out" with a young man for several weeks, without a
serious result.

They would go out once, maybe twice, and then the girl would   2
invite the boy to her house for dinner, and if he accepted, you could
consider the "deal" closed. Then, too, there was the matter of the
brothers of the girl. God help the young man who played fast and
loose with a girl on the Lower East Side if she had two or three
brothers. Perhaps this higher standard of boy-and-girl relationship
could be attributed to the more clearly defined separation between
"good girls" and "bad girls," and the existence of a definite "line of

demarcation" like the red-light district. Even sociologists do not seem to have the answer. Maybe what's going on now is better, who knows?

The Poets Were Paid

Harry Golden

My early morning impression of the East Side, and I mean six o'clock   1
in the morning, summer and winter, was of young boys streaming out of tenements to go to the synagogue to say kaddish for a departed parent before going to school, and maybe also carrying up a fifty-pound bag of coal before breakfast. Work, work, work.

Everybody worked all the time, and if there was no job, people   2
worked at something; they sorted rags or sewed garments, or fixed flowers and feathers for hat manufacturers. There were dozens and dozens of halls. Lodge halls, society halls, meeting halls. It was the "meetingest" place in the world. Every other building had space for meeting halls.

These fiction-fakers write about gangsters and they miss the   3
Free Loan Society. Where else did this happen? A man needed fifty dollars to go into some business or to tide him over, and he borrowed, without interest.

People scrabbled for a little living. They did anything for the chil-   4
dren. They wanted their children to enter the American middle class. My son will be a doctor, they'd say, or a lawyer, maybe a teacher. I never heard anyone express lesser hopes for his child. A man peddled fourteen hours, maybe, and brought home two dollars after he paid off his merchandise and his cart hire, or he brought home eleven dollars a week from the factory for fifty-four hours' work.

Who has ever seen such optimism anywhere on earth? The   5
night before the High Holy Days—everything would become quiet —that whole teeming district of hundreds of thousands of people in

tenements would suddenly come to a complete halt. You'd see work-ingmen with shiny faces coming out of the public baths and walking home and holding hands with their sons, and you've never seen its equal for brightness and happiness.

We had the Marshall Plan down there a half century ago. 6 Where else on earth, among the poorest people, did you see in every home a blue-and-white box where you were supposed to drop your pennies? Once a week an old woman would come around and empty it and off it would go somewhere overseas—the poorest of the poor helping still poorer ones across the Atlantic somewhere. Hundreds of sweatshop employees, men and women who sat at machines for nine and ten hours a day, came home, washed up, had supper, and went to the lodge hall or settlement houses to learn English or to listen to a fellow read poetry to them. Paid readers of poetry.

America gave them all hope and life, and they repaid America. 7 There has never been a more even trade.

5. State the main idea that all three essays share. Compare it to your prediction of the main idea.

Possibly your own impressions of city life agree with Golden's—or possibly they will agree more closely with the following essay by Tom Wolfe.

PREVIEW STEPS FOR "SLIDING DOWN INTO THE BEHAVIORAL SINK"

1. a. Read the title of the second essay (page 226). Name the topic. (Who or what is this essay about?)

b. Now predict the main idea. (What is the main point the author wants to make about this topic?)

   c. Read the first and last paragraphs of the essay. Revise your prediction if necessary. (*Note:* The main idea should sum up the smaller ideas of the essay.)

2. What in the author's background may have led him to the main idea? (See author's background, below title.)

3. Some words from the essay are listed below, accompanied by quotations. Mark any words you do not know and make an educated guess about their meanings using the context supplied by the quotations— and possibly Appendix A, Word Parts, on page 287. You may want to work with a small group of classmates.

   anthropologist "I just spent two days with Edward T. Hall, an *anthropologist*, watching thousands of my fellow New Yorkers. . . ."

   etiolate "The poor old *etiolate* animals were out there skidding on their rubber soles."

   connotations "The unhealthy *connotations* of the term are not accidental. . . ."

   aggravate ". . . a behavioral sink does act to *aggravate* all forms of *pathology*. . . ."

   pathology See above quotation.

   At the end of the Preview, you may want to go over any new features of style that occur in the following reading selection. For help, see Appendix B, Guide to Literary Terms (page 291), with accompanying exercises on individual features. You will need to know the terms *allusion, irony of situation, irony of wording, jargon, metaphor, overstatement,* and *simile*. You will also need the term *analogy*, which does not appear in the Guide. *Analogy* is an extended metaphor; here, analogy is a major part of the essay.

Before reading "Sliding Down into the Behavioral Sink," turn to pages 233–235 and skim the Reading Questions. Then read the essay to find answers to these questions.

Sliding Down into the Behavioral Sink

Tom Wolfe

Tom Wolfe, born in 1931, has a bachelor's degree from Washington and Lee University and a doctorate from Yale. He has written for several newspapers, beginning with The Washington Post, *and since 1968 has been a contributing editor for* New York *magazine. An artist as well as an author, Wolfe has also had several one-man shows of his drawings. His honors include two Washington Newspaper Guild awards and two honorary degrees—one for his art, the other for his writing.*

I just spent two days with Edward T. Hall, an anthropologist, watching thousands of my fellow New Yorkers short-circuiting themselves into hot little twitching death balls with jolts of their own adrenalin. Dr. Hall says it is overcrowding that does it. Overcrowding gets the adrenalin going, and the adrenalin gets them hyped up. And here they are, hyped up, turning bilious, nephritic, queer, autistic, sadistic, barren, batty, sloppy, hot-in-the-pants, chancred-on-the-flankers, leering, puling, numb—the usual in New York, in other words, and God knows what else. Dr. Hall has the theory that overcrowding has already thrown New York into a state of behavioral sink. Behavioral sink is a term from ethology, which is the study of how animals relate to their environment. Among animals, the sink winds up with a "population collapse" or "massive die-off. O rotten Gotham.

1

It got to be easy to look at New Yorkers as animals, especially looking down from some place like a balcony at Grand Central at the rush hour Friday afternoon. The floor was filled with the poor white

2

humans, running around, dodging, blinking their eyes, making a
sound like a pen full of starlings or rats or something.

"Listen to them skid," says Dr. Hall.   3

He was right. The poor old etiolate animals were out there skid-   4
ding on their rubber soles. You could hear it once he pointed it out.
They stop short to keep from hitting somebody or because they are
disoriented and they suddenly stop and look around, and they skid
on their rubber-sole shoes, and a screech goes up. They pour out
onto the floor down the escalators from the Pan-Am Building, from
42nd Street, from Lexington Avenue, up out of subways, down into
subways, railroad trains, up into helicopters—

"You can also hear the helicopters all the way down here," says   5
Dr. Hall. The sound of the helicopters using the roof of the Pan-Am
Building nearly fifty stories up beats right through. "If it weren't for
this ceiling"—he is referring to the very high ceiling in Grand Cen-
tral—"this place would be unbearable with this kind of crowding.
And yet they'll probably never 'waste' space like this again."

They screech! And the adrenal glands in all those poor white   6
animals enlarge, micrometer by micrometer, to the size of can-
taloupes. Dr. Hall pulls a Minox camera out of a holster he has on his
belt and starts shooting away at the human scurry. The Sink!

Dr. Hall has the Minox up to his eye—he is a slender man,   7
calm, 52 years old, young-looking, an anthropologist who has
worked with Navajos, Hopis, Spanish-Americans, Negroes, Trukese.
He was the most important anthropologist in the government during
the crucial years of the foreign aid program, the 1950s. He directed
both the Point Four Training Program and the Human Relations
Area files. He wrote *The Silent Language* and *The Hidden Dimension*, two books that are picking up the kind of "underground" following his friend Marshall McLuhan started picking up about five
years ago. He teaches at the Illinois Institute of Technology, lives
with his wife, Mildred, in a high-ceilinged town house on one of the
last great residential streets in downtown Chicago, Astor Street; has a
grown son and daughter, loves good food, good wine, the relaxed,
civilized life—but comes to New York with a Minox at his eye to
record—perfect!—The Sink!

We really got down in there by walking down into the Lexing-   8
ton Avenue line subway stop under Grand Central. We inhaled those
nice big fluffy fumes of human sweat, urine, effluvia, and sebaceous
secretions. One old female human was already stroked out on the

upper level, on a stretcher, with two policemen standing by. The other humans barely looked at her. They rushed into line. They bellied each other, haunch to paunch, down the stairs. Human heads shone through the gratings. The species North European tried to create bubbles of space around themselves, about a foot and a half in diameter—

"See, he's reacting against the line," says Dr. Hall.   9

—but the species Mediterranean presses on in. The hell with   10
bubbles of space. The species North European resents that, this male human behind him presses forward toward the booth . . . breathing on him, he's disgusted, he pulls out of the line entirely, the species Mediterranean resents him for resenting it, and neither of them realizes what the hell they are getting irritable about exactly. And in all of them the old adrenals grow another micrometer.

Dr. Hall whips out the Minox. Too perfect! The bottom of The   11
Sink.

It is the sheer overcrowding, such as occurs in the business sec-   12
tions of Manhattan five days a week and in Harlem, Bedford-Stuyvesant, southeast Bronx every day—sheer overcrowding is converting New Yorkers into animals in a sink pen. Dr. Hall's argument runs as follows: all animals, including birds, seem to have a built-in, inherited requirement to have a certain amount of territory, space, to lead their lives in. Even if they have all the food they need, and there are no predatory animals threatening them, they cannot tolerate crowding beyond a certain point. No more than two hundred wild Norway rats can survive on a quarter acre of ground, for example, even when they are given all the food they can eat. They just die off.

But why? To find out, ethologists have run experiments on all   13
sorts of animals, from stickleback crabs to Sika deer. In one major experiment, an ethologist named John Calhoun put some domesticated white Norway rats in a pen with four sections to it, connected by ramps. Calhoun knew from previous experiments that the rats tend to split up into groups of ten to twelve and that the pen, therefore, would hold forty to forty-eight rats comfortably, assuming they formed four equal groups. He allowed them to reproduce until there were eighty rats, balanced between male and female, but did not let it get any more crowded. He kept them supplied with plenty of food, water, and nesting materials. In other words, all their more obvious needs were taken care of. A less obvious need—space—was not. To

the human eye, the pen did not even look especially crowded. But to the rats, it was crowded beyond endurance.

The entire colony was soon plunged into a profound behavioral sink. "The sink," said Calhoun, "is the outcome of any behavioral process that collects animals together in unusually great numbers. The unhealthy connotations of the term are not accidental: a behavioral sink does act to aggravate all forms of pathology that can be found within a group." 14

For a start, long before the rat population reached eighty, a status hierarchy had developed in the pen. Two dominant male rats took over the two end sections, acquired harems of eight to ten females each, and forced the rest of the rats into the two middle pens. All the overcrowding took place in the middle pens. That was where the "sink" hit. The aristocrat rats at the ends grew bigger, sleeker, healthier, and more secure the whole time. 15

In The Sink, meanwhile, nest building, courting, sex behavior, reproduction, social organization, health—all of it went to pieces. Normally, Norway rats have a mating ritual in which the male chases the female, the female ducks down into a burrow and sticks her head up to watch the male. He performs a little dance outside the burrow, then she comes out, and he mounts her, usually for a few seconds. When The Sink set in, however, no more than three males—the dominant males in the middle sections—kept up the old customs. The rest tried everything from satyrism to homosexuality or else gave up on sex altogether. Some of the subordinate males spent all their time chasing females. Three or four might chase one female at the same time, and instead of stopping at the burrow entrance for the ritual, they would charge right in. Once mounted, they would hold on for minutes instead of the usual seconds. 16

Homosexuality rose sharply. So did bisexuality. Some males would mount anything—males, females, babies, senescent rats, anything. Still other males dropped sexual activity altogether, wouldn't fight and, in fact, would hardly move except when the other rats slept. Occasionally a female from the aristocrat rats' harems would come over the ramps and into the middle sections to sample life in The Sink. When she had had enough, she would run back up the ramp. Sink males would give chase up to the top of the ramp, which is to say, to the very edge of the aristocratic preserve. But one glance from one of the king rats would stop them cold and they would return to The Sink. 17

The slumming females from the harems had their adventures   18
and then returned to a placid, healthy life. Females in The Sink,
however, were ravaged, physically and psychologically. Pregnant rats
had trouble continuing pregnancy. The rate of miscarriages increased significantly, and females started dying from tumors and
other disorders of the mammary glands, sex organs, uterus, ovaries,
and Fallopian tubes. Typically, their kidneys, livers, and adrenals
were also enlarged or diseased or showed other signs associated with
stress.

Child-rearing became totally disorganized. The females lost the   19
interest or the stamina to build nests and did not keep them up if they
did build them. In the general filth and confusion, they would not put
themselves out to save offspring they were momentarily separated
from. Frantic, even sadistic competition among the males was going on
all around them and rendering their lives chaotic. The males began un-
provoked and senseless assaults upon one another, often in the form of
tail-biting. Ordinarily, rats will suppress this kind of behavior when it
crops up. In The Sink, male rats gave up all policing and just looked out
for themselves. The "pecking order" among males in the Sink was
never stable. Normally, male rats set up a three-class structure. Under
the pressure of overcrowding, however, they broke up into all sorts of
unstable subclasses, cliques, packs—and constantly pushed, probed,
explored, tested one another's power. Anyone was fair game, except
for the aristocrats in the end pens.

Calhoun kept the population down to eighty, so that the next   20
stage, "population collapse" or "massive die-off," did not occur. But
the autopsies showed that the pattern—as in the diseases among the
female rats—was already there.

The classic study of die-off was John J. Christian's study of Sika   21
deer on James Island in the Chesapeake Bay, west of Cambridge,
Maryland. Four or five of the deer had been released on the island,
which was 280 acres and uninhabited, in 1916. By 1955 they had
bred freely into a herd of 280 to 300. The population density was
only about one deer per acre at this point, but Christian knew that
this was already too high for the Sikas' inborn space requirements,
and something would give before long. For two years the number of
deer remained 280 to 300. But suddenly, in 1958, over half the deer
died; 161 carcasses were recovered. In 1959 more deer died and the
population steadied at about 80.

In two years, two-thirds of the herd had died. Why? It was not 22
starvation. In fact, all the deer collected were in excellent condition,
with well-developed muscles, shining coats, and fat deposits between
the muscles. In practically all the deer, however, the adrenal glands
had enlarged by 50 percent. Christian concluded that the die-off was
due to "shock following severe metabolic disturbance, probably as a
result of prolonged adrenocortical hyperactivity. . . . There was no
evidence of infection, starvation, or other obvious cause to explain
the mass mortality." In other words, the constant stress of overpopu-
lation, plus the normal stress of the cold of the winter, had kept the
adrenalin flowing so constantly in the deer that their systems were
depleted of blood sugar and they died of shock.

Well, the white humans are still skidding and darting across the 23
floor of Grand Central. Dr. Hall listens a moment longer to the skidding and the darting noises, and then says, "You know, I've been on
commuter trains here after everyone has been through one of these
rushes, and I'll tell you, there is enough acid flowing in the stomachs
in every car to dissolve the rails underneath."

Just a little invisible acid bath for the linings to round off the 24
day. The ulcers the acids cause, of course, are the one disease people
have already been taught to associate with the stress of city life. But
overcrowding, as Dr. Hall sees it, raises a lot more hell with the body
than just ulcers. In everyday life in New York—just the usual, getting
to work, working in massively congested areas like 42nd Street between Fifth Avenue and Lexington, especially now that the Pan-Am
Building is set in there, working in cubicles such as those in the editorial offices at Time-Life, Inc., which Dr. Hall cites as typical of
New York's poor handling of space, working in cubicles with low
ceilings and, often, no access to a window, while construction crews
all over Manhattan drive everybody up the Masonite wall with air-
pressure generators with noises up to the boil-a-brain decibel levels,
then rushing to get home, piling into subways and trains, fighting for
time and for space, the usual day in New York—the whole now-
normal thing keeps shooting jolts of adrenalin into the body, breaking down the body's defenses and winding up with the work-a-daddy
human animal stroked out at the breakfast table with his head
apoplexed like a cauliflower out of his $6.95 semi-spread Pima-
cotton shirt, and nosed over into a plate of No-Kloresto egg substi-
tute, signing off with the black thrombosis, cancer, kidney, liver, or

stomach failure, and the adrenals ooze to a halt, the size of eggplants in July.

One of the people whose work Dr. Hall is interested in on this score is Rene Dubos at the Rockefeller Institute. Dubos's work indicates that specific organisms, such as the tuberculosis bacillus or a pneumonia virus, can seldom be considered "the cause" of a disease. The germ or virus, apparently, has to work in combination with other things that have already broken the body down in some way—such as the old adrenal hyperactivity. Dr. Hall would like to see some autopsy studies made to record the size of adrenal glands in New York, especially of people crowded into slums and people who go through the full rush-hour-work-rush-hour cycle every day. He is afraid that until there is some clinical, statistical data on how overcrowding actually ravages the human body, no one will be willing to do anything about it. Even in so obvious a thing as air pollution, the pattern is familiar. Until people can actually see the smoke or smell the sulphur or feel the sting in their eyes, politicians will not get excited about it, even though it is well known that many of the lethal substances polluting the air are invisible and odorless. For one thing, most politicians are like the aristocrat rats. They are insulated from The Sink by practically sultanic buffers—limousines, chauffeurs, secretaries, aides-de-camp, doormen, shuttered houses, high-floor apartments. They almost never ride subways, fight rush hours, much less live in the slums or work in the Pan-Am Building.

We took a cab from Grand Central to go up to Harlem, and by 48th Street we were already socked into one of those great, total traffic jams on First Avenue on Friday afternoon. Dr. Hall motions for me to survey the scene, and there they all are, humans, male and female, behind the glass of their automobile windows, soundlessly going through the torture of their own adrenaline jolts. This male over here contracts his jaw muscles so hard that they bunch up into a great cheese Danish pattern. He twists his lips, he bleeds from the eyeballs, he shouts . . . soundlessly behind glass . . . the fat corrugates on the back of his neck, his whole body shakes as he pounds the heel of his hand into the steering wheel. The female human in the car ahead of him whips her head around, she bares her teeth, she screams. . . soundlessly behind glass . . . she throws her hands up in the air, Whaddya expect me—Yah, yuh stupid—and they all sit there, trapped in their own congestion, bleeding hate all over each other, shorting out the ganglia and—goddam it—

Dr. Hall sits back and watches it all. This is it! The Sink!

READING QUESTIONS FOR "SLIDING DOWN INTO THE BEHAVIORAL SINK"

Main Idea

1. State the essay's main idea in your own words. Compare it to your prediction of the main idea. (*Note:* The main idea should sum up the smaller ideas of the essay.)

Organization

2. a. Where in the essay is the main idea found?

   b. Why has the author placed the main idea there?

3. In what order are the paragraphs arranged? (Underline one.) Time / Least to most important / Most to least important / Simple listing / Logic: cause and effect / Other logic / Other

Style

4. How formal is the essay? (Circle your choice.)

   [Informal–1–2–3–4–5–6–7–8–9–10–Formal]

   What indicators convinced you? (For a list of possible indicators and two benchmark essays, see Appendix F, The Formality Spectrum, on page 307.)

5. Where do you see the following features of style? List one or two examples of each with their paragraph numbers.

Features (For definitions, see Appendix B, page 291.)

a. allusion

b. analogy

c. irony of situation

d. irony of wording

e. jargon

f. metaphor

g. overstatement

h. simile

i. other: _____

Content

6. Complete the chart below: Fill in paragraph numbers for any type of evidence Wolfe gives.

Enlarged Adrenals Linked to Increase in	Rats	Deer	Humans
Antisocial behavior			
Death rates			

7. a. Could antisocial behavior in cities be caused by anything else besides adrenalin poisoning? List other possible causes.

b. List other possible causes (besides adrenalin poisoning) of the higher death rates in cities.

8. Does Wolfe propose—directly or indirectly—any changes in American life? If so, what?

9. a. In the preview essays, how did Golden describe the crowded Jewish settlement in New York around 1900?

b. What kept that community from being a sink even though it was crowded?

10. Do you know of other cities besides New York—either in the United States or in another country—that cope with crowding differently? What differences seem most important?

If you have not already read the essay and answered the Reading Questions, be sure to do so before you proceed.

COMPOSITION QUESTIONS*

Listed below are the writing questions. Choose one and write an essay that answers it. Whichever question you choose, think of the person who will read your answer. The question may tell who your audience is. If not, think of a person you know and respect—preferably your instructor or a fellow student who will read your essay. Try to convince that person to believe you.

Bring in useful details from the selection(s) you have read and perhaps other incidents you know of. For ideas, review your answers to questions in the Preview and Reading Steps. When you first refer to a reading, give its title (in quotation marks) and the author's full name. Also, give the full name of anyone featured in the article the first time you mention that person.

Note: If you are assigned to write a one-paragraph essay, think of your answer to the question, and list several key points you could make to support your answer. Then choose just one of the points and explain it in detail.

1. Hall seems to imply that crowding is a major cause of the social problems of American cities. However, more than one influence may be at work at the same time. Evaluate Hall's theory in relation to rival explanations. Consider evidence (see your response to Reading Question 6) and alternative explanations (Reading Question 7). Some alternative explanations might include the justice system (see Unit 2); dilution of responsibility, as shown in the bystander effect (see Unit 3); and the drug problem (see Unit 16).

2. How likely is it that humans can live together in harmony even under crowded conditions? Consider any communities you know that have been crowded but peaceful. These could include communities in the United States (such as those described by Harry Golden) or in other countries (one example might be the Jewish ghettoes of Eastern Europe as described by Isaac Bashevis Singer). Some influences that

---

*You may want to refer to Golden's selections as a group ("Three essays by Harry Golden illustrate that . . .") In referring to the essay on overcrowding, identify both Tom Wolfe (the author) and Edward T. Hall (the anthropologist who was interviewed).

might overcome the ill effects of crowding are agreed-upon social rules, stable family life, and the high hopes of voluntary immigrants.

3. In your judgment, how hopeful is Wolfe that problems of over-crowding can be solved? Wolfe's paragraph 25 suggests that information may alert the public and cause them to solve the problem. Do you share his beliefs?

4. Does Wolfe suggest that the problem might be solved by the government or by private means? Which method do you favor? Tell why and/or how your preferred method would work. If you know about planned cities such as Columbia, Maryland, you might refer to them in answering this question. You might want to write your answer in the form of a letter to a public official or newspaper editor.

REVISION QUESTIONS

Once you have finished writing your essay, ask yourself the following questions.

1. Is there any statement the reader might not understand?
2. Is there any statement that might offend the reader?
3. Is there anything that's not very convincing?
4. Have I changed the subject and then changed it back again?
5. Have I said the same thing twice?
6. Do I want to try using any feature of style I've seen in the reading selection?

EDITING QUESTIONS

Once you've made changes, ask someone else to read your essay. Change it again as needed. Then read your essay out loud and answer the following questions.

1. Does every sentence make sense?
2. Does every sentence use the kind of language that most people consider "good English" these days? (*Hint:* Imagine a TV announcer reading it.)

3. Do the periods, commas, and other punctuation show the rise and fall of my voice?

4. Are the words spelled right?

If your instructor asks you to copy your paper over, proofread for copying errors before you hand it in.

UNIT
FIFTEEN

The Effects of Technology on Society

PREVIEW STEPS FOR UNIT FIFTEEN

In response to questions 1 and 2, try these steps: Write your answers, talk them over with three or four classmates, and then discuss them with the whole class.

1. What good effects has technology had on your life? Jot down whatever comes to mind for two or three minutes.

2. What bad effects has technology had on your life? Do you think the government should control advancements in technology? Again, jot down whatever comes to mind for two or three minutes.

3. a. Read the title of the first essay (page 241). Name the topic. (Who or what is this essay about?)

    b. Now predict the main idea. (What is the main point the author wants to make about this topic?)

    c. Read the first and last paragraphs. Revise your prediction if necessary. (*Note:* The main idea should sum up the smaller ideas of the essay.)

4. Some words from the essay are listed below, accompanied by quotations. Mark any words you do not know and make an educated guess about their meanings using the context supplied by the quotations— and possibly Appendix A, Word Parts, on page 287. You may want to work with a small group of classmates.

progressives "We have taken the distinction between *progressives* and *conservatives* so much for granted that it is now hard for us to think about politics in any other terms."

conservatives See above quotation.

status quo "Yet this way of looking at things was invented 200 years ago, at a time when modernization and progress were sweeping away entrenched privilege and challenging the *status quo*."

autonomy "Yet we have not come up with a new political direction that . . . relates to . . . our sense of personal *autonomy*."

paternalistic "Economic planners, urban planners, and social planners take over individuals' personal decisions by redefining them as technical problems that only 'the experts' can deal with. The tone is usually *paternalistic*."

5. Now read the following essay. As you read, jot down any questions that occur to you.

(*Note:* Question 6 appears after the essay.)

A New Declaration of Independence

Charles Siegel

America is at a crucial turning point. We have taken the distinction   1
between progressives and conservatives so much for granted that it is
now hard for us to think about politics in any other terms. Yet this
way of looking at things was invented 200 years ago, at a time when
modernization and progress were sweeping away entrenched privi-

lege and challenging the status quo. It is no longer relevant now that modernization and progress *are* the status quo. . . .

Our problem is not modernization itself but technocratic modernism, the blind faith that technology can do everything better. This fascination with technology and growth transformed America during the postwar period when we were the only country with a strong enough economy to move at full speed toward the technological ideal. Mamie Eisenhower would not serve fresh vegetables in the White House because she considered canned and frozen vegetables more modern. Federal, state, and local governments did all they could to promote the construction of freeways, housing subdivisions, and shopping malls rather than neighborhoods where people could walk. Suburban parents sent their children to nursery schools, where they could benefit from special programs designed by experts in educational psychology. 2

Without question, modernization has had great successes— among them, curing disease and reducing poverty—but now we can see that the modernist faith has also failed in many ways. For example, we spend more than twice as much on each child's education as we did in 1960 (after correcting for inflation), but standardized tests show that students learn less than they did then. Or consider this: America's per capita national income is about twice what it was in 1960 (after correcting for inflation), but Americans do not feel that they are twice as well off as they were in 1960. In many ways, we feel worse off. 3

Yet we have not come up with a new political direction that responds to the failures of modernization as it relates to four important aspects of our lives: the physical and social environment of our neighborhoods, our places of business, our families, and our sense of personal autonomy. Instead, we are still calling for more technology to solve the problems caused by technology itself. 4

We should take the opposite tack. Most environmental and social problems we face today exist only because we have had such faith in technology and economic growth in this century that we've rushed headlong to modernize every activity of life, even in many cases when it is obvious that modernization doesn't work. Rather than applying more expertise and spending more money to solve these problems, we should get at their root by limiting technology and growth. We should use modern technology where it works and get the inappropriate technology out of the way. 5

Revitalizing Our Neighborhoods

To build workable neighborhoods, we need to rein in the automobile—and the best way to do this is to reduce the speed limit. How low should we go? Consider the impact of reducing the speed limit to 15 miles per hour for private vehicles within the city limits. It would allow people to use cars for local errands but force them to take higher-speed public transportation for longer trips. As a result, automobiles would no longer dominate the environment, and bicycles and small electric vehicles could easily fit into the flow of traffic. Streets would be friendlier to pedestrians, and safe enough for children to play in them. We would also have to limit the scale of development to make room for slower forms of transportation. It is hard to get around on a bicycle or in an electric cart, and virtually impossible to walk anywhere, if you inhabit a landscape of tract housing and shopping malls.

6

Another possibility would be to cut the speed limit to 30 miles per hour. That would shift long-distance commuting from the freeways to high-speed rail systems. Commercial development would cluster around the rail stations to take advantage of the new customer base; freeway-oriented shopping malls would make way for mixed-use shopping and office complexes (with plenty of parking) at rail stations. Some of the suburban sprawl at the edges of metropolitan areas would also recede because it is totally dependent on high-speed freeway access.

7

Yet, if the city had a high-speed rail system, this change would still allow everyone to live in a suburban neighborhood. The big differences from today's suburbs would be that people would shop and work in mixed-use complexes, which are far more interesting than shopping malls and office parks, and most commutes would be less grueling. This change would also cut automobile use roughly in half, dramatically reducing the city's environmental problems.

8

Are these ideas a mere pipe dream? Not necessarily. Cities all over the world are "calming" traffic on residential streets. In the 1980s, Germany began an ambitious experiment that went further, slowing traffic on both residential and arterial streets in areas ranging from a neighborhood in Berlin with 30,000 residents to a small town of 2,300 residents. The government cut the speed limit in half but discovered that the time for the average trip increased by just a bit over 10 percent. Obviously, one result of traffic calming was to shorten the length of the

9

average trip. In addition, noise levels and injuries from automobile accidents dropped dramatically. The German automobile association, which was skeptical about the government's data, conducted its own interviews and found that, after speeds were lowered, 67 percent of motorists and even higher proportions of residents approved of the change. The experiment was so successful, in fact, that it has since been imitated in cities in Denmark, Sweden, the Netherlands, Italy, Switzerland, Austria, and Japan.

Protecting Our Small Businesses

To promote civic life, it would also be useful to phase out chain stores   10
and reduce the overall scale of retail outlets, so that national megastores could not displace locally owned businesses. Some cities already have zoning laws that restrict chains, but it would be more effective to have a national law limiting the number of stores that one company could own—to break up existing chains and reduce the mind-numbing sameness that now blankets most of the United States.

Eliminating chains would increase some costs. Obviously,   11
chains and superstores are more efficient than most independently owned stores because of their vast economies of scale. In some cases—supermarkets, for example—the economic benefits of chains might outweigh their social costs. But in others—most notably bookselling—quality, diversity, and the free flow of ideas are so important that it is urgent to get rid of the chains, even if the costs increase.

Replacing chains with small businesses would lower overall pro-   12
ductivity, but retailing is one of the few industries that can stay small without hurting a country's economic position internationally. Virtually all of Japan's retailing is done by mom-and-pop businesses, but it hasn't prevented Japan from becoming one of the most prosperous countries in the world.

Making Our Families Work

Moving from the storefront to the home front, it is clear that some of our   13
most deep-seated social problems result from the modernization of the family. Few would dispute that there is a "parenting deficit" in America today. Children are suffering not only because families are breaking up

but also because, even in intact families, both parents must work full time to keep up financially. The left generally ignores this new problem and continues to push for family policies from early in the century: more money for day care, Head Start, and schooling. These ideas made sense in the 1950s, when stable families were the norm and most people believed in progressive methods of raising children. But today even the left is disillusioned with them. They support these programs to help cope with family breakdown, but they have no vision of a better future.

By default, this territory now belongs to the conservatives who 14 rhapsodize about "the traditional family" (by which they really mean the early modern family, with a husband who goes to work in a factory or office and a wife who stays home). The conservatives strike a chord with many voters because they don't deny the damage done by the decline of the family during the past few decades, but they can't go any farther than that because they are also champions of economic growth.

The fact that parents no longer have time for their children is the 15 worst possible indictment of the modern economy. Rather than demanding more day care and schooling to help families conform to the economy, the left should be demanding radical changes in the growth economy to make it work for families. One practical approach would be to change the current tax laws—and corporate subsidy programs— which discriminate against parents who take care of their own children. Many parents already get tax credits and subsidies to help pay for day care. Why not give parents who forgo day care equivalent benefits? In many cases, equal benefits would make it possible for parents to cut back their work hours and raise their children on their own.

But larger economic changes are also needed. In 1950, one parent 16 working 40 hours a week was enough to support a typical family. If we had been more sensible, we could have used the phenomenal rise of women in the workforce from the 1960s onward to create families supported by two parents, each working 20 hours a week. The original promise of modernization was that higher productivity would give people more leisure, but the economy has not kept this promise.

Restoring Our Personal Autonomy

Technocratic modernism undermines autonomy in the same way that 17 it undermines the neighborhood and the family. Economic planners, urban planners, and social planners take over individuals' personal decisions by redefining them as technical problems that only "the experts" can deal with. The tone is usually paternalistic. The experts themselves believe they are using modern methods to "help" people, but, in reality, they are controlling people and increasing the feelings of powerlessness and dependence that are pervasive in modern society. To restore personal autonomy, we must limit the ability of technological organizations to control our everyday lives.

The most astounding example of the way that we allow bureaucracies to control our lives is our commitment to the idea that the economic system must "help" people by "providing jobs." This idea made sense in the early part of the century when most people needed more income to buy necessities. But now that we no longer have that problem, we need to give people the ability to choose their own standard of living. In a surplus economy, the idea that we must provide jobs for people forces us to promote economic growth, even if most of the products we produce are useless.   18

Not surprisingly, we think about work like consumers. We think in terms of *having* jobs, not in terms of *doing* jobs because they are useful. We demand more jobs just as we demand more transportation, education, health care, child care, and more of any "service" that we expect the system to provide. And, in the process, we lose sight of the fact that we are actually demanding to do unnecessary work.   19

It is reasonable to work until you produce what you want, then stop. But, as a culture, we believe in creating demand for products that people don't really want purely to create extra work for ourselves. To put the economy back on a rational basis, to produce the goods and services that people actually want, we need to offer job seekers more flexible work hours. One way would be to give employers tax incentives to create more part-time jobs and accommodate different work schedules without penalizing part-time workers with lower hourly pay, restricted benefits, or fewer promotion opportunities. Federal, state, and local governments should act as a model by offering their own employees work hours that are as flexible as possible.   20

We can't expect employers to take advantage of flexible work hours, though, unless we limit the demands that the consumer economy makes on them. In part, this would involve changing personal behavior—getting people to go beyond the "shop till you drop" mindset that makes Americans spend three to four times as many   21

hours shopping as Europeans do. But it also would require larger political changes, such as rebuilding American cities, where it now is
absolutely essential for most families to own two cars.

Humanizing the Economy

We can use the law to control growth if we learn to think about tech- 22
nology in human terms, rather than focusing on the abstractions that
only "the experts" can work with. As long as we think of transportation, land use, and pollution control as "urban problems," we will
surrender to the city planners and let them decide what kinds of
neighborhoods we live in. But if we can focus on the human purpose
of our cities—they are the places where we live—it will become obvious that the people themselves should make the political and personal decisions that will shape the city's design.

Similarly, as long as we think of unemployment and inflation 23
as "economic problems," we will allow economists to decide what
our standard of living should be. But when we think about the
human purpose of the economy—to produce things that we actually want—it becomes obvious that workers should get to choose
their own work schedules and standard of living. Planning is useful to control the business cycles and fine tune the economy, but
this planning should be subordinate to the human question of what
we want to consume, which individuals should decide for themselves.

The bias of the consumer economy has crippled our politics. 24
Real change will be possible when people act as citizens who use the
law to govern themselves—not as clients demanding more services
from the system and voting for the politicians they think will do the
best job of providing them with more education, more health care,
more transportation, and, most important, more jobs. The moral advantage of limiting technology is that it increases individual freedom
and responsibility, which have been eroded by modernization. Someone always objects that limiting technology is unrealistic—for example, that Americans will never vote to lower the speed limit. That
may be true today, but only because people believe that building livable cities is a technical problem that the planners must solve for
them, and that their role is just to demand services from the planners.
People will act differently if they see that, in order to have decent

cities to live in, well-educated children, and an economy that produces things they want, they must consume less and do more for themselves.

6. State the essay's main idea in your own words. Compare it to your prediction of the main idea. (*Note:* The main idea should sum up the smaller ideas of the essay.)

PREVIEW STEPS FOR "ON THE EDGE OF THE DIGITAL AGE: THE HISTORIC MOMENT"

1. a. Read the title of the second essay (page 251). Name the topic. (Who or what is this essay about?)

   b. Now predict the main idea. (What is the main point the author wants to make about this topic?)

   c. Read the first and last paragraphs of the essay. Revise your prediction if necessary. (*Note:* The main idea should sum up the smaller ideas of the essay.)

2. What in the author's background may have led him to the main idea? (See author's background, below title.)

3. Some words from the essay are listed below, accompanied by quotations. Mark any words you do not know and make an educated guess about their meanings using the context supplied by the quotations—

and possibly Appendix A, Word Parts, on page 287. You may want to work with a small group of classmates.

agrarian "The *agrarian* economy was completely restructured, and social and political institutions transformed to fit the new realities."

precursor "And the Internet is the *precursor* to the information superhighway, which will be the pipeline for the vital flow of the information of the Digital Age."

obsolescence "The failure of our schools is rooted in the *obsolescence* of a system that mass-produces brains in an era in which the world's knowledge doubles every four years."

redundant "Information technologies will make millions of working people *redundant* and send them scattering to retool their skills and seek new work."

hierarchical "The centralized, *hierarchical* organization characteristic of the Industrial Age will shift into the more decentralized organization that will be the hallmark of the Digital Age."

infrastructure "By then your home may have 50 of these tiny computers connected to the information *infrastructure*, much as you now have 50 electric motors tied to the electrical grid powering your refrigerator, washing machine. . . ."

ubiquitous "These *ubiquitous* computers finally may have the power to bring a sense of tranquillity back to our lives, allowing us to live in less-crowded surroundings, more integrated with nature."

inauspicious "For a revolution, [the creation of the microprocessor] was a pretty *inauspicious* beginning. At the time, many people didn't see it as much of an improvement over the existing mainframe computers."

quasipublic "But soon they [local area networks] were connecting different companies or institutions through such *quasipublic* computer networks as the Internet."

superfluous "But the white collars, too, were becoming *superfluous* in an office environment pervaded by information technologies."

cadres "You don't need *cadres* of middle managers making reports and shuffling information to the executives when personal computers on networks can do the job."

consummate "Our national government is paralyzed largely because it's a *consummate* product of the Industrial Age."

extraneous "They are trying to define their essential core services and get out of delivering *extraneous* services. They are trying to adopt new technologies and shed unneeded levels of managers, in their case, bureaucrats."

imploded "But what happened in the 1980s, the dawn of the Digital Age? . . . The Soviet Union's entire system completely *imploded* in less than 10 years."

totalitarian "But in a much more fundamental way, that *totalitarian* system could not function in a world of digital technologies and global telecommunications. And so we watched the Soviet empire collapse."

ascendant "The *ascendant* industries are ones in which the United States leads the world: computers, telecommunications, entertainment, media."

Renaissance "The first *Renaissance* came about largely because the printing press enabled all the isolated minds of medieval Europe to finally connect."

synergy "What kind of *synergy* will be created this time around [during the second Renaissance], as all the minds on the planet become wired together through the Net?"

tenured "*Tenured* professors and teachers' unions face not minor pay cuts, but radically new roles."

4. At the end of the Preview, you may want to go over any new features of style that occur in the following reading selection. You will need to know the terms *allusion, metaphor*, and *simile*. For help, see Appendix B, Guide to Literary Terms (page 291), with accompanying exercises on individual features.

5. Before reading "On the Edge of the Digital Age: The Historic Moment," turn to pages 261–262 and skim the Reading Questions. Then read the essay to find answers to these questions. As you read, jot down any questions that occur to you.

On the Edge of the Digital Age: The Historic Moment

Peter Leyden

Peter Leyden (1959–), now the managing editor of Wired *magazine, was the Minneapolis–St. Paul's* Star Tribune's *information technologies reporter when he wrote the article below. Having joined the newspaper in 1990, he covered the urban affairs beat before moving to the technologies assignments. He has also worked as a newspaper reporter and as a special correspondent in Asia for* Newsweek *magazine and several newspapers. He has master's degrees in journalism and comparative politics from Columbia University and a degree in intellectual history from Georgetown University.*

We are living through an extraordinary moment in human history.   1

Historians will look back on our times, the 40-year span between 1980 and 2020, and classify it among the handful of historical moments when humans reorganized their entire civilization around a new tool, a new idea.   2

These decades mark the transition from the Industrial Age, an era organized around the motor, to the Digital Age, an era defined by the microprocessor—the brains within today's personal computer.   3

The mid-1990s . . . may come to be viewed as the defining moment when society recognized the enormity of the changes taking place and began to reorient itself.   4

The last time humans went through such a wrenching transition was during the Industrial Revolution of the late 18th and 19th cen-   5 turies. The agrarian economy was completely restructured, and social and political institutions transformed to fit the new realities.

The trauma was severe: Peasants were driven off their fields and into factories. Industrialists became fabulously rich overnight. Rustic village life was replaced by an urban one. Political revolutions flared. 6

Our transition will be every bit as brutal. Once-secure professionals will find their skills obsolete. Washington's government bureaucracies will see much of their power eroded. Cities will face accelerating population losses. 7

And when the trauma subsides, the changes in our daily lives will be just as profound as those between a rural peasant and an urban factory worker. It may sound preposterous, but that's the best way to describe the scale of changes that we're facing. 8

You've heard the talk about how the Digital Revolution will change the way you work and live. 9

Start believing the hype. 10

**Digital Age's Next 10 Years May Be More Traumatic
Than the Great Depression**

From this historical perspective, much of the confusion of our tumultuous times begins to make more sense. 11

Why is it that our federal government seems paralyzed, our schools dysfunctional, our society fracturing into thousands of subgroups? Why do we have so much anxiety when the economy is so strong? 12

And what's driving this boom in computers and telecommunications? Sales of personal computers, CD-ROMs, cellular phones, you name it, are off the charts. Just two years ago, you never heard the word "Internet" or had any concept of e-mail. Today everyone seems to be going online. 13

Here's one way to think about it: We're at a point in the transition where almost everything associated with the old Industrial Age is falling into dysfunction and everything associated with the new Digital Age is booming. 14

This boom is just the beginning of the spread of microprocessors—tiny computer chips that will be installed in almost all the tools and appliances that we'll use in our lives, making those tools more in- 15 telligent and useful. And the Internet is the precursor to the information superhighway, which will be the pipeline for the vital flow of the information of the Digital Age.

Even our seemingly intractable social and political problems 16 can be reinterpreted in this new light: That gridlock in Washington is more about the inability of our old centralized political institutions to adapt to the decentralized, fast-moving realities of our time. The failure of our schools is rooted in the obsolescence of a system that mass-produces brains in an era in which the world's knowledge doubles every four years.

The economic anxiety comes from the rapid restructuring of 17 the economy and workplace, which puts everyone's career and livelihood at risk.

The early signs of this transitional trauma have been around for 18 the last 15 years, from the displacement of manufacturing workers in the early 1980s to the downsizing of office staffs that started in the early 1990s.

And the next 10 years may be the most disruptive and difficult 19 period that any of us have lived through—including those who lived through the Great Depression. We'll see the rise and fall of entire sectors of the economy, the disappearance of whole professions, not just individual jobs. Information technologies will make millions of working people redundant and send them scattering to retool their skills and seek new work.

The advent of widespread home shopping will reduce the need 20 for sales clerks. Intermediaries such as travel agents will be cut out of many business transactions when consumers can make their own travel arrangements with airlines and hotels via "intelligent" software agents.

Even professional salespeople with specialized skills—like real 21 estate agents—may find their services less in demand when consumers themselves can easily tap into real-estate listings and mortgage information databases.

The centralized, hierarchical organization characteristic of the 22 Industrial Age will shift into the more decentralized organization that will be the hallmark of the Digital Age. Look at your own workplace: It's probably already started. "Empowerment" of employees is the watchword as layers of managers are eliminated and decision making is pushed closer to where the actual work gets done.

Computers May Have the Power to Make World
a More Placid Place to Live by 2020

By about the year 2020, all this will have largely played itself out. The   23
new digital network will be in place, and we'll have absorbed microprocessors in all their myriad forms into our lives.

By then your home may have 50 of these tiny computers con-   24
nected to the information infrastructure, much as you now have 50
electric motors tied to the electrical grid powering your refrigerator,
washing machine, dishwasher, blender, right down to the clocks on
your wall.

In 25 years, the trauma will have largely subsided and the world   25
could well have become a more placid place to live. These ubiquitous
computers finally may have the power to bring a sense of tranquillity
back to our lives, allowing us to live in less-crowded surroundings,
more integrated with nature.

Imagine a world where the bulk of people work out of their   26
homes and don't have to live within a 30-minute drive from their
employer. You like the mountains? The ocean? A small middle-
American town? Move there.

Imagine children gathering in neighborhood schools of no   27
more than a dozen kids where parents can pick them up for lunch.
Think about governments relying on the diversity and intelligence of
entire communities by letting people debate and vote on all the
major issues that affect their lives.

Imagine regular folks actively participating in the news cover-   28
age of their communities. Imagine those who hate shopping using
digital models online and getting tailormade clothes. How about a
world where physical money—from dollars to dimes—disappears?

Sound far-fetched? It's already begun. We're already seeing   29
the baby steps of trends leading in those directions—whether it's
custom-made Levi's jeans, the rise in telecommuting or experiments
in electronic direct democracy.

Every 18 Months Microprocessors Shrink
as Power Doubles, Price Drops

The story really starts in the early 1970s with the creation of the mi-   30
croprocessor. For a revolution, it was a pretty inauspicious begin-

ning. At the time, many people didn't see it as much of an improvement over the existing mainframe computers.

However, the integrated circuits of microprocessors were smaller   31
and cheaper than the mainframe computers. The development process was such that, eventually, every 18 months or so the microprocessors could double in power, shrink in size, and drop in price.

That has allowed a microprocessor coming out this year to be   32
50 times more powerful than a 1975 IBM mainframe computer. The computer that used to fill a room now fits in a small video game—and the price has fallen from $10 million to $500.

That same dynamic can be expected to boost the power of   33
today's microprocessors a hundredfold in the coming decade.

The 1980s marked the beginning of the introduction of the mi-   34
croprocessor into mass society, primarily through the personal computer. Throughout the decade, personal computers took over the business world, which had the money to invest in the relatively expensive new technologies.

By the early 1990s, a crucial development took place: Comput-   35
ers began to get tied together. At first, the connections were made within the same company in what are called LANs, or local area networks. But soon they were connecting different companies or institutions through such quasipublic computer networks as the Internet.

The key change was that personal computers went from being   36
calculators to being communicators that allowed people to interact, via electronic mail or bulletin boards, for example. People like to communicate. They don't use the telephone because it's a cool gadget; they use it to speak to other human beings.

Increasingly throughout the 1990s, the personal computer came to   37
be seen as a totally new way to communicate. And so it began to leave the confines of the business world and make its breakthrough into the home.

If the story of the 1980s was the personal computer, then the   38
story of the 1990s is the Net. The developments are of equal importance because the Digital Age needs both the microprocessors in place and the infrastructure to tie them together. Only when they are tied together does the Digital Age take off.

And has it ever taken off. Since 1990, anything to do with com-   39
puter networks has exploded. The Internet was growing 10 percent per month throughout last year. The World Wide Web, the subset of the Internet that handles multimedia images, grew more than 10 percent per week.

Technology Life Cycle Shows That Fastest Growth Is Yet to Come

Technology companies in California's Silicon Valley use a recurring   40
image: a marketing curve that describes the rate at which a market
absorbs a new product or a society absorbs a new technology.

The curve inches up slowly as trendsetters buy the new technol-   41
ogy. Then it jumps at a steep angle as more people buy in. That steep
growth continues until most people in the society own the technology, and then the curve flattens at the top. That absorption rate has
occurred again and again in the history of technologies—television,
radio, you name it.

When you plot the growth of almost anything related to these   42
digital technologies over the last five years, you see the same unmis-
takable curve ramping up. . . .

Any key technology comes to a point when its usefulness be-   43
comes so apparent that its absorption into society is inevitable. It tips
the balance from the iffiness of a gadget to the certainty of a key tool.
All signs say that the microprocessor has passed that point.

This growth is likely to continue for another 25 years. By the   44
year 2020, the 40-year technology adoption life cycle will be complete. An entire generation will have grown up in the Digital Age and
will take it for granted. And that generation will be running the
world. . . .

Microprocessor Is to This Era What Motor Was to Industrial Age

The microprocessor is a very powerful tool. It can perform the calcu-   45
lations of many minds put together, and it can do those calculations
at speeds that humans simply can't achieve. When linked, they become vastly more powerful.

Like motors, microprocessors have the power to transform. The   46
same decade that marked the introduction of the microprocessor into
society also marked the beginnings of some severe economic disloca-
tion. A strong argument can be made that they're directly related.

One of the big stories of the early 1980s was the downsizing of   47
the U.S. manufacturing economy—the closing of factories across the
American Rust Belt. At the time, we blamed foreign competition: We
couldn't compete with Japan.

But the much less visible story was the spread of digital tech- 48
nologies into factories. Microprocessors were not only housed in personal computers; they were finding homes in robots and other tools
on shop floors. Information technologies allowed firms to reorganize
work flow more efficiently; advanced telecommunications allowed
whole factories to be moved to foreign lands. It was largely these digital developments that allowed for the huge layoffs.

One of the big stories of the early 1990s was the 1990–92 reces- 49
sion. What made the recession remarkable was that many of those
being laid off were middle managers, clerks, and secretaries. Historically, recessions have primarily hit blue-collar workers.

But the white collars, too, were becoming superfluous in an of- 50
fice environment pervaded by information technologies. You don't
need cadres of middle managers making reports and shuffling information to the executives when personal computers on networks can
do the job. You don't need as many secretaries answering phones
when you have voice mail.

We've heard the stories of our era's human tragedies that rival 51
those of the peasants torn from the fields: the blue-collar worker who
had spent 30 years on the assembly line only to be thrown out of
work for good; the white-collar worker who gave her life to the corporation only to find she now has to strike out on her own as a consultant.

And we have our rags-to-riches stories as well. We have our An- 52
drew Carnegie of the Digital Age: His name is Bill Gates. He went
from a bright kid with some good ideas about software to the richest
man in the country as the head of Microsoft. He was worth almost
$10 billion before he reached age 40.

That kind of dramatic making of fortunes is a pretty good indi- 53
cation that a new wide-open economic system is taking shape, and
the rules have yet to be made.

Digitalization Leaves Centralized Government in Gridlock

It's not just the economy that's feeling the trauma. Once the econ- 54
omy changes, our public institutions inevitably come under the same
pressures. And for the last 15 years, our political and social institutions have come under increasing stress and fallen into increasing
dysfunction.

Take a look at Washington, DC. It's become a standard lament   55
among Americans of all political persuasions that our federal government simply does not work. No one seems to be able to figure a way
out of the legislative gridlock and general paralysis.

Here's one way to view it: Our national government is para-   56
lyzed largely because it's a consummate product of the Industrial
Age. In fact, our Constitution was hammered out at the very dawn of
that age, more than 200 years ago. And modern Washington is a
creature of the mass, centralized, bureaucratized society that was the
crowning achievement of that age. The logic of that age was to cen-
tralize. And the post–World War II Washington establishment and
federal government did that very well.

One of the defining features of the emerging Digital Age is de-   57
centralization. The spread of powerful microprocessors, tied together
through an infrastructure that moves information at the speed of
light, tends to empower the extremities of organizations of all kinds.

Seen in that light, modern Washington is completely at odds   58
with the conditions of this new world. It's a centralizing government
in a decentralizing world.

Taking that same historical perspective, many of the major polit-   59
ical events of last year make more sense. We're seeing the very beginnings of a changeover from a highly centralized system of government
built up since the New Deal in the 1930s to a more decentralized system in tune with the emerging age.

For the first time in 60 years, government appears to be funda-   60
mentally shifting course. In 1994, the party consistently holding to
the philosophy of less government and more decentralized government—the Republicans—captured control of the Congress after
decades out of power. The Democrats, the party clearly associated
with big activist government, face the prospects of becoming the nation's minority party after controlling Washington and the bureaucracies since the New Deal.

That's not to say that voters consciously voted for the party   61
more in tune with the emerging Digital Age. But when you step back
from the minutiae of individual issues, it's apparent that our federal
government—and all levels of government—are beginning to go
through what businesses have been going through for years.

They are trying to define their essential core services and get out   62
of delivering extraneous services. They are trying to adopt new technologies and shed unneeded levels of managers, in their case, bureau-

crats. And they are trying to push decisionmaking down to lower levels of their organizations—and ultimately to the voters themselves.

Businesses call it "reengineering" the corporation. Politicians   63
call it "reinventing" government. They're the same thing.

Digital Age Spurred Soviet Collapse While Playing to American Strengths

To underscore the power of these historical forces, it's worth looking   64
at the fate of the one other industrial superpower of the 20th century.

The Soviet Union took a very different path of industrialization   65
than the United States, but it carried off a pretty impressive feat. In 1917, it was a vast nation of peasants. Sixty years later, in the 1970s, it was a highly industrialized nation in a global struggle for control of the world.

But what happened in the 1980s, the dawn of the Digital Age?   66

The Soviet Union's entire system completely imploded in less   67
than 10 years. The Soviets had built an extraordinarily centralized economy and bureaucratized society. Their system was an extreme manifestation of the centralizing tendencies of that era.

They had no way to cope with an era of instantaneous commu-   68
nication. Faxes and computer networks helped circulate information within that closed society and get word out to the world. But in a much more fundamental way, that totalitarian system could not function in a world of digital technologies and global telecommunications. And so we watched the Soviet empire collapse.

Is the United States doomed to share the fate of the Soviet   69
Union? Far from it. Just as the Industrial Revolution was born in England, the most advanced and powerful country at the time, the Digital Revolution is being born in the last remaining superpower, the United States. We're the first country making this transition into the Digital Age.

We're way ahead of Japan and Europe in this process. We have a   70
much higher penetration of personal computers in the workplace and the home. We own 40 percent of all the world's personal computers used in business. The next closest country is Japan, with 7 percent.

We dominate the world's Internet and early development of the   71
information superhighway: At the start of this year, the United States had almost 26,000 computer networks hooked up to the Internet, compared to about 1,600 each for Japan and Germany.

At a conference called the Networked Economy last fall in   72
Washington, DC, the Japanese government representative said Japan
considers itself about 10 years behind the United States in building
its information superhighway.

This Digital Age should play to many of America's strengths.   73
The ascendant industries are ones in which the United States leads
the world: computers, telecommunications, entertainment, media.
And on a deeper sense, the Digital Age will reward qualities that
often characterize the American worker: creativity, innovation, autonomy, initiative, and speed.

More importantly, the Digital Age will lend more importance to   74
the individual. Digital technologies can empower individuals in profound ways. And the United States, far more than any other country
in the world, has built its entire economic and social system on the
individual.

Worldwide Synergy Via the Net Could Spur Creativity—or Even a Second Renaissance

The Digital Age offers immense possibilities: We may see a time   75
when these digital technologies bring about huge productivity increases that lead to much higher levels of prosperity and a halving of
our 40-hour work week.

We may even see a flowering of human creativity in something   76
like a second Renaissance. The first Renaissance came about largely
because the printing press enabled all the isolated minds of medieval
Europe to finally connect. What kind of synergy will be created this
time around, as all the minds on the planet become wired together
through the Net?

Yet getting from here to there will require an ordeal the likes of   77
which we have never experienced.

The corporation that year in and year out has paid your wages   78
and handed you benefits packages—from health plans to pensions—
may not be around for long, or you won't be on for the ride.

Talk of educational reform may be nothing compared to scrap-   79
ping traditional lectures while beginning long-distance, individualized learning through computers. Tenured professors and teachers'
unions face not minor pay cuts, but radically new roles.

And reinventing government takes on new meaning in this light. We're having a hard enough time trimming back the military. We haven't even contemplated dismantling the U.S. Postal Service as most physical mail turns into digital bits. 80

You think it's confusing and tumultuous now? Just wait for the coming trauma. 81

READING QUESTIONS FOR "ON THE EDGE OF THE DIGITAL AGE: THE HISTORIC MOMENT"

Main Idea

1. State the essay's main idea in your own words. Compare it to your prediction of the main idea. (*Note*: The main idea should sum up the smaller ideas of the essay.)

Organization

2. a. Where in the essay is the main idea found?

   b. Why has the author placed the main idea there?

3. In what order are the paragraphs arranged? (Underline one.) Time / Least to most important / Most to least important / Simple listing / Logic: cause and effect / Other logic / Other

Style

4. How formal is the essay? (Circle your choice.)

   [Informal—1—2—3—4—5—6—7—8—9—10—Formal]

What indicators convinced you? (For a list of possible indicators and two benchmark essays, see Appendix F, The Formality Spectrum, on page 307.)

5. Where do you see the following features of style? List one or two examples of each with their paragraph numbers.

   Features (For definitions, see Appendix B, page 291.)

   a. allusion

   b. metaphor

   c. simile

   Content

6. Does the author propose any change? If so, what do you think would be the result of such a change?

7. Do you agree with the author's main idea? Why or why not?

If you have not already read the essay and answered the Reading Questions, be sure to do so before you proceed.

COMPOSITION QUESTIONS

Listed below are the writing questions. Choose one and write an essay that answers it. Whichever question you choose, think of the person who will read your answer. The question may tell who your audience is. If not, think of a person you know and respect—preferably your instructor or a fellow student who will read your essay. Try to convince that person to believe you.

Bring in useful details from the selection(s) you have read and perhaps other incidents you know of. For ideas, review your answers to questions in the Preview and Reading Steps. When you first refer to a reading, give its title (in quotation marks) and the author's full name. Also, give the full name of anyone featured in the article the first time you mention that person.

Note: If you are assigned to write a one-paragraph essay, think of your answer to the question, and list several key points you could make to support your answer. Then choose just one of the points and explain it in detail.

1. What Siegel and Leyden describe will produce trauma. While Leyden discusses the traumatic effects leading to the Digital Age, Siegel focuses more on the good effects of his proposed changes. Describe the transitional periods for Siegel's plans: (1) lowering highway speed limits to 30 miles per hour, especially in rural areas (par. 7); (2) substituting mixed-use complexes for shopping malls (par. 7); (3) phasing out chain stores and superstores, thus increasing prices and the cost of living (par. 11); (4) getting people to participate more in federal, state, and local governmental planning (par. 15, 18, 22). Which do you think will be the most difficult period?

2. Siegel's plan would raise the cost of goods (par. 11). Can the American consumer make a decision in favor of Siegel's plan if that plan cuts into his or her buying power? He says that Japan prospers on less-efficient small businesses instead of superstores. Are Americans willing to accept the enormous cost of living that exists in Japan? Will Americans let factors other than money be the determining ones in making decisions? Explain.

3. Which traumatic experience do you think would be more palatable to you, Siegel's or Leyden's? Why?

4. Leyden predicts a traumatic transition from the Industrial Age to the Digital Age. How do you think this transition will affect you personally?

5. The changes that both Siegel and Leyden describe would help the environment by reducing use of the automobile. Siegel proposes legislating lower speed limits in order to make a market for high-speed rail service (par. 6–9). Leyden suggests letting technology take its course so that most people will work out of their homes and will not need to use cars as much. Which idea do you favor? Why?

6. Siegel advocates and Leyden predicts a decentralization in human lifestyle (Siegel: whole article; Leyden: par. 16, 22, 54 on). Explain the differences in the way these two men see the decentralization process.

7. The decentralization in both articles will also affect education (Siegel: par. 13, 15, 24; Leyden: par. 16, 27, 76, 79). How do you envision the educational process either for public schools or for colleges 10 to 20 years from now?

8. Both Siegel and Leyden have proposals that would improve children's lives. Siegel's plan would change federal and state laws (par. 15); Leyden's plan would have parents working at home with flexible hours. Compare and contrast the two plans. Which one do you think would improve family life more?

9. Both Siegel and Leyden look forward to more independence for the individual. Of their two approaches for shaping the future, which one do you think will more likely result in this goal?

10. Take one factor in society during the Renaissance and compare and contrast it to what you think that factor will be like in what Leyden calls the second Renaissance.

11. Siegel is concerned that "we think in terms of *having* jobs, not in terms of *doing* jobs because they are useful" (par. 19). How is that attitude a problem? If people were paid by achievement rather than by a time basis, would this attitude change for the better? Why or why not?

12. In paragraph 29, Leyden talks of "experiments in electronic direct democracy." What is that, and how can it be accomplished?

13. In his last paragraph, Siegel describes what has "crippled our politics." What, according to Siegel, must be done to get our electorate walking on healthy legs? Predict whether Americans will be willing to make this happen.

14. Compare and contrast the politics discussed in Siegel's last paragraph with the centralized/decentralized concepts of politics discussed by Leyden (par. 54 on). How do these two men see technology affecting politics differently?

15. Both Siegel (par. 1) and Leyden (par. 56) write about how a political system that was formed 200 years ago at the beginning of the Industrial Age is hampering progress now. Must we change just the political ideas of progressive versus conservative or centralization versus decentralization, or must we take larger steps in rewriting the Constitution? Explain.

16. Both Siegel (par. 16) and Leyden (par. 75) favor cutting the 40-hour work week in half. Whose ideas do you think have the best chance of bringing about a 20-hour work week? Why?

17. According to Leyden, those who know how to use computers will work from home. Robots will be running much of industry. What kind of work will people do if they do not have computer skills? Is the Western world destined to become an even more widely-split society of haves and have-nots? What can be done to help the have-nots live a meaningful existence during the Digital Age?

18. In what ways can the ideas of Siegel and Leyden be integrated effectively for a better society?

REVISION QUESTIONS

Once you have finished writing your essay, ask yourself the following questions.

1. Is there any statement the reader might not understand?
2. Is there any statement that might offend the reader?
3. Is there anything that's not very convincing?
4. Have I changed the subject and then changed it back again?
5. Have I said the same thing twice?
6. Do I want to try using any feature of style I've seen in the reading selection?

EDITING QUESTIONS

Once you've made changes, ask someone else to read your essay. Change it again as needed. Then read your essay out loud and answer the following questions.

1. Does every sentence make sense?
2. Does every sentence use the kind of language that most people consider "good English" these days? (*Hint:* Imagine a TV announcer reading it.)
3. Do the periods, commas, and other punctuation show the rise and fall of my voice?
4. Are the words spelled right?

If your instructor asks you to copy your paper over, proofread for copying errors before you hand it in.

UNIT
SIXTEEN

◆

Reducing the
Threat of Drugs

PREVIEW STEPS FOR UNIT SIXTEEN

In response to questions 1 and 2, try these steps: Write your answers, talk them over with three or four classmates, and then discuss them with the whole class.

1. Jot down any words or phrases that come to your mind when you hear the phrase "war on drugs."

2. List some possible advantages and disadvantages of legalizing drug use.

   Advantages   **Disadvantages**

3. a. Read the title of the first essay (page 270). Name the topic. (Who or what is this essay about?)

   b. Now predict the main idea. (What is the main point the author wants to make about this topic?)

   c. Read the first and last paragraphs. Revise your prediction if necessary. (*Note:* The main idea should sum up the smaller ideas of the essay.)

4. Some words from the essay are listed below, accompanied by quotations. Mark any words you do not know and make an educated guess about their meanings using the context supplied by the quotations—

and possibly Appendix A, Word Parts, on page 287. You may want to work with a small group of classmates.

illicit "The most compelling argument against the legalization of *illicit* drugs lies in . . . our nation's experiences with those drugs that are legal. . . ."

ratification ". . . the *ratification* of the eighteenth amendment led to a decrease in the number of hospital admissions for alcoholism. . . ."

repeal "Increasing public concern over . . . disrespect for the law . . . combined with the growth of organized crime were responsible for . . . pressure to enact the *repeal* of prohibition."

mandatory "It did not designate any *mandatory* tax on alcohol. . . ."

revenues ". . . [allocate] any tax *revenues* from alcohol to specific purposes."

per capita ". . . *per capita* consumption of alcohol returned to the pre-prohibition levels."

relevance "What can we learn from these experiences that has *relevance* to the recent public debate. . . ?"

discourse "The point of relevance for this *discourse* is that as these 'prohibitions'. . . were removed there was a dramatic increase in the numbers of individuals who engaged in the use of these drugs."

adverse "Accompanying this dramatic increase . . . were the *adverse* consequences that result from drug use."

project "We can *project* that if legalization were to be enacted the numbers of [users] would increase significantly."

civil "During the late 1970s laws were changed in 11 states to classify possession of marijuana . . . for personal use as a '*civil*' rather than a 'criminal' violation."

diffusion "Many expected a rapid *diffusion* of this 'decriminalization' mood throughout . . . the United States."

5. Now read the following essay. As you read, jot down any questions that occur to you.

(*Note*: Question 6 appears after the essay.)

Past Experience with Legalization

Kim Edward Light

The most compelling argument against the legalization of illicit drugs lies in a close examination of the realities of our nation's experiences with those drugs that are legal—specifically, alcohol and tobacco. Upon close analysis, the experiment of alcohol prohibition was not entirely without its lessons regarding the behavior of people and society. Although framed as a failure, the ratification of the eighteenth amendment led to a decrease in the number of hospital admissions for alcoholism and a decrease in the death rate from alcohol-related problems. This decline began sharply at the initiation of prohibition and decayed gradually during the 1920s as the widespread and publicized disrespect for the law grew. Nevertheless, at the end of prohibition the death rate from alcoholism and alcohol related problems was lower than before the ratification of the eighteenth amendment. 1

Increasing public concern over the widespread and highly published disrespect for the law regarding the consumption of alcohol, combined with the growth of organized crime, were responsible for the increasing pressure to enact the repeal of prohibition. Added to this pressure were the realities of the depression and the notion that alcohol, once legal, could be taxed and thus, pay for the damage it causes in some individuals. These are the same arguments currently offered for the legalization of illicit drugs. 2

The twenty-first amendment repealed the eighteenth amendment and returned control of alcohol availability to the states. It did not designate any mandatory tax on alcohol or [allocate] any tax revenues from alcohol to specific purposes. Subsequently, sales of alcohol in- 3 creased rapidly. However, it was not until after World War II that per capita consumption of alcohol returned to the pre-prohibition levels. Thus, prohibition did succeed in reducing alcohol availability, use, and related problems. Taxes on alcohol products currently account for over 50% of the consumer's cost for alcohol beverages. However, these tax revenues, approximately $13.5 billion per year, do not even begin to offset the $136 billion (1990) per year economic impact of alcohol and alcohol-related problems in our society.

Finally, one must consider the enormous industry that has 4 arisen to design, develop, produce, market, advertise, and lobby the government concerning alcoholic beverages. Similar industries would predictably develop over time with the legalization of illicit drugs.

Comparable experiences have occurred with the other legal 5 drug in the form of tobacco. Although never strictly prohibited, there has been considerable activity in the past to regulate, and discourage, use. . . . During the early 1900s there was considerable pressure against, if not outright prohibition of, smoking by women. In 1919 the first advertisement appeared showing a woman smoking. Seventy years later, smoking-related lung cancer surpassed breast cancer as the leading cause of premature death among women.

The point of relevance for this discourse is that as these "prohi- 6 bitions" against the use of alcohol and tobacco in various forms were removed there was a dramatic increase in the numbers of individuals who engaged in the use of these drugs. Accompanying this dramatic increase in the numbers of people using these drugs were the adverse consequences that result from drug use. Currently, tobacco kills more Americans in seven weeks than the total number of American servicemen and women who died during the Vietnam War. This despite the fact that only 25 to 30 percent of Americans use tobacco.

What can we learn from these experiences that has relevance to 7 the recent public debate regarding the legalization of drugs? We can project that if legalization were to be enacted the numbers of individuals who use these drugs would increase significantly. That is the lesson of history, and it is not likely that we can legalize drugs such as marijuana, cocaine, heroin, or amphetamines and avoid a corresponding increase in the use of these drugs especially by young people.

Along with this increase in the numbers of persons using these 8 drugs, there will be an increase in the adverse consequences that are the direct result of use. Such adverse consequences are recognizable in the medical and physical health of the person. However, physical health is often a later adverse consequence. Early problems which result from the use of drugs (including alcohol and tobacco) include problems in working, driving, and relationships with others.

Proponents of legalization point to the potential revenues to be   9
obtained from the taxation of these new products. They even go so far as to suggest that these generated revenues would offset the economic damage resulting from the legalization and concordant increase in use. However, to be a realistic option, taxes applied to the newly legalized drug products would need to be set so high that the underground economy for sales of these drugs would still find sustenance.

During the late 1970s laws were changed in 11 states to classify   10
possession of marijuana in various amounts for personal use as a "civil" rather than a "criminal" violation. One of the stated goals of this policy was a decrease in the number of criminal court cases being tried. Many expected a rapid diffusion of this "decriminaliza-tion" mood throughout the remainder of the United States. In fact no states have "decriminalized" marijuana since 1978. Although advocates insisted that such decriminalization would not increase use, an increase in use is exactly what occurred. During the period of 1972 to 1978, marijuana use rose 125 percent among high school seniors, 200 percent among older adults, and 240 percent among teenagers. Marijuana use in the U.S. peaked one year after the eleventh state enacted its decriminalization laws.

6. State the essay's main idea in your own words. Compare it to your prediction of the main idea. (*Note:* The main idea should sum up the smaller ideas of the essay.)

PREVIEW STEPS FOR "THE WAR ON DRUGS SHOULD BE ABANDONED"

1. a. Read the title of the second essay (page 275). Name the topic. (Who or what is this essay about?)

b. Now predict the main idea. (What is the main point the authors want to make about this topic?)

c. Read the first and last paragraphs of the essay. Revise your prediction if necessary. (*Note:* The main idea should sum up the smaller ideas of the essay.)

2. What in the authors' backgrounds may have led them to the main idea? (See authors' backgrounds, below title.)

3. Some words from the essay are listed below, accompanied by quotations. Mark any words you do not know and make an educated guess about their meanings using the context supplied by the quotations—and possibly Appendix A, Word Parts, on page 287. You may want to work with a small group of classmates.

dissuaded "First, the drug warriors believe that drug consumers can be permanently and effectively *dissuaded* from *ingesting* their drugs of choice. . . ."

ingesting See above quotation.

psychoactives "For casual users of *psychoactives*, this *stance* is no doubt basically correct. . . ."

stance See above quotation.

deterrent ". . . death is not the only *deterrent* to drug use by addicts."

abstain "Addicts . . . who are forced to *abstain* from their drug of choice due, say, to imprisonment . . . are, in the *nomenclature* of the field, 'dry' rather than 'sober.'"

nomenclature See above quotation.

incarceration "... *incarceration*, or the threat thereof, at best produces abstinence; it does not produce recovery...."

draconian "Truly *draconian* measures, including punishment, will induce some addicts to temporarily *forgo* their drug of choice...."

forgo See above quotation.

fallacy "Another *fallacy* underlying the current approach ... is the belief that ... the market for psychoactives will collapse."

infrastructure "This core demand is sufficient to keep the basic *infrastructure* of the drug market profitable and in place."

proponents "... not even the most ardent *proponents* of today's policies claim that we have eliminated casual drug use."

resilience "Despite seventy-five years of all-out war on heroin in this country, the suppliers and addicts remain.... The *resilience* of [the problem] ... is not unique to the United States...."

unabated "Meanwhile, the rehabilitation camps ... continue to grow in size, and hangings continue *unabated*."

aggrieved "An illegal drug transaction involves a voluntary exchange between buyer and seller ... 'victimless' ... in the sense that there is no *aggrieved* party who is likely to serve as a criminal witness."

covert "... the drug warriors typically must rely on *covert* operations, including the use of informants and undercover activities...."

excised "Drug use in the United States is not confined to some narrowly defined, easily *excised* subculture."

4. At the end of the Preview, you may want to go over any new features of style that occur in the following reading selection. You will need to know the terms *allusion* and *metaphor*. For help, see Appendix B, Guide to Literary Terms (page 291), with accompanying exercises on individual features.

5. Before reading "The War on Drugs Should Be Abandoned," turn to pages 280–282 and skim the Reading Questions. Then read the essay to find answers to these questions. As you read, jot down any questions that occur to you.

The War on Drugs Should Be Abandoned

Daniel K. Benjamin and Roger Leroy Miller

Daniel K. Benjamin, former Chief of Staff at the U.S. Department of Labor, is Professor of Economics at Clemson University. Roger Leroy Miller is Research Professor of Economics at Clemson University and Adjunct Professor of Law at the University of Miami. He is also the producer of a 20-part series for NBC-TV called America: The Super Market. *Together they wrote* Undoing Drugs: Beyond Legalization.

The current federal approach to fighting the war on drugs, which is essentially identical to that used during Prohibition seventy years ago, is based on two fundamental errors concerning drug use, abuse, and addiction. First, the drug warriors believe that drug consumers can be permanently and effectively dissuaded from ingesting their drugs of choice if the costs of doing so are high enough. For casual users of psychoactives, this stance is no doubt basically correct; most casual users will respond to an increase in the cost of an activity by doing less of that activity. Thus, Prohibition reduced alcohol consumption in America, and the fear of being arrested today induces many casual users to "just say no." 1

In principle, this theory also applies to addicts whether the costs are self-inflicted or externally imposed. After all, a dead addict is no longer a practicing addict. And there is evidence to suggest that death is not the only deterrent to drug use by addicts. For example, 2 during Prohibition, the number of actively practicing alcoholics probably fell by as much as 20 to 30 percent, a (very) rough estimate based on the observed decline in cirrhosis deaths and other alcohol-related deaths during Prohibition. World War II proved even more disruptive to practicing heroin addicts in America, whose numbers may have fallen by as much as 50 percent during the war due to the worldwide disruption of heroin supplies.

Addiction Is a Disease

Nevertheless, the approach of the drug warriors ignores a fact that is recognized by every specialist in the field of drug and alcohol treatment: Addiction and alcoholism are diseases. Addicts and alcoholics who are forced to abstain from their drug of choice due, say, to imprisonment or threat thereof are, in the nomenclature of the field, "dry" rather than "sober." They are still addicts and alcoholics, whose practice of their addiction has merely been interrupted. Short of being executed or physically isolated from their psychoactive of choice, the overwhelming majority will sooner or later (and more likely sooner than later) return to drugs or alcohol, thereby starting the cycle anew. Involuntary incarceration, or the threat thereof, at best produces abstinence; it does not produce recovery from the underlying disease. 3

Addicts and alcoholics are not hopeless cases, however, fit only for abandonment or permanent incarceration. Treatment programs have been developed (and are steadily being improved) that empower these individuals to refrain completely from consuming their psychoactive of choice, and to do so in a manner that enables them to live "as though" they are not addicts or alcoholics. These programs, which generally require a lifelong commitment to self-monitored follow-up programs (such as Alcoholics Anonymous or Narcotics Anonymous), help addicts and alcoholics become recovering addicts or alcoholics—sober (or "clean") rather than merely dry. Those treated remain at risk of returning to the depths of practicing addiction if they resume drug or alcohol use, but they learn how to establish an effective set of barriers against such resumption of use, barriers that the dry addict or alcoholic does not have. 4

The current approach to the drug wars is imperiled by its refusal to acknowledge addiction as a disease rather than a crime. 5

When it comes to their psychoactive of choice, addicts (and alcoholics) simply don't respond to incentives the way rational people do, because they are not—in this dimension—rational. By the very definition of the term, an addict has "given himself up" to his drug. Truly draconian measures, including punishment, will induce some addicts to temporarily forgo their drug of choice, but most will refuse or simply switch to legal substitutes (such as alcohol) while awaiting the opportunity to return to their drug of choice. Unless they obtain treatment (and not just punishment), they are at best "just one hit away from their next high."

Drug War Fallacies

Another fallacy underlying the current approach to the drug wars is the belief that if casual users can be prevented from consuming drugs, the market for psychoactives will collapse. Let's consider the facts. The consumption of psychoactives generally follows the lognormal distribution, which means that the vast majority of the population either does not use the psychoactive or uses it only casually, and a small minority of the population accounts for the vast bulk of the total consumption of the psychoactive. Consider alcohol. About 80 percent of all adult Americans either don't drink, or drink in such moderation that, as a whole, this part of the adult population drinks only 20 percent of the alcohol consumed in the United States. The other 20 percent of the adult population—the "heavy drinkers"—consume the remaining 80 percent of the alcohol. In fact, the 10 percent of adult Americans who drink the most consume more than 50 percent of the total amount of alcohol drunk in the United States.

This pattern has been true in the United States for as long as such statistics have been kept, and holds (plus or minus a few percentage points) in all countries for which statistics are available. And although the percentages that fall into each category differ across different psychoactives, the character of the lognormal distribution generally holds true: Most people consume drugs either not at all or casually, but most of the consumption is accounted for by a small percentage of people, who systematically either abuse or are addicted to the psychoactive in question. This pattern is true not just when most people are nonusers, as with heroin. *Even when casual use is widespread, as it is with marijuana and cocaine, most of the drug in*

6

7

question is being consumed by the abusers and addicts. This point cannot be overemphasized. Casual users ingest less than half of the illegal drugs in question, while the bulk of all illegal drug consumption
(between 60 percent and 80 percent) is engaged in by abusers and
addicts. And it is these individuals who are the least responsive to the
measures advocated by today's drug warriors.

The upshot is sad but simple. If we spend enough money and   8
deprive enough people of their liberties, we can, in principle, dissuade people from casual use, and even induce some addicts to give
up. But a core of abusers and addicts will remain who, though small
in number, will keep overall consumption high. This core demand is
sufficient to keep the basic infrastructure of the drug market profitable and in place. *We can dissuade 70 percent of the users; we cannot
eliminate 70 percent of the use.* And achieving even this would require efforts on a scale far beyond what we are trying now; after all,
not even the most ardent proponents of today's policies claim that
we have eliminated casual drug use. Perhaps more importantly, and
distressingly, even a 30 percent reduction in total consumption by
means of today's policies would require significant additional resources permanently devoted to this task. The moment we lessen our
efforts or relax our constraints, casual users will return to the market,
and drug dealers will immediately leap into the breach, ready, willing, and able to supply all comers.

Prohibition History

History is clear on this point. Despite fourteen years of all-out war   9
against alcohol during Prohibition, the suppliers survived, and when
Repeal brought a resumption of legal production, the cocktail hour
returned to millions of homes across the country. Despite seventy-
five years of all-out war on heroin in this country, the suppliers and
addicts remain. One out of 400 Americans is addicted to heroin
today, just as roughly one out of 400 was addicted eighty years ago.
The faces and names have changed, but the addiction has not.

The resilience of users, addicts, and suppliers is not unique to the   10
United States, nor does it exist simply because we haven't been "tough
enough." Malaysia and Singapore, for example, both impose the death
penalty for drug trafficking. For run-of-the-mill drug users, the penal-

ties range from whipping to two years in boot-camp-style "rehabilitation" facilities, where pushups and hard labor are the order of the day.

"Punishment must be strict, or otherwise the penalty has no meaning," says Roh Geok Ek, the director of Singapore's central narcotics bureau. The assistant director of the Malaysian antinarcotics force, Tey Boon Hwa, claims that "we hang anyone convicted who exhausts their appeals." Apparently, officials in both countries mean what they say. Since Malaysia introduced the death penalty for trafficking in 1983, some 235 people have been sentenced to death; as of early 1990, 81 had been hanged. Singapore, whose population is about the same as that of Dallas or Boston, has imposed the death penalty for drugs since 1975. Thirty-seven people have received the death sentence for trafficking; at last count, twenty-five of them had been executed. According to the prime minister of Singapore, Lee Kuan Yew, "death is the best deterrent we have." It's difficult to argue with the prime minister's logic, but drugs have not disappeared from the streets of his nation. Despite the prospect of whipping and forced labor, the arrest rate for drug possession in Singapore is still only about 30 percent below that in the United States. Meanwhile, the rehabilitation camps in both Malaysia and Singapore continue to grow in size, and hangings continue unabated.

1984 in the Making

An illegal drug transaction involves a voluntary exchange between buyer and seller. The sale, purchase, and consumption of illegal drugs therefore constitute what are commonly labeled "victimless" crimes, in the sense that there is generally no aggrieved party who is likely to serve as a criminal witness. As a result, the legal authorities must do without the most important ingredient in a successful prosecution—the victim. Without victims to report drug deals and drug use, and to serve as material witnesses at trial, the drug warriors typically must rely on covert operations, including the use of informants and undercover activities, in their endeavors. Most Americans rightly regard such operations as suitable perhaps against foreign spies, but surely not appropriate for everyday police work. Unfortunately, covert operations have quickly transformed the federal government's war against drugs into a war against its citizens.

War Is Hell

Drug use in the United States is not confined to some narrowly de-   13
fined, easily excised subculture. Tens of millions of Americans use illegal psychoactives each year, and they come from all walks of life. If
we are to undo drugs in America, our policies must reflect the fact
that *we* are the users, the abusers, and the addicts.

Although the bulk of all users of psychoactives are casual users,   14
the bulk of all use is by abusers and addicts. And most of the damage
done to and by users occurs as a result of addiction and abuse. This
is true whether we focus on the adverse health consequences for the
users (such as lung cancer for nicotine addicts), adverse health consequences for third parties (such as people killed by drunk drivers), or
other adverse effects (such as crimes committed by heroin addicts).
Thus, only if we materially alter the behavior of addicts and abusers
will our policies yield substantial benefits.

Unless and until public policy is shaped to yield a permanent   15
and substantial reduction in use rather than users, few beneficial consequences are likely to result from drug policy.

READING QUESTIONS FOR "THE WAR ON DRUGS SHOULD BE ABANDONED"

Main Idea

1. State the essay's main idea in your own words. Compare it to your
   prediction of the main idea. (*Note:* The main idea should sum up the
   smaller ideas of the essay.)

Organization

2. a. Where in the essay is the main idea found?

   b. Why have the authors placed the main idea there?

3. In what order are the paragraphs arranged? (Underline one.) Time / Least to most important / Most to least important / Simple listing / Logic: cause and effect / Other logic / Other

Style

4. How formal is the essay? (Circle your choice.)

[Informal—1—2—3—4—5—6—7—8—9—10—Formal]

What indicators convinced you? (For a list of possible indicators and two benchmark essays, see Appendix F, The Formality Spectrum, on page 307.)

5. Where do you see the following features of style? List one or two examples of each with their paragraph numbers.

Features (For definitions, see Appendix B, page 291.)

a. allusion

b. metaphor

Content

6. Explain Benjamin and Miller's statement: "We can dissuade 70 percent of the users; we cannot eliminate 70 percent of the use" (paragraph 8).

7. In the first sentence of the article, Benjamin and Miller refer to two "fundamental errors" or fallacies. What are they?

8. Read the following chart of reasons to treat drug use as either a crime or an addiction. Where there are blanks, supply paragraph numbers and examples (give a label in one or two words). The first two boxes are done for you. Add any arguments you think of.

Should We Treat Drug Use as a Crime or an Addiction?

Treat as a Crime (Light's overall position)	Treat as a Medical Problem (Benjamin & Miller's overall position)
L: Drug laws reduce drug use—and related drug problems (**par.** 1). **Example:** Prohibition.	B&M: Drug laws reduce use—temporarily—but not addiction (**par.** 3). **Example:** Prohibition.
Drug problems relate to casual use as well as addiction; also, some casual users become addicts.	B&M: Most drug problems result from addiction, not casual use (**par.**). **Example:**
L: Legalization would lead to open advertising and therefore increase use (**par.**). **Example:**	
L: Although legalization makes a sales tax possible, money gained would not pay costs of increased drug problems (**par.**). **Example:**	
B&M: Some say that without casual use, the drug market would collapse (**par.**)*	B&M: About 70% of the market would remain: Addicts would still buy (**par.**). **Example:**
	L: Some say widespread demand for illegal drugs feeds organized crime (**par.**).
	L: Some say widespread disobedience of a law leads to disrespect for other laws (**par.**).
	B&M: Getting tougher won't work (**par.**). **Example:**

(continued)

Should We Treat Drug Use as a Crime or an Addiction? (continued)

Treat as a Crime (Light's overall position)	Treat as a Medical Problem (Benjamin & Miller's overall position)
	B&M: Spying and informing are not the American way (**par.**)
Addiction is hard to cure; we might better prevent addiction by restricting casual use.	B&M: Casual use is hard to eliminate (**par.**); we might better treat addiction (**par.**).

*Here, B&M have set up a straw man and then knocked it down—they have offered an argument against their own position and then said it is false.

9. Do the authors propose any change? If so, what do you think would be the result of such change?

10. Do you agree with Benjamin and Miller's main idea? Why or why not?

If you have not already read the essay and answered the Reading Questions, be sure to do so before you proceed.

COMPOSITION QUESTIONS*

Listed below are the writing questions. Choose one and write an essay that answers it. Whichever question you choose, think of the person who will read your answer. The question may tell who your audience is. If not, think of a person you know and respect—preferably your instructor or a fellow student who will read your essay. Try to convince that person to believe you.

Bring in useful details from the selection(s) you have read and perhaps other incidents you know of. For ideas, review your answers to questions in

---

*To avoid writing a "true confessions" paper, try to disguise any personal material—or keep it brief.

the Preview and Reading Steps. When you first refer to a reading, give its title (in quotation marks) and the author's full name. Also, give the full name of anyone featured in the article the first time you mention that person.

Note: If you are assigned to write a one-paragraph essay, think of your answer to the question, and list several key points you could make to support your answer. Then choose just one of the points and explain it in detail.

1. Benjamin and Miller admit in paragraph 3 that drug laws do reduce use, even for addicts, while prohibitions are in effect. They also admit that serious health problems result from use (paragraph 14). Argue that restrictive drug laws are worthwhile even though they do not cure addiction.

2. According to Light (paragraph 2), Prohibition was repealed partly because people felt that demand for illegal alcohol fed organized crime. On the one hand, legalizing drugs may reduce organized crime (Mafia or gangs). On the other hand, legalizing may raise use and in turn raise nonprofessional violence such as abuse and impulse crime. Argue that legalizing drugs will reduce or increase crime overall.

3. Light (paragraph 8) disagrees with Benjamin and Miller (paragraph 14) about whether casual drug use causes drug-related problems such as illness, driving accidents, work errors, or crime. Argue that casual use does or does not cause these problems.

4. Benjamin and Miller argue that we should quit fighting casual use and instead focus our efforts on treating addiction (paragraphs 14 and 15). However, if casual use increases, addiction may increase as well. Argue that an increase in the number of casual users will or will not lead to increased numbers of addicted users.

5. Benjamin and Miller argue in paragraphs 10 and 11 that getting tougher will not work; they give examples from Malaysia and Singapore. Yet in paragraph 12 the same authors state that spying and informing are not the American way. Evaluate how well a lesson from one culture applies to another.

6. According to Benjamin and Miller (paragraphs 8–12), the U.S. cannot eliminate casual use—we don't have the money, won't spy and inform, and aren't deterred even by harsh punishments. Argue that the U.S. can or cannot greatly *reduce* casual use either by the war on drugs or by other means (education, counseling, etc.).

7. According to Benjamin and Miller (paragraphs 14 and 15), drug policies will not be effective unless they focus on reducing addiction. In paragraph 4, the same authors mention some key characteristics of effective treatment programs: life-long commitment, self-monitoring, involvement in a group such as Narcotics Anonymous, and other internal or external barriers against resumption of use. Create a model for an effective treatment program and explain it.

8. Legalization could increase use by allowing open advertising (Light, paragraph 5) or by reducing fear of punishment (Benjamin and Miller, paragraph 1). Yet casual drug use is already so widespread in the U.S. that it may not increase further. Judge whether legalization would increase the casual use of drugs.

9. Benjamin and Miller want the U.S. to focus efforts on treating addicts but do not say what they would do about existing drug laws. Some possibilities are legalizing drugs, decriminalizing them (punishing violations by a fine but not jail), or simply not enforcing the drug laws. Which of these options seems to fit best with treating addicts? (For some details about decriminalization, see paragraph 10 of Light.)

10. Benjamin and Miller refer in paragraph 12 to "victimless" crimes, involving "a voluntary exchange between buyer and seller." No one has a complaint, so no one will act as a witness. Some would say that these crimes are victimless in a larger sense: The exchange occurs between consenting adults and no harm is done to anyone else. Argue that drug use is or is not society's business.

REVISION QUESTIONS

Once you have finished writing your essay, ask yourself the following questions.

1. Is there any statement the reader might not understand?
2. Is there any statement that might offend the reader?
3. Is there anything that's not very convincing?
4. Have I changed the subject and then changed it back again?
5. Have I said the same thing twice?

6. Do I want to try using any feature of style I've seen in the reading selection?

EDITING QUESTIONS

Once you've made changes, ask someone else to read your essay. Change it again as needed. Then read your essay out loud and answer the following questions.

1. Does every sentence make sense?
2. Does every sentence use the kind of language that most people consider "good English" these days? (*Hint:* Imagine a TV announcer reading it.)
3. Do the periods, commas, and other punctuation show the rise and fall of my voice?
4. Are the words spelled right?

If your instructor asks you to copy your paper over, proofread for copying errors before you hand it in.

APPENDIX

A

Word Parts

Below is a list of word parts to be used in defining the meaning of words in this book that may be new to you. Each word part is given with its meaning and an example word in parentheses.

A

a- = without (asexual)
ab- = from (absent)
-able/-ible = capable of (breakable)
ad- = to (adjust)
-al = related to (sexual)
anti- = against (antisocial)
aud- = related to hearing (audible)
auto- = self (automobile)

C

-cern = to perceive (concern)
co- = having something in common (co-workers)
con- = with/together (consult)

D

de- = down/away (depressed) or reverse (deactivate)
deca- = ten (decade)
-duct = carry/lead (conduct)

E

electr- = electric (electricity)
-er = doer (fighter)
-escent = becoming (adolescent)
-ette = small form of something (kitchenette)
ex- = out of (exit) or former (ex-wife)

F

fatu- = foolish (infatuation)

G

-graph = a picture/writing (photograph)

H

holo- = whole (holocaust)
hyper- = over (hyperactive)
hypo- = under, hidden (hypo–crite)

I

-ible/-able = able to (audible)
-ic/-istic/-itic = characteristic of, or related to (artistic; arthritic)
in- = not (incapable) or into (input)
-ion = action or act of (suction) or condition (qualification)
-ist = expert/specialist (artist)
-ity = state of being (purity)

J

-ject = throw (reject)
-jug = to join, joined (conjugal)

L

lex- = word (dyslexia)

-logy, -logi = science of (anthropology)

luc- = light (lucid)

M

manu- = hand (manual)
micro- = very small (microscope)
mobil- = moving (automobile)
mono- = one (monologue)
mort- = death (morgue)

N

nephr- = kidney (nephritis)
neuro- = nerve (neurotic)
non- = not (nonprofit)
nov- = new (novelty)

O

-ode = way or path (electrode)

P

path = feeling (sympathy) or disease (pathology; psychopath)
per- = through or throughout (pervade)
-phone = sound (telephone)
-pol = to sell (monopoly)

-pos- = to put (compose)
pre- = before (pre-war)
-prehend = to grasp (comprehend)
pro- = forward (progress) or favoring (pro-abortion)
proto- = the first of something; the parent (prototype)
psycho- = mind (psychology)

R

re- = again (redo)

S

socio- = society (sociology)
-spir- = breathe (expire)
sub- = under (submarine)

T

temp- = time (temporary)
-ten = hold (intent, contend)

U

un- = not (unhappy)

V

-vade = to go (invade)
vest- = clothes (vest, vesture)

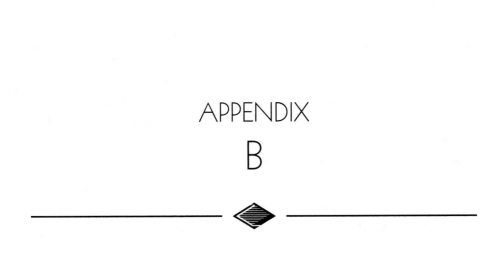

APPENDIX

B

Guide to Literary Terms

Allusion—brief mention of a famous person, event, document, piece of literature, or quotation.

> *Ex.:* "That's a regular James Bond car" (referring to trick gadgets on the movie character's car).

> *Note:* If a person or event is described in the essay, the reference is not an allusion.

Cliché—a tired expression, once colorful but now overused and stale.

> *Ex.:* "Put your shoulder to the wheel," "pretty as a picture"

Connotation—the emotional meaning of a word.

> *Ex.:* The word *childish* reminds us of the unpleasant qualities of a child, who may be self-centered, demanding, and so forth.

Denotation—the dictionary meaning of a word.

> *Ex.:* The word *childish* means "like a child."

Irony—a contradiction.

> *Irony of wording:* wording that is the opposite of what is meant.
>> *Ex.:* "a lovely scab"
> *Irony of situation:* a situation that is the opposite of what we would normally expect.
>> *Ex.:* Doctors often take poor care of their own health.

Jargon—specialized language that is hard for an outsider to understand (often meant more to impress us than to tell us anything).

> *Ex.:* "Multiple contusions" (several bruises)

Metaphor—See *simile,* below.

Overstatement—saying more than one means.

> *Ex.:* "When Bob yells, he can be heard for miles."

Restraint—a low-keyed, not-too-emotional style.

> *Ex.:* "If we had been called when he first attacked, the woman might not be dead now."

Sentimentality—appeal to the emotions.

> *Ex.:* "If only we had been called when the madman first appeared out of the shadows to grab little Kitty. . . ."

Simile or **metaphor**—a comparison of two unlike things to create an image.

Simile—a comparison using *like*, *as*, or *than*.

Ex.: "The windows of the empty house looked like blank eyes."

Metaphor—a comparison not using *like*, *as*, or *than*.

Ex.: "The windows of the empty house stared blankly."

Note: A comparison of two people or things that really are alike is not a simile or a metaphor.

Ex.: "John looks like his sister."

Symbol—one thing that stands for something greater than itself.

Ex.: A traffic light may stand for the law and its authority.

Tone—the writer's attitude toward his or her subject and audience. The tone may be sad, angry, humorous, and so on.

Ex.: The following two statements mean the same but differ in tone:

"I solemnly swear to bring our cause to the attention of the administration." (serious, formal)

"I'll make the prez sit up and take notice if I have to cut off his tie." (humorous, informal)

Understatement—saying less than one means.

Ex.: As a neighbor, Count Dracula was a bit different.

APPENDIX
C

Allusion

A. In each sentence below is at least one allusion. Explain its meaning. (The first two are done for you.)
   1. Mark was literally swept off his feet by *the local Arnold Schwartzenegger.* (A strong and forceful man.)
   2. Just before the election, the candidate studied the latest poll for the last time—he had *seen the handwriting on the wall.*
      (Had seen a prediction of defeat. *Note:* Just before Babylon fell, its king saw a hand write a message on his wall. Not understanding it, he called in the prophet Daniel, who told the king that his kingdom was going to fall to the enemy.)
   3. Discouraged, the police chief said, "What we need is *Sherlock Holmes.*"

   4. When his civics teacher, Miss Johnson, asked Jack if he had thrown the paper airplane, he *pleaded the Fifth Amendment.*

   5. From what her teasing friends had told her, Jill thought her blind date was going to be *Dracula*; but when she opened the door and saw a *Keanu Reeves*, she felt a lump in her throat.

   6. Pete was as cheery as *Walter Matthau.*

   7. Andy Rooney named one of his essays *"In and of Ourselves We Trust."* (What famous quotation does this remind you of? What do you think the essay is about?)

   8. As Jack walked out of a two-hour examination, he told a friend, "I think I just *met my Waterloo.*"

B. (Optional) Write two allusions and explain each.
1.

2.

C. Define *allusion*.

D. Why do people use allusions?

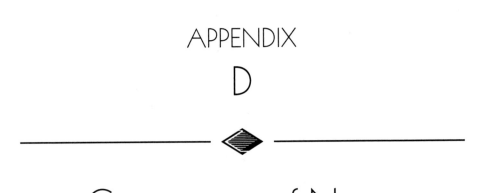

APPENDIX
D

Connotations of Names

A. Match the name to its connotation.

Name		Connotation
1. Ebenezer Scrooge	_____	a. interested in nature
2. Brenda Starr	_____	b. miserly
3. Morning Glory	_____	c. glamorous
4. Daddy Warbucks	_____	d. tough
5. Rocky	_____	e. rich

B. Give the connotation(s) you have in mind for each name below.

Name	Connotation
1. Joe	_____
2. Lola	_____
3. Nellie	_____
4. Brunhilda	_____
5. Brock	_____
6. Junior	_____
7. Your own name	_____

C. Suppose you want to change your name to give yourself a new image. Supply a possible name for each image.

Name	Connotation
1. _____	tough, popular leader
2. _____	macho cowboy
3. _____	strong, romantic man
4. _____	wealthy woman
5. _____	flinty, aristocratic judge
6. _____	glamorous woman
7. _____	wise doctor

D. (Optional) Give an example of a real name change and the reason.

E. Define *connotation*.

F. In what occupations might people be particularly aware of the connotations of names?

Figures of Speech: Metaphors, Similes, and Clichés

A. Match the colorful word or phrase on the left with the "plain English" version on the right. The first two are done for you.

**Figure of Speech
(Metaphor or Simile)**   **Plain English**

1. bulldog	__d__	a. energetic person
2. silky	__g__	b. blank look
3. ball of fire	_____	c. jumbled words
4. holy worm	_____	d. football lineman
5. face of corpse three hours old	_____	e. conniving preacher
6. squirming sea of language	_____	f. flowing hair
7. leaves of a willow tree	_____	g. soft

B. Now write your own plain English version of each figure of speech below.

**Figure of Speech
(Metaphor or Simile)**   **Plain English**

1. beanpole   _____

2. walrus   _____

3. political polar winds   _____

4. wounded knight   _____

5. "No man is an island."   _____

C. Why do people use figures of speech?

D. Figures of speech may be either metaphors or similes. Inspect the examples below; then state the difference.

Simile: Their french fries taste like cardboard.
Metaphor: Their french fries are made of cardboard.

Simile: Her eyes were as sharp as knives.
Metaphor: Her eyes cut into me.

Simile: The child's hair was softer than silk.
Metaphor: The child's hair was silk.

1. Define a *simile*.

2. Define a *metaphor*.

3. Label the following as either "M" (metaphor) or "S" (simile).
   a. His beard was white as snow. ___
   b. I weeded out my mistakes. ___
   c. My room looks like a disaster area. ___
   d. If I keep eating five meals a day, I'll be a whale. ___
   e. You smoke more than a chimney. ___

E. One problem that some people have with similes is distinguishing them from simple comparisons. Below is a list of sentences, some having similes and some having simple comparisons. Put an "S" before any sentence with a simile (a colorful expression, not meant to be realistic); put an "SC" in front of any with a simple comparison (a real comparison); put "NC" for no comparison.
   _____ 1. Jack is five inches taller than Jill.
   _____ 2. After Jack fell down the hill and into the swamp, he looked like Jill's pig.
   _____ 3. I am as hungry as a man stranded on an island with nothing but coconuts.
   _____ 4. As the next mayor, I will fight air pollution.
   _____ 5. Bill felt as strong as any man.
   _____ 6. Shakespeare wrote like a genius.
   _____ 7. Shorty is taller than the Empire State Building.

F. Sometimes a metaphor gives two images at once (for example, "the hand of God leaves footprints"). Thus it is called a *mixed metaphor*. Before each example below, put "M" for metaphor (consistent, meaningful comparison) or "MM" for mixed metaphor (inappropriate, inconsistent comparison).
   _____ 1. That's just gravy on the cake.
   _____ 2. After the explosion below deck, the ship suddenly became an anthill with workers scurrying out of every hole.

_____ 3. With red in his eyes, the congressman hoofed the dust for several moments, ready to charge the reporter, but finally restrained himself and offered a bullish grin.

_____ 4. There's no use locking the door after the horse is stolen.

_____ 5. He tried to sell some hot ice.

G. Metaphors and similes are invented to give color and even humor to a message. But like a twice-told joke, they can lose their punch if repeated often. An overused expression is known as a *cliché*. Mark each expression below with a "+" (fresh and colorful) or a "−" (overused). (Your answers may be different from your instructor's and still be all right: An old expression may still be new to you because you have not yet done as much reading.)

_____ 1. She gave him the cold shoulder.

_____ 2. Hurry up. You're slow as molasses.

_____ 3. It's as bright as new nail polish.

_____ 4. I'll leave when hell freezes over.

_____ 5. With that short, dyed hair, she looks like a dandelion.

_____ 6. His eyes are bigger than his stomach.

_____ 7. Wash up. You've got a bad case of ditchdigger's hands.

H. (Optional) Write a metaphor of your own.

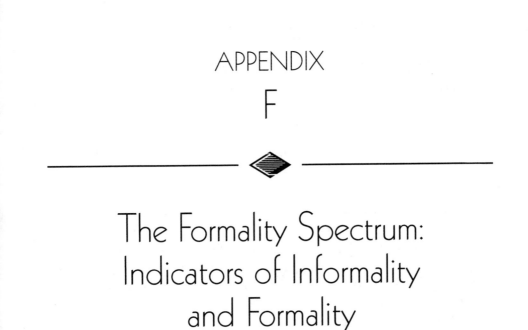

The Formality Spectrum: Indicators of Informality and Formality

Informality ⟵—————————⟶	Formality
Humor	Serious tone or mood

Informal wording or slang
  kid
  put in jail
	Formal vocabulary
	  juvenile
	  incarcerate

Short sentences and paragraphs overall	Long sentences and paragraphs overall
Use of first person (I) or second person (you)	Use of third person (he, she, it, one, they)
Contractions	Few or no contractions

Below are two sample passages, one very informal and one very formal. First read both quickly and compare them to get an overall impression of their formality. Label one with an "I" for informal and the other with an "F" for formal. Then list some indicators of informality or formality that you notice in each passage.

Equality and Speech

Catharine A. MacKinnon

Canada's new constitution, the Charter of Rights and Freedoms, includes an expansive equality guarantee and a serious entrenchment of freedom of expression. The Supreme Court of Canada's first move was to define equality in a meaningful way—one more substantive than formal, directed toward changing unequal social relations rather than monitoring their equal positioning before the law. The positive spin of the Canadian interpretation holds the law to promoting equality, projecting the law into a more equal future, rather than remaining rigidly neutral in ways that either reinforce existing social inequality or prohibit changing it, as the American constitutional perspective has increasingly done in recent years. . . .

We argued that group defamation in this sense is not a mere expression of opinion but a practice of discrimination in verbal form, a link in systemic discrimination that keeps target groups in subordinated positions through the promotion of terror, intolerance, degradation, segregation, exclusion, vilification, violence, and genocide. We said that the nature of the practice can be understood and its impact measured from the damage it causes, from immediate psychic wounding to consequent physical aggression.

Why We Must Put Up with Porn

Susan Isaacs

If you and I were sitting together, listening to a little Vivaldi, sipping herbal tea, chatting about men and women, arguing about politics and art, we might get around to what to do about the porn problem—at which point you'd slam down your cup and demand, How can you of all people defend smut-peddling slimeballs who portray women being beaten and raped?

Well . . .

You're the one (you'd be sure to remind me) who hates any kind of violence against women. You're the one who even gets upset when James Cagney, in *The Public Enemy*, the 1931 classic, smashes a grapefruit into Mae Clarke's face, for heaven's sake!

That's right, I'd say.

So? Don't you want to protect women? Why not ban books and films that degrade women?

Let's have another cup of tea and I'll tell you.

1. Which passage is more formal? What characteristics give it formality?

2. What characteristics of informality do you see in the other passage?

APPENDIX
G

Irony of Situation

A. Complete the following sentences. The first three are done for you.
1. Your driver-training teacher has <u>hit a tree</u>.
2. The writer F. Scott Fitzgerald couldn't <u>spell</u> very well.
3. A great South American patriot is named <u>O'Higgins</u>.
4. Your English teacher says _____.
5. A college student goes to sleep at _____ in the evening.
6. On M.A.S.H., Hawkeye once considered _____.
7. Monet painted some of his most famous pictures after losing some of his _____.
8. The composer Beethoven was _____.
9. John F. Kennedy, a wealthy president, sponsored laws to help _____.
10. A famous football player had the hobby of _____ _____.

B. (Optional) Write two sentences showing irony of situation.
1.

2.

C. Define *irony of situation*.

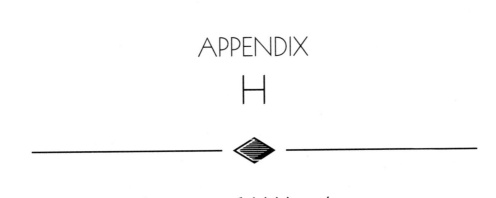

APPENDIX
H

Irony of Wording

Read the student editorial below. Then answer the questions that follow it.

Life Off Campus

Living off campus is a fantastic experience. No RLO rules to worry   1
about; no cafeteria meals to choke on; no fumbling for your I.D. just
to get into your dorm.

When you live off campus, you can experience independence   2
and self-respect (hey, I like burnt toast!). And no one ever tells you
what you can or can't do.

But what about the other side of this wonderful living experi-   3
ence? Have you ever tried living with eight girls while one girl thinks
she owns the freezer? What about your roommate's boyfriend or
girlfriend who conveniently calls at three o'clock in the morning (and
the phone is next to your room)? Ah, and then there's the favorite
roommate who allows you to clean up her dog's gift to the rug since
she is never home to train it.

Everyone's favorite job is cleaning up. When dishes start hitting   4
the ceiling, everyone invariably denies ever eating at home. If you
have a Felix in your house, you've got it made. If you don't, well,
good luck, Oscar.

If roommates are great, then the house conditions are even bet-   5
ter. Ever have the bathroom leak right in your room? Or a gas oven
that nearly blasts you every time you light it?

Bet most of you off-campus lovers have the most tasteful wall-   6
paper you've ever seen (yes, even better than mom's). Not to mention
the most decorative (and comfortable) couches. Sway-back mat-
tresses take some getting used to, but you can learn to mold into a
V-position.

Yes, all in all, off-campus living is most enjoyable. I wouldn't   7
trade it for the world! (And you were thinking of moving off
campus?)

A student editorial. Published October 13, 1983, in *State* (student newspaper of Frostburg
State University).

1. What is the author's *stated* main idea?

2. What is the author's *real* main idea?

3. What details convince you of the real main idea? Note the paragraph number here and make a check in the margin by each.

4. a. Where does the author say just the opposite of what's meant?

   b. How can you tell the author does not mean these words?

5. Why do you think the author chose to say one thing and convince you of just the opposite?

6. How would you define *irony of wording*?

APPENDIX

I

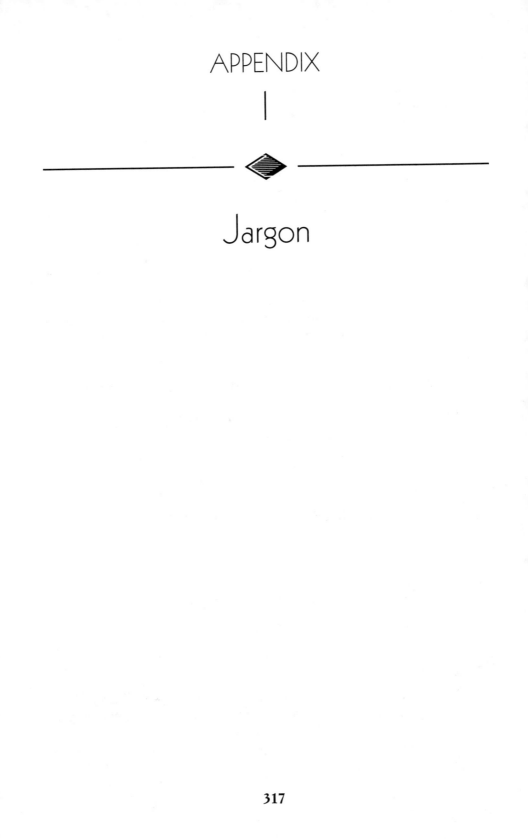

Jargon

A. Match the jargon with the plain English word that has the same meaning.

	Jargon		**Plain English**
(Business)	1. utilization	_____	a. heroin
(Drug slang)	2. horse	_____	b. back
(Medicine)	3. posterior	_____	c. poor
(Sociology)	4. underprivileged	_____	d. use
(Teen slang)	5. dissing	_____	e. speaking or acting disrespectfully to (a person)
(Black slang)	6. honky	_____	f. paper copy
(Computers)	7. hard copy	_____	g. white person

B. At the left of each number above, state where that kind of jargon is used (among lawyers or drug dealers, for example).

C. List three jargon words you know and their plain English versions.

Jargon   **Plain English**

1. _____   _____
2. _____   _____
3. _____   _____

D. How would you define *jargon*? (*Note:* Are all jargon words long?)

E. There are at least three reasons why people use jargon. Name one.

"Little Miss Muffet" is an old nursery rhyme. Below, Russell Baker shows how people from several fields would discuss it in their own jargon. To identify the person's field, fill in the blank with one of the following: editorial writer, psychiatrist, sociologist, militarist (military specialist), child, book reviewer.

Little Miss Muffet

Russell Baker

Little Miss Muffet, as everyone knows, sat on a tuffet eating her   1
curds and whey when along came a spider who sat down beside her
and frightened Miss Muffet away. While everyone knows this, the
significance of the event had never been analyzed until a conference
of thinkers recently brought their special insights to bear upon it.
Following are excerpts from the transcript of their discussion:

_____We are clearly dealing with a prototypical illustration of a   2
highly tensile social structure's tendency to dis- or perhaps even de-
structure itself under the pressures created when optimum minimums do not obtain among the disadvantaged. Miss Muffet is nutritionally underprivileged, as evidenced by the subminimal diet of
curds and whey upon which she is forced to subsist, while the spider's cultural disadvantage is evidenced by such phenomena as legs
exceeding standard norms, odd mating habits, and so forth.

In this instance, spider expectations lead the culturally disad-   3
vantaged to assert demands to share the tuffet with the nutritionally
underprivileged. Due to a communications failure, Miss Muffet assumes without evidence that the spider will not be satisfied to share
her tuffet, but will also insist on eating her curds and perhaps even
her whey. Thus, the failure to preestablish selectively optimum norm
structures diverts potentially optimal minimums from the expecta-
tion levels assumed to . . .

_____Second-strike capability, sir! That's what was lacking. If Miss   4
Muffet had developed a second-strike capability instead of squander-
ing her resources on curds and whey, no spider on earth would have
dared launch a first strike capable of carrying him right to the heart
of her tuffet. I am confident that Miss Muffet had adequate notice
from experts that she could not afford both curds and whey and, at
the same time, support an early-spider-warning system. Yet curds
alone were not good enough for Miss Muffet. She had to have whey,
too. Tuffet security must be the first responsibility of every diner. . . .

_____Written on several levels, this searing and sensitive explo- 5
ration of the arachnid heart illuminates the agony and splendor of
Jewish family life with a candor that is at once breathtaking in its sim-
plicity and soul-shattering in its implied ambiguity. Some will doubt-
less be shocked to see such objects as tuffets and whey discussed
without flinching, but hereafter writers too timid to call a curd a curd
will no longer. . . .

_____Why has the Government not seen fit to tell the public all it 6
knows about the so-called curds-and-whey affair? It is not enough to
suggest that this was merely a random incident involving a lonely spider and a young diner. In today's world, poised as it is on the knife
edge of . . .

_____Little Miss Muffet is, of course, neither little nor a miss. These 7
are obviously the self she has created in her own fantasies to escape
the reality that she is a gross divorcee whose superego makes it impossible for her to sustain a normal relationship with any man, sym-
bolized by the spider, who, of course, has no existence outside her
fantasies. Little Miss Muffet may, in fact, be a man with deeply re-
pressed Oedipal impulses, who sees in the spider the father he would
like to kill, and very well may some day unless he admits that what he
believes to be a tuffet is, in fact, probably the dining room chande-
lier, and that the whey he thinks he is eating is, in fact, probably . . .

_____This is about a little girl who gets scared by a spider. (The 8
child was sent home when the conference broke for lunch. It was
agreed that he was too immature to subtract anything from the sum
of human understanding.)

ANSWERS: Paragraphs 2 and 3: Sociologist; 4: Militarist; 5: Book reviewer; 6: Editorial writer; 7: Psychiatrist; 8: Child.

APPENDIX

J

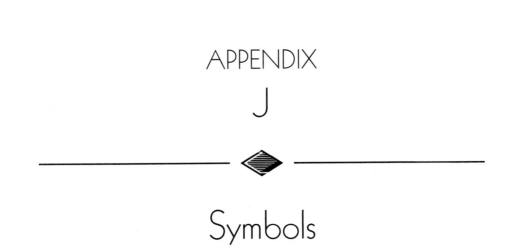

Symbols

A. Note each symbol on the left. Then at the right, state what that symbol stands for. The first two are done for you. *Note:* if your answers are not the same as other people's, you are not necessarily wrong. It may be that the symbol has a special personal meaning for you.

Symbol	Meaning
1. dove	<u>peace</u>
2. traffic light	<u>the law</u>
3. lion	_____
4. rainbow	_____
5. dog	_____
6. thunderclouds	_____
7. heart	_____
8. fire	_____
9. wind	_____
10. sun	_____
11. blue	_____

B. (Optional) Symbols 7–11, repeated below, appear in well-known songs. Name the song.

7. heart   _____
8. fire   _____
9. wind   _____
10. sun   _____
11. blue   _____

C. A personal symbol means different things to different people. Fill in the blanks below to show the personal meanings of some symbols. The first two are done for you.

A car: To a sixteen-year-old, a car can mean <u>power and independence</u>.

To her parent, a car can mean <u>danger and loss of authority</u>.

To a poor person, a car can mean _____.

A house: To a child, a house can mean _____.

To a parent, a house can mean _____.

(Optional) Add one or two personal symbols and tell what they mean to you.

_____

_____

D. Define a *symbol:*

_____

_____

APPENDIX
K

$$\diamond$$

Spelling List

Here is a place for you to make a personal spelling list, one that will save you much time and effort when you edit. Add to this list after you finish each paper: Write in any words that gave you trouble—even if you find you guessed them right and even if you "really knew better." File them by first letter so you can find them easily.

Even if you use a computer program to correct your spelling, you'll still need this list for problems the computer can't catch: the one-word/two-word problem (the word *maybe* means *possibly*, but *may be* means *might be*) and other words that sound alike but are spelled differently (*their, there, they're*). Record these with their meanings.

As your list builds, it will become a handy reference, quicker to use than the dictionary because it is so much shorter.

A

advice
advising
affect = to influence (verb)
all right
a lot (two words)
all together = as a group
altogether = completely
argument

B

belief
believe
buy
by

C

choose (now I choose)
chose (then I chose)
cite = refer to
commitment
committing

D

do
due
doesn't

E

effect = the result (noun)
every day = each day
everyday = ordinary

F

G

H

have (could have, should have,
     will have)

I

imply = to hint
infer = to guess
in turn (two words)
it's = it is (or it has)
its = belonging to it

J

K

knew = past tense of *to know*

L

less = smaller in amount
fewer = lower in number
loose (rhymes with goose) = not
     tight
lose = not win

M

N

necessary
new = not old
now = not then

O

occur
occurred

P

presence
privilege

Q

R

receive

S

T

than = comparison (more than,
    rather than)
then = not now OR if . . . then
their = belonging to them
they're = they are
there = in that place OR stating a
    fact (there are three)
today's world
tomorrow
too = also OR overly (too much,
    too small)
two = 2
to = use whenever *too* and *two*
    don't fit (to the store/ to see)
truly

U

V

view

W

whether = comparison (whether
    or not)
weather = outdoor conditions
where = in what place? (Where is
    it?)
were (We were taking the car.)
we're = we are
while
who's = who is OR who has
whose = belongs to
writing

X

Y

Z

APPENDIX
L

---◆---

Discussion Grading Sheet

Following is one possible grading scheme for class discussion, based in part on the task and maintenance roles described in the introduction.

(Sample)

Section Date NAMES											
Brought text											
Listened act.											
Cited text											
Gave info/op.											
Asked info/op.											
Started disc.											
Summarized											
Diagnosed											
Evaluated											
Relieved tens.											
GRADE											

A = 4 pts.   D = 1 pt.
B = 3 pts.   F = 0 pt.
C = 2 pts.
NC (No Credit) = Excused abs.

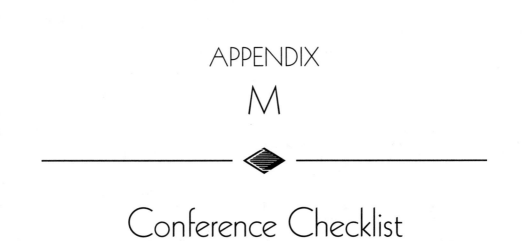

APPENDIX

M

Conference Checklist

Bring this checklist, filled in for the essay, to your conference.

	Essay				
Title	**1**	**2**	**3**	**4**	**5**
1. Title that shows your main idea and is different from the title of the reading—no underlining or quotation marks†					
Introduction (Background)					
2. Title of each reading selection from textbook the first time you refer to it, in quotes*					
3. Each author's first and last names with first mention in your text**					
4. Thesis/assertion (question to be discussed—or its answer); use key content words from question					
Body (Evidence)					
5. Develops the thesis					
6. Uses evidence from the reading(s) in the textbook					
7. Analyzes the issues					
8. Shows original thought					
Conclusion					
9. Answers the question clearly—uses key words again (reread introduction and conclusion)					
10. Closes the essay—no new material					

† **Title:** Capitalize the first word (and first word after : or ;). Capitalize the last word. Capitalize all middle words, even short ones, except these:

Articles	**Short Joining Words**	**Short Prepositions (2–4 letters)**
a, an, the	and, but, or, nor, so	as, at, by, for, from, in, into, near, of, on, over, to, up, with

Referring to the readings

*1. The first time you refer to an essay, give its title and the author's full name.

Example 1: In the essay "Old Before Her Time," Katherine Barrett says that old people often are overlooked.

Example 2: Katherine Barrett, the author of "Old Before Her Time," says, "The old are often ignored" (p. 55).

*2. Summarize the author's ideas in your own words (see Example 1, above) or use the author's words—**sparingly**—in quotation marks (see Example 2, above).

**3. Place the apostrophes correctly.

Example 3: The essay by Miguel Braga . . . OR Miguel Braga's essay . . .

Example 4: Miguel Braga's and George Smith's essays . . . (separate essays)

Example 5: Joe Green and Al Rosen's essay . . . (one essay written jointly)

Coherence or continuity

1. Arrange your ideas in logical sequence.
2. Show how your ideas are related.
   - Combine sentences.
   - Use transitions (*however* / *so* / *for example*).
   - Use pronouns. Be sure the reader can tell what they refer to.

Proofreading

1. To hear your ideas, read your paper forward, preferably out loud.
2. To check for sentence structure, read from back to front, sentence by sentence.
3. Read once through for each type of error you tend to make.

Conferences

1. To conferences, bring:
   - class text and class handouts, especially the conference checklist and your editing checklist.
   - complete essay, typed double-spaced, with approximately one-inch margins on all four sides. Keep all your prewriting and successive drafts; turn these in with your final copy.

2. First draft conference feedback focuses on content and organization.
3. After the final draft conference, be sure to update your spelling and editing checklists. Show them to your instructor right away.

What is effective content?

- answers the question
- formulates concepts thoughtfully
- shows awareness of two sides of an issue
- avoids generalizations in place of supporting detail
- uses specific examples
- varies the use of examples or evidence
- shows critical thinking (analysis, synthesis, original thought)
- uses sources appropriately
- uses appropriate formality (see Appendix F, pp. 307–309, *Controversy*)

What builds an arresting introduction?

- startling statistics
- an anecdote, short story, fable, or personal experience
- a question or series of questions
- history
- the importance of the subject
- song or relevant quotation (from the reading or elsewhere)

What is effective organization?

- arresting introduction
- thoughtful thesis
- well-developed paragraphs
- appropriate conclusion
- overall unity (all parts support the thesis and relate to each other)
- overall coherence (readers can see the relations between thoughts and move easily from one to the next; transitions and consistent tense will help)

What builds an appropriate ending?

- concluding the anecdote
- history and future implications
- statement of the importance of the subject
- a quotation